W9-BUF-896

ADVANCE PRAISE FOR

What Your ADHD Child Wishes You Knew

"Short enough for a busy parent to actually read and use; utterly reliable and authoritative but never pedantic; wise, kind, and teeming with the chirping voices of children who have ADHD; this cornucopia of a book will feed you over and over again. Wonderfully written, infused with positive energy and solid information. All parents of children who have ADHD should buy it."
—EDWARD HALLOWELL, MD, bestselling
author of *Delivered from Distraction*

"We have many effective treatments and strategies to help kids with ADHD better manage daily life, but this book will provide that equally important intervention: feeling understood. I love how this book helps parents create a deeper relationship with their kids so that the whole family can thrive."
—ARI TUCKMAN, PsyD, MBA, author of
More Attention, Less Deficit and *Understand Your Brain, Get More Done*

"Dr. Saline helps parents understand the negative and positive thought patterns in their families and expose the components of unhelpful behaviors, and then, using her 5 C's approach, guides them toward workable solutions. I highly recommend this book to assist parents in tuning up their abilities to see and hear their children's signals more accurately, untie the knots of miscommunication, and improve everyone's coping strategies for living with ADHD."
—AARON T. BECK, MD, psychiatrist and professor emeritus,
University of Pennsylvania, Perelman School of Medicine

"When I give presentations for parents of children with ADHD and executive skill challenges, my message to them is *Most of these kids turn out fine!* This book is an excellent blueprint for parents who want to make that happen. Dr. Saline is a skilled therapist who has learned to listen to her clients. This book teaches us to do the same."
—PEG DAWSON, EdD, psychologist and
coauthor of *Smart but Scattered*

"Dr. Saline provides compassionate, consistent, and comprehensive guidance around the broad impact of ADHD on individuals and families. Her 5 C's provide a practical foundation for overcoming the wide-ranging challenges of living with ADHD."
—MARK BERTIN, MD, developmental pediatrician and author of *How Children Thrive* and *Mindful Parenting for ADHD*

"Sharon Saline is a rare commodity—a psychotherapist who 'gets it!' Not only does she understand complex kids, but she speaks to parents in a kind, straightforward, clear way that helps them improve their communication with their kids—in the heat of the moment, when they need it most. Creatively developed, constructive in its advice, and compassionately written, this is the kind of book I'd recommend to the parents in my community."
—ELAINE TAYLOR-KLAUS, cofounder of ImpactADHD.com and author of *Parenting ADHD Now!*

"Dr. Saline does an excellent job of bringing compassion and insight to address the struggles children with ADHD face. She infuses each of her concepts with quotes from children of all ages as they share the impact ADHD has on them. The book will leave you feeling positive and inspired to face the challenges together with your child."
—CINDY GOLDRICH, EdM, ACAC, ADHD parent coach and teacher trainer, PTS Coaching

"After making a diagnosis of ADHD, parents often ask me 'What do we do now?' Finally, there is a resource I can recommend that gives concrete advice on how to help their children, illustrated with stories, examples, and the science behind the advice."
—JONATHAN SCHWAB, MD, medical director, Northampton Area Pediatrics

"As a school psychologist, I recognize the struggles of these children and am grateful for the wisdom they share. As a parent, my first reaction to reading this book is 'Here we are, in print!' My mom take-home message is that by following Dr. Saline's sage advice, we parents can become the champions our ADHD kids really need."
—KATHY CASALE, school psychologist and parent of two kids with ADHD

"I wish I'd had this insightful and compelling book when my children were younger. A must-read for the parent of a child with ADHD."
—AYELET WALDMAN, author of *A Really Good Day*

"This book is a treasure trove for any parent of a child diagnosed with ADHD. I will return to it over and over, as a parent, a teacher, and a fellow-sufferer of 'bullet brain.'"
—NERISSA NIELDS, singer/songwriter and cofounder of The Nields Band, author of *How to Be an Adult*

"As a teacher and a parent, I know how often our children's frustrations become our own. Dr. Saline helps children, caregivers, and educators feel supported and equipped for success."
—AMY MELTZER, award-winning teacher and parent of a teen with ADHD

"This book is a treasure in how it simplifies what parents need to do to best support kids with ADHD. Frustrated parents can exhale and learn how to create a positive, collaborative dynamic at home using Sharon Saline's many helpful tips and strategies."
—DEBBIE STEINBERG KUNTZ, LMFT, founder of Positive Impact Family

"This book is a gift for ADHD kids and their parents, packed full of wisdom and practical tips from kids and adults alike. The five C's are tools I use and teach in my own practice all the time."
—CHRISTOPHER WILLARD, PsyD, faculty, Harvard Medical School, and author of *Growing Up Mindful* and *Raising Resilience*

What Your ADHD Child Wishes You Knew

Working Together to Empower Kids for Success in School and Life

Dr. Sharon Saline

Foreword by
DR. LAURA MARKHAM

A TarcherPerigee Book

tarcherperigee

An imprint of Penguin Random House LLC
375 Hudson Street
New York, New York 10014

Copyright © 2018 by Sharon Saline
Penguin supports copyright. Copyright fuels creativity, encourages diverse voices,
promotes free speech, and creates a vibrant culture. Thank you for buying an
authorized edition of this book and for complying with copyright laws by
not reproducing, scanning, or distributing any part of it in any form
without permission. You are supporting writers and allowing
Penguin to continue to publish books for every reader.

Illustrations page 37, 147: © Sarina Hahn
Illustration page 97: Rhymes with Orange © 2016 Hilary B. Price—Distributed by
King Features Syndicate, Inc.
Illustration page 181: Rhymes with Orange © 2011 Hilary B. Price—Distributed by
King Features Syndicate, Inc.

TarcherPerigee with tp colophon is a registered trademark of Penguin Random
House LLC.

Most TarcherPerigee books are available at special quantity discounts for bulk
purchase for sales promotions, premiums, fund-raising, and educational needs.
Special books or book excerpts also can be created to fit specific needs. For details,
write: SpecialMarkets@penguinrandomhouse.com.

Library of Congress Cataloging-in-Publication Data

Names: Saline, Sharon, author.
Title: What your ADHD child wishes you knew : working together to empower
kids for success in school and life / Dr. Sharon Saline ; foreword by
Laura Markham.
Description: New York City : TarcherPerigee, 2018. |
Identifiers: LCCN 2018017661 (print) | LCCN 2018026790 (ebook) |
ISBN 9780525504375 (e-book) | ISBN 9780143132394 (paperback) |
ISBN 9780525504375 (ebook)
Subjects: LCSH: Attention-deficit hyperactivity disorder. |
Attention-deficit-disordered children. | Attention-deficit hyperactivity
disorder—Social aspects. | Parent and child. | BISAC: PSYCHOLOGY /
Psychopathology / Attention-Deficit Disorder (ADD-ADHD). |
FAMILY & RELATIONSHIPS / Children with Special Needs.
Classification: LCC RJ506.H9 (ebook) | LCC RJ506.H9 S254 2018 (print) |
DDC 618.92/8522—dc23
LC record available at https://lccn.loc.gov/2018017661
p.   cm.

Printed in the United States of America
5   7   9   10   8   6   4

Book design by Katy Riegel

This book is dedicated to all of the kids who trusted me enough to share their stories and to my mother, who believed in this project from the very start.

Contents

Part Three:
Life at Home and Beyond

Foreword

PARENTING ANY CHILD is hard. But parenting a child with an ADHD brain is the kind of hard that can make you want to throw yourself on the floor and join your child in his or her tantrum.

And truth be told, it doesn't get easier as kids hit the preteen and teen years—it gets harder. That's because you won't be there to keep them on track when your son needs to keep his locker organized and remember to turn in his homework or your daughter scrambles to get herself to each class on time while navigating complicated peer dramas. ADHD brains develop a bit more slowly, and school gets more pressured for young people every day.

If you're wondering how to teach your child or teen the executive functioning skills that are essential to their success as they become more independent in school and in life, then this empowering book is for you. Dr. Sharon Saline has worked with children and teens with ADHD for more than twenty-five years and convincingly demonstrates that they have one essential ally, one irreplaceable tool as they move through their preteen and teen years and into adulthood: you.

From teaching executive functioning skills to modeling emotional self-regulation, you the parent are your child's most important teacher.

Think of this book as your road map. In it, you'll find clear routes to becoming the parent—the capable, kind, helpful parent—that your child or teen needs *you* to be, so your child can become their own personal best.

Above all, Dr. Saline offers concrete, practical tools for building the relationship that both you and your child want and deserve. Her Five C's—self-Control, Compassion, Collaboration, Consistency, and Celebration—add up to a program that supports parents, while helping kids develop the skills they need to thrive.

Dr. Saline knows full well how challenging family life can be when ADHD is on the scene. She brings uncommon clarity and an open heart to difficult topics like the shame that both child and parent alike often feel as they struggle together with the challenges of ADHD. But she also helps us celebrate the strengths—the energy, the imagination, and the fun—of kids with ADHD. Reading this book reminds parents that other families have successfully grappled with ADHD and helped their children develop hard-won skills to handle adult life.

What is most moving about this book, and most helpful to parents, are the voices of the many ADHD children and teenagers themselves who fill these pages. Dr. Saline's secret power, and your secret weapon, are the same: listening. If you really listen to your child and see the world through his or her eyes, if your child feels seen and heard by you, you can build a relationship of love and compassion that will see you both through the hard times.

You will not always find it easy to be the parent of a child with an ADHD brain. You will sometimes despair, wondering, "How will my child turn out?" Fortunately, you'll see in this book, and hear in these young people's voices, that they will turn out to be themselves and more, and that their struggles are immeasurably helped when they see you intervening at school on their behalf, sitting with them when they hurt, supporting them through academics and chores, and believing in them even when they don't believe in themselves.

The harder the struggle, the sweeter the victory. Dr. Saline's relationship-based model gives you the practical wisdom to create that sweet, supportive relationship with your child that gives your child the skills they need to thrive. You'll each grow as the lessons and insights in the book become part of your everyday lives. And what does a child, or a parent, desire more than that?

Dr. Laura Markham
author of Peaceful Parent, Happy Kids:
How to Stop Yelling and Start Connecting

Introduction

"School is okay, but homework, especially with my mom, is the worst thing. She just doesn't understand what it's like for me. We get my stuff done, but we argue a lot. I want to do it myself, but I can't, so I'm stuck."

—Oliver, age 9

"I'm very in the moment. I am very good at forgetting, which is honestly one of my favorite qualities. Small things don't bother me a lot."

—Ella, age 16

"After school, I go outside or do PlayStation by myself or with my friends. . . . By myself it's hard to stop. But if I'm with another person and my dad yells that it is time to get off, we do something else. Like when I'm by myself, uh, what's to do?"

—Logan, age 11

"Having ADHD is like you're trying to pedal uphill on a bike, but it's not in gear so you're going backward. You're trying, but it's just not going. Sometimes I get so irrational and angry because I try so hard."

—Amari, age 17

If you are the parent of a child or teen with attention-deficit hyperactive disorder (with or without hyperactivity), these stories, or ones like them, might seem familiar to you. You may know that school is challenging for your son and that the two of you argue too much. You may know that your daughter is forgetful and needs multiple reminders to remember her soccer practice and her chores. But do you really understand what having ADHD is like for them? What difference would that make in your daily parenting struggles to help them grow into responsible, competent, and happy adults? Based on interviews with dozens of kids from various ethnic and socioeconomic backgrounds, this book gives you insights into the minds and feelings of children and teens with ADHD. Their stories unlock a rich trove of feelings, thoughts, and ideas about themselves and what it means to have ADHD. Their perspectives open up the extraordinary opportunity for parents to better understand their minds, emotions, and actions. These tales, along with decades of clinical experience helping more than a thousand youths and families, have informed my distinctive approach, the Five C's of ADHD Parenting. With these tools, you learn how to create lasting solutions to daily challenges in your family.

Through my work with children, teens, and their families—in my psychotherapy practice and as a consultant to schools, a keynote speaker, and a workshop facilitator, I have observed that families dealing with ADHD seem to miss one another's signals and wind up angry, frustrated, hurt, and disconnected. Kids repeatedly tell me things that they don't share with their parents but would like to discuss. Parents tell me they want to understand what is going on with their children but need practical strategies to meet their daily challenges. My Five C's method (self-Control, Compassion, Collaboration, Consistency, and Celebration) offers you an effective, evidence-based road map for reducing family stress and improving the loving connections that everyone wants.

The voices in this book echo the sentiments and behaviors of your own son or daughter, offering a window into what you might not know about them. Some of the kids have been in therapy with me or other clinicians; some of them have never been to therapy at all. All of them share their experiences with surprising honesty, humor, and poignancy. As you read, you'll learn effective ways to figure out what *your child* is telling you—with their words and actions. You'll become more skilled at navigating the complicated issues they bring to you. Instead of focusing on how to fix your child or teen, the Five C's build connection and improve working together as the basis for effective change. Most kids share a similar desire to feel seen, heard, and understood. You'll create win-win situations where they *want* to work with you. Many books about ADHD tell parents what to do and how to discipline. This one explains how being an empathic ally creates the lasting changes you and your child long for. I have found from years of working with families that this collaborative approach is what works best.

Each chapter begins with a vignette or excerpts from interviews to set the tone for our journey together, with personal stories threaded throughout the book. In Part One, we go over the model of the Five C's of ADHD parenting. We look at living with ADHD and learning differences, understanding the ADHD brain and executive functioning, getting an accurate diagnosis, and accepting life with an ADHD brain (for you and your child). In Part Two, we delve into various aspects of school, including academic issues, homework, and self-advocacy. In Part Three, we examine life at home by exploring tantrums and worries, organization, friendships, and technology. With useful exercises and easy-to-remember techniques, you'll learn a variety of practical strategies that *really* work.

Throughout this book, I refer to attention issues as ADHD in part because ADHD/ADD seems cumbersome, and it is clinically and medically called "ADHD, inattentive, hyperactive or combined type."* In order to respect the spectrum of gender diversity, I use the plural "they/them" as much as possible instead of "he/she or him/her" to

---

* Although the issues and behaviors for hyperactivity and inattention differ, for most kids, their experiences of living with ADHD are actually more similar than not. For this reason, I use the term "ADHD."

refer to a child or teen. I call kids "boys," "girls," "sons," and "daughters" for the ease of language rather than an intention to exclude transgender or gender-nonconforming youth. All the names and identities of the children, teens, and parents have been disguised to protect their privacy.

Finally, I have a personal connection to ADHD that is different from most authors. I grew up in a family with a younger brother who was hyperactive and impulsive. When he was five years old, he started therapy, which helped with anger management but ultimately missed the mark. The main issues of attention difficulties and executive functioning challenges were not addressed because information about ADHD in the early '70s was scant. He struggled, my parents struggled with him, and I watched it all unfold. They used a top-down, authoritative model of parenting that just did not work. Sometimes I avoided getting involved in their conflicts; at others, I attempted to mediate them. It was tough for all of us, especially my brother.

My perspective as a sibling—living with untreated ADHD from the inside out and seeing how it affected everyone—initially drew me to child and family therapy and now to writing this book. I want kids with ADHD to share their stories and know that their words matter to the adults who care for them and that we are listening. I envision families who have less conflict and stress and more ease in their daily interactions. I hope parents will share any familiar-sounding voices in this book with their son or daughter as reassurance that they are not alone. I believe that this book paves the way for essential dialogues and successful interventions between parents and kids. The Five C's of ADHD parenting provides a valuable map for doing this as well as building closeness and cooperation. With these tools in hand, your child or teen will be better positioned to grow up with the competency, self-esteem, and resiliency they need to lead meaningful and productive lives.

PART ONE

Life with ADHD

Chapter 1

....

The Five C's of ADHD Parenting

Meet Drew, age 12, *as he says to his dad: "Don't open my locker! Just help me get to class on time."*

They make an odd but not unusual pair. The boy is tall and gangly with wavy black hair that perpetually falls over his eyes, wearing a wrinkled T-shirt and black Converse sneakers whose size matches his age–12. His father, a squat, balding man a few inches shorter than his son, limps alongside him. Their mission: go to the middle school after the students have left the building on this autumn afternoon and map out the best route to classes so that Drew, recently diagnosed with ADHD, won't be late anymore.

It's weirdly quiet when they enter the school. Bill, who never really liked school, looks around warily. He takes a deep breath and reminds himself that he is here to help his son. He turns to Drew and grumbles, "Let's start with your locker." They make their way through the empty hallways in silence until arriving at Locker 152.

"Open it."

"Dad, seeing my locker wasn't our deal. We're here to figure out

how I can get to classes without being late, which isn't going to work anyway because I'm just slow. I'm a slow walker."

Bill's eyes narrow, and his throat tightens. "Drew, open your locker. I want to see how you keep your things. Your progress report says that you're late to classes and you forget to turn work in. So open it up. Let's see what's going on in there."

Drew reluctantly turns the dial on the combination lock, and, as the door pops open, a notebook, several sheets of paper, and an empty soda can fall to the ground.

"Drew, you can't keep your stuff like this. It's a mess, just like your room." Bill bends over and starts picking up the various papers strewn on the floor. "These need to go in folders, and these books should be stacked up, not shoved in here. Hey, what's this?" He picks up a half-eaten candy bar that's melted onto a notebook. "Haven't I taught you better than this?" He starts pulling everything out of the locker onto the floor.

"Dad, will you just stop? Dad! This is why I didn't want to open my locker. It's my stuff. I don't even need half those papers. . . ." Drew raises his voice: "Stop touching my stuff! You don't know what you're doing!"

Bill continues, mumbling about responsibility. Drew pounds his fists on a nearby locker and, when that does not stop his dad, throws himself on the floor before finally storming away. He hates when his dad flat-out ignores him, and besides, they were supposed to figure out how he can get to classes faster, not organize his locker. This is stupid. Bill yells after him, "Where do you think you're going?"

"Away."

"I'm your ride home."

"I'm walking."

Confused and frustrated, Bill watches Drew leave and wonders how he can help his son.

Sound familiar? If you are a parent of a kid with ADHD, you've probably been through a scenario similar to this many times. You ask yourself over and over, *What's so difficult? Why does he keep making the same mistakes? What doesn't she get?* You feel as though you're living in the movie *Groundhog Day* because the same negative behaviors occur over and over while nothing you try seems to make a difference. You love your child, but you are repeatedly frustrated, and at a deeper level, you're frightened. You ask yourself, *What will become of my child if they can't get it together? Are they destined to spend their life working at a low-paying, dead-end, and unfulfilling job?* Parenting any child is hard enough. But parenting a child with ADHD sometimes feels like peaks of progress are regularly followed by intense backslides.

Why is daily life often harder for kids with ADHD? They seem to struggle academically, socially, and psychologically. They forget things, can't slow down, find it hard to focus, space out regularly. They are disorganized; they feel overwhelmed; they can't control their emotions; they miss the nuances of peer interactions. While they like their creativity, their "out of the box" thinking, and their energy, they are usually ashamed of their shortcomings, want to avoid dealing with them, and often feel powerless to change them. Similar to all kids, they just want to be "normal." They certainly don't want to have a "disorder," and no matter how many times you tell them that everyone's brain is different, they think it is definitely more than a "focus problem." As a parent, how can you feel competent and effective in assisting them to overcome the daily challenges they face and embrace the brain they have? How can you listen to what they are telling you about their experiences and offer them the empathy and guidance they need?

These two questions are fundamentally linked. It's as difficult for them as it is for you. It's crucial to remember that kids with ADHD are doing the best they can with their skills—skills that are compromised by the inherent complexities of having ADHD (such as challenges with working memory, impulse control, and concentration). They do the best they can with their personal resources and know, either outright or internally, when they are

> It's as difficult for them as it is for you.

falling short. You, as their caretakers, witness their efforts. You see them triumph one day and flop the following. You try to make things better for them, sometimes offering suggestions that work while others are rebuffed before you can finish your sentence. Too often, you end up doing an '80s slam dance: colliding into each other and then bouncing away, bruised and overheated.

While children and teens with ADHD often feel misunderstood and criticized for things they can't help doing, they also want to be connected to others, loved, and accepted for who they are. They want to be skilled and successful, they want to feel as though they belong, and they especially want to be heard. Instead, kids often feel just the opposite: incompetent, insecure, worried, angry, silenced. Sometimes they cling to parental help, and sometimes they push it away. Despite any actions and words otherwise, kids with ADHD, like all young people, desperately crave their parents' approval and support. They also want the acceptance of their teachers and peers.

While you love your kids, as their parent, you may be more often exhausted by their antics than amused by them. Although you may value their creativity, intelligence, or athletic prowess, you probably struggle with maintaining patience, balance, and humor in the face of strife or chaos. You want more cooperative, responsible behaviors. You don't want to remind your son to put away his laundry for the third time as the clean stuff slowly mixes with the dirty on the floor. You don't want to attend another meeting with your daughter's teacher about her spaciness in class and failure to turn in assignments. And most of all, you don't want to feel incapable and clueless as a parent about how to guide your child to become a fully functioning adult. You, like all parents, want to feel capable and competent.

The goal of this book is to give you a road map to be that capable parent via the voices of children and teens with ADHD. You'll elicit and listen to your child's stories about having ADHD and respond empathically, supportively, and calmly. You'll notice what your son or daughter is communicating to you with their words and actions. You'll work together toward solutions for everyday challenges. Your son or daughter will learn to see you as an ally. They will be more open to your suggestions because they feel seen and heard. You'll feel less stressed, and your child or teen will begin to thrive.

I call this road map the Five C's of ADHD Parenting:

....

■ **self-Control:** Learning to manage your own feelings first so you can act effectively and teach your child with ADHD to do the same.

"I lost it with him yesterday before we left for dinner with my parents. After three reminders to put on his shoes, when he still didn't have them on, I yelled, 'Terrell! *Shoes!*' I wish I had more patience, but I have my limits too." —Monica, the mother of Terrell, age 8

"I am an emotional person, and sometimes I don't have any control over my feelings. It's like being a volcano that's ready to explode at all times." —Martina, age 17

....

■ **Compassion:** Meet your child where they are, not where you expect them to be.

"He works so hard to make it through a day at school. It blows my mind how he does that. I try to remember this when we are fighting about doing his homework the way I think it should be done." —Eva, the mother of Marco, age 10

"I don't like how my parents try to help me because they talk too much and ask too many questions. It pressures me when I don't have the answers, but I don't say nothing because I don't want them to get mad at me." —Angel, age 11

- **Collaboration:** Work together with your child and other important adults in their life to find solutions to daily challenges instead of imposing your rules on them.

"I coach my daughter's basketball team, and because she has trouble remembering directions, people end up frustrated or yelling at her, which she doesn't like. We made a plan: I give her a calm reminder, and she asks for help more often. Yesterday, when she missed the warm-up directions, she quickly ran over, asked someone what we were doing, and got started. No drama! This was huge for her."

—Eric, the father of Sheena, age 12

"Sometimes there's some bumps in the road—like in the mornings. Mom said I can play video games if I am ready for school early, but then I don't want to stop when it's time to leave and I get really mad. We got a timer now that gives a reminder and final bell. I don't like it, but I don't yell so much. She likes that." —Jack, age 8

- **Consistency:** Do what you say you will do; aim for staying steady, not for perfection. Nurture their efforts to do their best, and do the same for yourself.

"We use screens as incentives and consequences, but we can't always stick with a plan. Sometimes we forget or something happens or we just feel tired. I know we give mixed messages, but we are trying our best." —Scott, the father of Darren, age 15

"What my mom does, which I really don't understand, is that she cleans up and complains. She'll say, 'I'm going to leave the next mess I see you make and tell you to clean it up,' and then goes in, cleans it up, and tells me about it. I tell her, 'Let me do it next time,' but she never does."

—Stella, age 14

....

■ **Celebration:** Notice and acknowledge what's working by contin-
uously offering words and actions of encouragement, praise, and
validation.

"I want Nolan to do his best effort at school and home, so I get upset
when he doesn't. He told me last week what he hears from me is that
he's never good enough. I'm surprised that Nolan doesn't hear me telling him how smart he is and could do better because of that."
                                    —Michael, the father of Nolan, age 11

"My mom taught me to think positively. If you can ask yourself questions during the day, like, 'What am I doing right now? What can I do to
make this situation a little better?' then you can turn around a crappy
situation. When we do this together, she helps me find something good,
which I really appreciate."   —Martina, age 17

MY FIVE C'S model relies on two things: **strength-based thinking** and
attentive awareness. With **strength-based thinking**, you focus on your
child's capabilities to help them build competence, self-confidence, and
pride. **Strength-based thinking** means identifying traits, or behaviors
they excel at, and nurturing those skills. These abilities may be either
obvious or obscure, but they are there, and your job is to identify them.
If things have been tough at home and all you can see is how your seven-
year-old son is good at building with LEGOs and snuggling with the
dog, then those strengths are your starting point. *"Shawn, that's a fancy
house you built with your LEGOs. Look at all of those rooms." "It's so nice how
you like to cuddle with our puppy. I know that you really love him."* Pay equal
if not more attention to these qualities instead of how he is a slow
reader and a reluctant soccer player. Focus on and appreciate their
strengths, however idiosyncratic they may be. *"Wow, you set the table by
putting the silverware in the glasses. That's different." "Hey, you cleaned your
bathroom and arranged all your makeup according to color. Looks cool."* When

parents use **strength-based thinking**, they cultivate self-confidence, resilience, and motivation in their kids because you are working from a place of competency instead of failure.

Attentive awareness involves observing, listening to, and acknowledging what your child is saying. This serves as the starting point for any desired changes. If your thirteen-year-old daughter is racing around on Sunday night in a panic because she forgot to do the math project due on Monday, she is showing several things. Not only is she disorganized about keeping track of her assignments and unable to remember them, she is scared, worried, and overwhelmed. Instead of angrily saying, *"How many times have I told you that you need to do a better job doing your homework before the eleventh hour? Your bedtime is in thirty minutes,"* or *"Why can't you learn to keep up with things and follow directions like your sister?!"* use **attentive awareness** and respond empathically. For example, you might say: *"I see how worried and overwhelmed you are about your math. Let's slow everything down and figure out what would be helpful. You'll get through this, and I'll help in whatever way I can."* Getting mad at her won't help either of you. She is emotionally overloaded and needs your support. **Attentive awareness** guides you to aligning with her in solving the problem.

The next day, when things are calmer, you can brainstorm a different approach to weekend homework. *"I think we need a plan to help you avoid these incidents in the future. What do you think? When can we talk about this?"* Then ask for her opinion about what happened, share your observations, and create solutions together. When a kid with ADHD fails at a task he or she should be able to perform, it's usually because they don't know what else to do or can't access what they know they should do. Dr. Ross Greene, founder of Lives in the Balance (www .livesinthebalance.org) asserts that "kids do well if they can," and they prefer to do well if they have the skills to do so.[1]

When kids meet with defeat, it's because they don't see other choices for themselves in that moment. This perspective can be hard for our adult minds to grasp. How can it be that your teen son doesn't see other choices when he shoplifts a Mike's Hard Lemonade? There are lots of reasons: poor impulse control, peer pressure, denial of real consequences, fun of risk-taking behavior. His thinking brain wasn't available to him in that moment, but that doesn't mean that he likes to do "bad things." Frequently kids with ADHD don't make effective choices because they have missed the environmental, visual, or verbal cues that would help them slow down and figure out an alternative. Sometimes they fail so much that they don't believe they can succeed anymore. Darren, a fifteen-year-old boy in my therapy practice, refused to talk to his biology teacher about his failed exam: "*I failed the class last year, and I'm failing again. What's the point? It won't help.*" After some digging, we remembered he had spoken to her recently about a difficult class assignment and she had been helpful. He reconsidered. They reviewed his errors, and she ended up giving him some credit for his corrections.

Strength-based thinking and **attentive awareness** counteract kids' pattern of failure. Challenges that are frequently frustrating, overwhelming, or isolating become manageable because you have faced them together. Sometimes they approach you for advice or help with a problem. They share their stories, listen to your words, and watch your actions. They see and feel what connection looks like. They realize that they are not as alone as they may have felt because you are sharing in their successes and their flops. At other times, you bring up a trouble spot, often a trickier but necessary part of your parenting job. In these moments, you create the platform for discussing issues by your approach, your tone, and your attitude.

When you put your heads together to invent alternatives and explore new choices about an issue that matters to you, the Five C's Parenting kicks in. You calmly share what you see or hear, your point of view and feedback. By including your child in the process of addressing a problem that you have identified either on your own or together, you are demonstrating basic respect for them—even if they don't always show this to you. That's part of their development into adults. Mutual input is the key, but, as the parent, you obviously have the final say. If your son doesn't think dirty dishes left overnight in his room is a problem, or your daughter refuses to call when she is going to be an hour late, as the responsible adult, you get to insist on a change.

Many parents stare in disbelief when I talk about this approach to raising kids with ADHD. *"Why do we have to 'negotiate' things? Why can't she just do what I tell her to do? I'm her mother. That's how I was raised. Do what I say or else."* For many of us, the "or else" usually included rageful yelling; spanking with hands, belts, or paddles; or time spent in isolation (being sent to our rooms for hours). But this "my way or the highway" style of parenting doesn't really fit with Generation X or Millennial parents, who don't want to squelch their kids—either because of philosophical beliefs or rejection of the restraints they felt as children.[2] Fifty years ago, psychologist Diana Baumrind labeled this forceful type of parenting "authoritarian,"[3] and researchers have since found that being punitive and controlling does not assist parents in increasing their child's cooperation.[4] In fact, it's the parent/child relationship that motivates kids to chip in and comply. Alfie Kohn, international parenting expert and author, writes:

> On balance, the kids who do what they're told are likely to be those whose parents don't rely on power and instead have developed a warm and secure relationship with them. They have parents who treat them with respect, minimize the use of control, and make a point of offering reasons and explanations for what they ask.[5]

My conversations with kids with ADHD wholeheartedly support Kohn's opinion. Teaming up with your child to deal with trouble spots produces better results all around, but the back-and-forth can be maddening. As parents, you, like your child, are trying to do the best you can given *your* resources. Naturally, all parents want to help kids flourish and will usually do whatever they can to assist them. You teach your sons and daughters life skills, offer suggestions, repeat instructions, and then hopefully watch them move along, sometimes fluidly and sometimes fitfully. Last week, your six-year-old daughter was miraculously ready for school on time on Monday and Tuesday, listening to your reminders and following the routine. On Wednesday, you were rushing madly to get to work and school on time. While you were hurriedly getting dressed for work, she was supposed to be brushing her teeth and putting on her shoes. Instead, she was hopping around on one foot with a hat over her eyes pretending to be a blind kangaroo. One step forward and two steps back. Sometimes you are amused; other times, you are just disheartened. It's in these moments, when you are stressed, fed up, and demoralized, that you need my Five C's parenting approach.

> **One step forward and two steps back.**

How many times have you experienced the following scenario? Your thirteen-year-old daughter comes home from school, simultaneously eats a snack, watches TV, does her math homework, and leaves her snack dishes and books on the sofa with the TV on while she wanders upstairs to Facebook her friends. You have probably told her a thousand times not to study and watch TV and not to eat on the sofa. In spite of agreements about house rules, you come home from work and are again greeted by the familiar mess. You likely think, *"What is* wrong *with her?"* You may lose it and scream at her, *"Pick things up immediately or you'll lose electronics for the next five days."* You may even tell her that she is *"a space cadet and a slob."* You may ask her if she knows anything about the rules of your house, and when she grudgingly says yes, you demand to know why she can't follow them. She has no answer. Maybe she knows but refuses to tell you, or maybe she honestly doesn't know.

What her behavior is showing you is that, given her ADHD and her level of development, she simply doesn't make positive choices consistently. Of course she knows the house rules, but because she is a teenager with ADHD, her impulsive desires, her inability to finish one thing before starting another, and her failure to remember to do things have trumped the rules. Most likely she feels ashamed about that, but you won't see that embarrassment if you are yelling; you will be met by a defensive, angry girl. Any productive conversation has disappeared, and there's no actual listening either. You have hit a wall.

You both need different skills and new ways of behaving and you need them *now!*

My Five C's model of *self-Control, Compassion, Collaboration, Consistency,* and *Celebration* will help you build on what you do that already works while offering you new ideas and perspectives to help you through difficult parts. The five components, examined carefully in the rest of this chapter, will strengthen your natural parenting skills while building warmer family connections and reducing stress and disharmony.

1. self-Control

"Yesterday at breakfast, I called my dad an idiot when he took out the OJ for my cereal instead of the milk. It was funny. He didn't think so. He slammed the milk on the table, which made it spill, grabbed my arm, and yelled in my face that I had no right to talk to him that way. Then he stormed out of the kitchen and I had to clean up the spilled milk, which wasn't even my fault."
—Carly, age 12

NO PARENT CAN interact effectively with anyone, let alone their son or daughter with ADHD, in the midst of a conflict (or any other situation) if they are momentarily disconnected from themselves, emotionally triggered, or feeling out of control. Most kids are particularly adept at engaging in behaviors that can drive their parents crazy. Kids who have ADHD—with their inherent poor impulse control, forgetfulness, and emotional intensity—repeatedly set off their parents in ways that wear them down. Your ability to function thoughtfully and calmly can stop episodes from recurring. **How many times have you felt as though you are at the end of your rope, feeling the fibers slip through your fingers as you yell at your son again?**

Realistically, you can't deal with any situation effectively until you get yourself under control. Being aware of your feelings and what is bubbling inside you is the first step toward a positive alliance with your child or teen. Take deep breaths, pause, get in touch with what you are feeling. Any of the following exercises will cool the fire inside you.

EXERCISE 1: BREATHING

Here are my favorite, *really simple* breathing techniques that kids with and without ADHD seem to love. Together, with your son or daughter, give each one a try and choose your favorites.

Nostril Breathing

This comes from yoga. Place your right finger on your right nostril, and breathe in and out with your left one. Then switch. Do this five to ten times. Notice how you feel.

Chest Breathing

Place your hand on your chest or the top of your diaphragm, and take a deep breath. Exhale. Repeat this five times. Notice how you feel.

Flower/Candle Breathing

One of my clients, Zora, age 16, told me about this third option—"Sniff the flower, blow out the candle"[6]—that she learned in school, and we adapted it. Extend your pointer finger, and hold it about six inches from your face. Take a long, deep breath, as if you are smelling a beautiful rose. Then, exhale it like you are blowing out a candle on a birthday cake. Do this three times. Notice how you feel.

NOW THAT YOU are calmer, you have a chance to figure out a way to handle the situation before you do something that escalates it. This process of mindfulness is the opposite of losing your temper. Dr. Laura Markham observes:

> Being mindful means that you pay attention to what you're feeling, but don't act on it. . . . Acting on it mindlessly, with words or actions, is what compromises our parenting.[7]

Choosing mindfulness leads to responding instead of reacting. It keeps a situation from spiraling into a confrontation and leads to the creation of the positive parent/child alliance at the heart of the Five C's approach.

> Choosing mindfulness leads to responding instead of reacting.

We all have times when we say something in frustration and wish we could take it back. Most likely, those words are part of a knee-jerk response when your emotional brain has hijacked your thinking brain. Reacting with explosive feelings and inappropriate actions speeds up interpersonal disconnection and throws kindling on the flames of a growing escalation. As adults, our developed prefrontal cortex—the seat of the thinking brain—is capable of reestablishing *self-Control* and getting our explosive emotions back in check. However, your child and teen, whose prefrontal cortex is still maturing (until at least age twenty-five), lacks this important level of self-regulation.[8] They need guidance with managing their big feelings. For them, the emotional and physical reactions happen fast. One teen boy told me that his anger *"is like a huge wave, a tidal wave. I am doing fine and then 'POW!' Suddenly I am struggling to keep my head above water."* Probably you, too, have felt this powerful wave of emotion at some time or another in your life. But as an adult you have the skills to subdue it and rein yourself in.

Reacting generally involves criticism and blame, followed by regrets. Criticism is an outlet for spontaneous adult anger or intolerance that all children interpret instantaneously. For kids with ADHD, it is the sandpaper that rubs regularly against their skin. *"Sit still like Jamie and Tyler during morning meeting!"* *"Can you stop leaving your smelly soccer socks in the kitchen every day and put them in the laundry where they belong?!"* "Why don't you have any capital letters in your report? You can't turn it in like this." Even when you are trying to give them helpful reminders or positive feedback, the tone and delivery can make whatever you say feel like criticism. Many kids—those with ADHD and those without it—question the concept of "positive feedback." But children and teens with ADHD just don't seem to believe in it. As Chloe, age ten, said to me while wriggling upside down in the striped chair in my office, *"There is no such thing as positive feedback. There is nothing good about feedback. It's all bad. I don't know why you adults won't admit that."* It's all criticism to them: a constant reminder of how they've messed up again.

Blame teaches kids that the adult being right is more important than their being understanding: that it is acceptable to put someone down when they have made a mistake and that something wrong is usually someone's fault. Blaming a child reduces their ability to take responsibility for their actions, encourages lying, and breeds fear. When children worry about being blamed, they consciously avoid owning their actions. When her parents found ants in her bedroom, Ruby, age nine, denied eating there because she knew it was expressly against her father's wishes. But Ruby likes to eat when she reads, and she often reads in her bedroom. Finally, she admitted to snacking while reading in her bed:

> I just go into the kitchen to get something to eat with my book, and then I wander into my bedroom. I am thinking about the book, not the food. My parents told me that food in my room could bring bugs, but I didn't really believe them. I am really sorry, but apparently parents don't take it that way. They're like, "Oh, this kid messed up our house and it cost us money; she's going to get punished." Why would I tell them?

Blame increases low self-esteem by finding fault with behaviors and choices, even though kids with ADHD sometimes can't control what they do.

Responding is what's called for here, and it can be tough to do. A parent or caregiver needs to acknowledge what their child is expressing, either verbally or nonverbally, in a nonjudgmental way. You can't be dismissive: *"It shouldn't be such a big deal to get off your iPad. You've been on it for an hour!"* This only exacerbates tension and negates that it *is* a big deal for your son to turn it off. You need to marshal all your *self-control* to be patient and let your words reflect only what you see and hear going on around you. *"I see that it is hard to get off your iPad when you are having fun using it. But the hour we agreed on is up."* By responding instead of reacting, you validate whatever is going on and then, if necessary, open up the space to create an alternative solution: *"I understand that you think it isn't fair and you aren't ready to stop. What can we do about that?"* Talk it over, and set up a different plan for the next day. They may still get upset, but they will likely feel comforted by knowing that their opinions were heard and they are part of the decision-making process. Responding does not mean that you are "giving in," only that you are hearing their feelings and making a plan for the future.

Responding is especially challenging in families where things happen very quickly, often escalating within seconds. Much as you would like to manage everyone's behavior and avoid a blowout, all you can really control is yourself. The big difference in any provocative situation is whether you react or respond. When you trudge into the house after a long day at work with two big bags of groceries that have to be magically transformed into something delicious and your twelve-year-old daughter rushes toward you, emphatically waving a pink piece of paper in your face, shouting, *"You need to sign this so I can go on the field trip on Friday! It's really important, my teacher said so. Can you sign it now?"* you have two choices. You can react and yell, *"What are you doing?! Can't you see that my hands are full?"* Or, you can respond and say, *"Hey, I see this is important, but my arms are full. Why don't you give me a hand and then we can take care of it?"* If you choose the first option, you will, in all likelihood, be met by an even bigger reaction in return. By choosing the second option, you will likely avoid an eruption and maybe even get some cooperation along the way.

Willie, age thirteen, and his dad, David, share how they improved their relationship by practicing thoughtful *self-Control*:

> DAVID: Now, we communicate better, and we listen to each other without emotional excitement. I like things a certain way. I have strong opinions. When they aren't that way, I try to control them. Usually unsuccessfully.
>
> WILLIE: Yeah, general communication. Dad's not doing the one thing he used to do a lot, just automatically assuming I am lying. That's how quite a few of our fights got started. He would accuse me and yell, and I would say, "No I'm not" and get mad at him. Sometimes I didn't do what he wanted just to get back at him. I didn't care if I got punished.
>
> DAVID: I am trying to stay calmer and listen more. It's not always easy. I think Willie knows that. I see him not digging his heels in as much or stomping off, so that helps too.
>
> WILLIE: It's simple. Don't tell me I'm lying and then not listen to me. I don't have to get so angry now because he isn't accusing me as much.

Practicing *self-Control* doesn't mean perfection; it's a continuous process. You will still get upset at times—don't beat up on yourself. Just try to bring yourself back.

Those moments when you are most frustrated are the ones when you most need to remember to slow down and use your thinking mind. Take time for two minutes of nostril or chest breathing. Then, you can simply reflect back to your child what you notice is going on. When you observe and listen carefully and exert *self-Control* and steady behavior, you demonstrate to your child that there are other options available for them when they are fired up. As one father of a fourteen-year-old boy told me, *"The power of example is all any of us can do for our kids."*

2. Compassion

....

"When I get overwhelmed, it's hard to use words. Like, if I am disappointed in myself, I don't really say so. Sometimes I do. The thoughts are racing in my head. Then I just lie down and not do anything and pretend I don't hear anyone. My mom tells me she gets frustrated because I don't ask for help, but I just can't."   —James, age 11

WHAT DOES COMPASSION look like when you are parenting a child with ADHD or teen? The Dalai Lama believes that love and *Compassion* are necessities, not luxuries, for human survival.[9] *Compassion* in parenting means being able to see your child *where they are*: with empathy and patience in the context of their cognitive, social, emotional, and physical development. When your ten-year-old son is cooperating with you and clearing the dinner dishes, being kind is not really a problem. When your sixteen-year-old daughter is crying in your arms because her girlfriend broke up with her, showing her love and understanding is not really too hard. But when your nine-year-old daughter takes her shampoo and rubs it all over the shower walls to see how sudsy they can get and then sprays water to clean off the bubbles, which spreads the mess all over the bathroom, you are not likely to react to her curiosity with sensitivity. In fact, you're furious. It's moments like these when you have to dig deep, remind yourself about the necessity of *Compassion*, and find some.

Like *self-Control*, the first step in having *Compassion* for others is to cultivate some for yourself. If adults who parent kids with ADHD can accept themselves for who they are, warts and all, it will be easier to accept their children's foibles. Can you do this? If not, what gets in the way? *Compassion* is a frame of mind that withholds judgment and embraces others for who they are at a given moment, even if it's not who you want them to be. This is especially true when you consider your children. You can hold on to the possibility that your child will change as long as it's not an expectation. Expectations often breed disappointment; hope leads to opportunity.

Many of the kids with ADHD interviewed for this book repeatedly spoke about how their parents were their main supports. When asked "What gets you through tough times?" they replied:

- "I get a lot of support from my family, even when I have been failing."
- "I think the relationship with my parents; I owe a lot to them."
- "My mom is the main person I talk about this stuff with."
- "Having my mom there to keep me on task nicely."
- "They tell me things like, 'You're not dumb,' not like the negative things that I say to myself."
- "Me and my dad talk when we do stuff on the farm. Me and him have a pretty open line of communication, which is nice."
- "My dad helped keep me get organized with school stuff, which is huge because I don't know how to do it at all by myself."

These children feel seen and heard by their parents; bolstered by them; understood by them. They do not feel pitied or labeled as "stupid" or "defective." They see their parents intervening with school on their behalf, sitting with them and wading through their struggles with academics or chores and believing in them, even when they didn't believe in themselves. Sometimes this means that their parents put aside some of their own desires, frustrations, or disappointments in the service of what serves their children best at a given point in time. At other times, parents have to push their children to reach beyond what they see as their inabilities. It can be hard to know when to hold your ground and when to let go.

A few months ago, in my office, Rick was arguing with his bright fourteen-year-old son, Kevin, about his schedule for ninth grade. The boy did not want to take Honors English as a freshman. Even though his dad said he was smart, English was hard for him, especially writing. Rick acknowledged that writing was hard for his son, but he was concerned that not taking Honors English would look bad for college applications later on. He was even willing to pay for a tutor to help, although it was stretch financially. But Kevin would not budge. They were going around and around.

KEVIN FUMED: "Dad, I'm signed up for Honors Math. I love math. Why isn't that enough? You always want me to be perfect. Well, I'm not. I'm nervous about going to high school. Do you get that? Remember what it was like when I started middle school? I couldn't fall asleep at night."

RICK PAUSED AND SAID QUIETLY: "I don't want you to be overwhelmed and anxious. I just don't want you to give up on yourself. You are a smart kid. I want you to have opportunities that I didn't. If you take Honors English, you will learn to write well, and that's an important skill in life, one I wish I had more of."

Kevin looked at his father. "Well, I'm not you. I can learn to write fine in regular English, which is hard enough for me."

RICK SIGHED: "That may be true. I will talk to your guidance counselor about that. But I still think having another Honors class is important on your transcript. What about an Honors science? You like science."

KEVIN REPLIED: "If Honors classes are so important to you, I guess I could just take Honors Biology. Then you could help me, not some guy we have to pay.

Rick considered his idea. "That seems fair. If we can switch you to Honors Biology, that's okay. And let's see how English goes. If the writing portion isn't sufficient, maybe we'll get you help anyway."

KEVIN SMILED. "Works for me."

Kevin and his father each altered their ideas to create a new plan that met both of their needs. Rick led the way: he met his son where he was—a kid who likes math and science but is scared about the transition to high school. Summoning up empathy and personal insight, Rick focused on what was most important—his son having challenging classes and a strong transcript that reflected his intelligence. He listened carefully to what Kevin was saying, offered a different solution to the problem they faced, and then decided to talk to the guidance counselor to get more information. They stopped arguing. Ultimately, they came up with an alternative schedule that supported Kevin and reflected Rick's parental goals too.

Compassion also encompasses forgiveness. The ADHD brain, with its focus on the present, doesn't tend to hold grudges: what happened yesterday or last week is long forgotten in the face of what is going on right now. As a parent, your adult mind remembers incidents that your child has happily left behind. One week later, you may still be annoyed about cleaning up that bathroom after its spontaneous redecoration with shampoo, but your daughter is focused today on whether you are going to get her the sparkly sneakers that she wants. Forgiveness, the companion to *Compassion*, necessitates being able to move on. You don't stuff your feelings down until something else occurs so they can come roaring out; you genuinely move on. I bet you are wondering, "How in the world can I do this in the face of all the irritating and unresolved incidents that pop up each day?"

Parents know that it can be hard to forgive or move on when there is little or no accountability from their kids or genuine apologies. Their kids want to get it over with, say a quick sorry, and move on. The best option for you is to have a conversation with your son or daughter in a quiet moment, within their twenty-four-hour memory window, about what happened. Say what you need to say, see that it is heard, and ask for some accountability. When the conversation is over, you are finished; you reset and move forward.

Compassion creates alliances that are the heart of successful parenting. Drs. Edward Hallowell and Peter Jensen, in their book *Superparenting for ADD*, emphasize its importance:

It is the feeling of positive connection, a feeling of being cared for no matter what, a preverbal sense of belonging to something positive that's larger than yourself.[10]

This bond makes up the foundation for feeling close as a family and cooperating to face anything that comes your way.

3. Collaboration

"It doesn't work when my parents take things away because I will keep on asking for it or do other things that annoy them. Now that I'm in high school, I wish they would trust me more so we could talk about stuff."

—Jackson, age 14

COLLABORATION, AT ITS core, involves listening and mutual respect. This is not the feedback that children with ADHD usually receive. Typically, they are told that they are doing something wrong and they should do something else instead. Like all of us, kids with ADHD do not like it when other people tell them what to do, yet this is what they experience most of the time at school, at sports, at home. They don't really want other people's solutions to their challenges. They would rather avoid thinking about their problems if they can; they just want to get through them and be like everyone else. But they know they need help sometimes, and despite their protests, they probably want you to work with them to figure out what to do, how to make lasting changes.

When you collaborate with a youngster with ADHD, you are approaching problems with a "we" attitude instead of a "you" attitude. You are working together to address concerns that you both have. This means that you and your ADHD son or daughter acknowledge a problem but you, the parent, are not going to dictate the solutions. Here's what the "we" looks like in real life. You and your ten-year-old daughter agree that she has difficulty getting off the computer when her allotted thirty minutes on a school night are over. She is supposed to help you set the table when she is done. When you tell her that her time is up, you frequently have a major battle. She keeps asking for another minute to finish something while you are rushing around trying to finish cooking dinner and the table is still not set. You end up yelling at her, she screams and cries, and the meal arrives cold on the table. Sometimes the rest of the evening goes poorly too; bath and bedtime are stressful and unpleasant. You are both unhappy about this sequence of events. What can you do that is *Collaborative*?

The first thing is to have a conversation at a planned, specific time: a talk during which you both share what is happening in your family. Describe your frustrations, and then ask your child for her perspective. You share your unhappiness with yelling and your desire to have a nice, warm meal for the family. She tells you how hard it is to just get off the computer when she may not have finished the level of her game. You each talk, and you each listen. Identify areas of agreement about what isn't working. Then brainstorm ideas (hearing all of them without judgment), and choose one or two changes that you both think are possible to try. Perhaps you both agree that a timer, with a two-minute warning, would be a better signal than having you tell her several times to get off the computer. Perhaps she would like you to come and get her when the timer goes off and give her a hug when she stops. Perhaps she wants to make setting the table a game or a race to make it more fun. Together you agree to go to the drugstore and buy a cheap timer. You are willing to try these things for a week; then review them and see how they are working.

A family collaborative model of solving problems with kids with ADHD invites participation from your kids that fosters their cooperation. When you include your child in the process of addressing challenging behaviors and listen to what they are saying both verbally and behaviorally, you become their ally, not their adversary. They feel seen, heard, and valued. They are more likely to buy into whatever you are trying to accomplish because they are part of the process. Of course, there are crisis moments when safety and health concerns mean you step in and make the decisions. If your newly licensed teenage son comes home Saturday night after the curfew of the state's Cinderella driving laws, then you have to make a choice about giving him the car next weekend. If your six-year-old daughter wakes up in the middle of the night and watches television, then you have to intervene. These moments call for you to be the parent and adult that you are. I am not suggesting giving a youngster with ADHD authority over house rules or allowing them to determine the parameters of acceptable behavior.

Your children need you to be their parents, not their friends. They want limits, and they need direction. They learn about moral and ethical behavior from you and your values. The point here is to involve your child with ADHD in the process of creating solutions to challenges in their lives and in your family. You ask questions and listen to their answers, even when you don't agree. When your seven-year-old son tearfully tells you in the car on the way to school after another disastrous morning departure that mornings go better with Mama because she helps him more than you do, his complaint has valuable information. He is not just criticizing you. He is telling you that he is overwhelmed and can't follow through on what he knows he is supposed to do when you are in charge. Your job is to uncover exactly what your wife does that works better and decide if you can do something similar. This is more important than taking the remark personally, as a slight on your parenting skills. Then you negotiate a plan with him that allows him to feel supported and nurtures the independence you want him to have. You are conveying to him that his opinion and feedback matter. Together, you face the demons of disastrous mornings and create solutions that work.

4. Consistency

"We have a list on the refrigerator of our chores, but if my mom doesn't remind us to look at it, then sometimes we forget. How can we remember if she doesn't? Then she gets mad at us, which doesn't seem fair. Everybody forgets things. It's not such a big deal."   —Chloe, age 10

CONSISTENCY MEANS DOING what you say you are going to do over and over again—as best you can. It entails responding similarly to recurring behaviors and standing firm in the face of pressure to change. It doesn't mean being perfect or shaming yourself when you can't do it. It means writing yourself reminders about family agreements or ground rules if you need them and not giving consequences that you can't enforce. *Consistency* lies in sticking with a plan more often than not—while allowing for flexibility when you have no other options.

How do you build the foundation for *Consistency?* Start by establishing clear guidelines for behavior with your son or daughter that mean something to them and to you. *"When you come home from school, you have to eat your snack, as we have agreed on, and do your homework before computer games. Otherwise, your work doesn't seem to get finished."* *Consistency* depends on reliability. Kids with ADHD like to know what is coming, and predictability helps guide their choices. They learn from their experiences and start to understand that their actions have consequences. (This cause-and-effect relationship is exactly where their executive functioning skills can be weak.) If your daughter knows that she will lose her phone for the evening if she doesn't clean up her room by 6:00 p.m. per your earlier agreement but then you let her keep it because you want to be able to reach her, there is no *Consistency.* What she learns is that you don't mean what you say and that her actions have no consequences.

Consistent parents return to the plan when there are setbacks. Setbacks are part of any learning process and are not permanent derailments. They are teaching and learning opportunities for both you and your child. A setback occurs when a plan has been working and then—oops, there's a bump in the road. It happens when your sixteen-year-old daughter forgets her lunch after bringing it every day the week before. It's when your nine-year-old son refuses to pick up the LEGOs that are all over the living room after doing well with cleaning up for the past two weeks. These moments are not failures. They are days when you say: *"Oh well, no one is perfect. You can try again."* This is as true for them as it is for you: when there's a lapse, you all regroup instead of throwing out your game plan and declaring defeat.

> Setbacks are part of any learning process.

Exceptions to *Consistency* differ from being inconsistent. Exceptions are used when you want to send a clear message or when an accepted family rule can be broken because of an unplanned occurrence or an emergency. They don't permanently alter anything and don't mean that you are resorting to an erratic parenting style. Let's say that your seven-year-old daughter is allowed to watch thirty minutes of television each day while you make dinner. Yesterday, you accidentally dropped a glass on the floor, which needed to be cleaned up and prolonged the meal preparation, so you told her to watch an extra thirty minutes while you cleaned up and finished cooking. Then you told her why you made this choice. That's a purposeful exception and doesn't interfere with the general rules around television. When you give her an extra thirty minutes because you are tired of dealing with her and listening to her whining about how unfair your rules are, you are not making a purposeful exception. You are teaching her that pestering you enough can get her what she wants and that family rules can be easily broken.

Consistent limits are loving teaching tools. Kids learn how to tolerate disappointment, build resilience, and understand predictability.

> Consistent limits are loving teaching tools.

Consistent parents are compassionate but firm. Even though it may be hard to teach your kids what you struggle with personally, you do the best you can. Maybe you put yourself on the same program and work alongside them on a shared challenge. When your child is unhappy with your decisions, consistent parents acknowledge their feelings but do not give in to them unless it's an exception situation. You maintain your boundaries and stay the course because you know, in the long run, it's the only way to nurture a competent, independent adult.

5. Celebration

"I like dancing, cheerleading, reading, knitting, and crocheting. There's so many other things that I do that are productive and good about me. I love my family and my friends. I don't let ADHD get in the way of that anymore. My parents tell me when I do something good, and I can see that they are really happy for me. They also help me when I mess up. Now I say 'Okay, I'll just try harder next time,' and I move on."

—Ana, age 16

HAVE YOU EVER noticed how your child or teen with ADHD remembers the negative things people say to them more than the positive? While all humans are wired for remembering the negative more than the positive, (psychologists call this the negativity bias),[11] the minds of youngsters with ADHD are particularly vulnerable to holding on to what is "bad" about them, especially when they hear it from adults. Most likely, this pattern evolved over years of having been criticized for not remembering things, not doing things properly, not controlling themselves, etc. While our ancestors needed the ability to learn and remember lessons from tough experiences for survival, people today also need to learn how to retain lessons and feedback from good experiences to build morale and self-confidence. This is especially true for children and teens.

Self-esteem is a pivotal issue for young people with ADHD. Low self-worth contributes to depression and anxiety and leads to giving up, not caring, and failing. Positive experiences and rewarding relationships nourish inner strengths. In order for those good memories to outnumber the bad ones, they have to take up permanent residence in the brain's neural structures. Typically, this process begins with holding on to that good stuff in what is called your "working memory" long enough for it to be picked up by your short-term memory and then consolidated into your long-term memory. Since people with ADHD usually struggle with working-memory impairments, their brains often can't seem to hold on to information, positive or negative, long enough to transfer into long-term storage. With lots of repetition, time, and physical development, however, material can be effectively moved down the memory line. This is how learning occurs. For youth with ADHD who receive so many corrections and suggestions about what they could be doing differently, the negative messages often dominate their sense of who they are. Ideally, these would be offset by positive ones.

In more than twenty-five years of working with kids and teens with ADHD, I have seen one sad constant emerge: every single person has a deep-seated sense of shame about having ADHD and/or being "different" from their peers. Sometimes this shame is obvious: your daughter can't seem to make friends, can't write as well or easily as her peers, and spaces out at her desk at school. Sometimes it is more hidden: your son boasts about his accomplishments at video games and basketball but hides his tests from you or procrastinates endlessly before starting his homework. Either way, this shame often starts early in life and continues into adulthood. Many of them expect to hear negative comments about themselves. When I asked Kyle, age twelve, in a family session how he would like to receive feedback about his behavior, he interrupted before the words "good" or "constructive" came out and said, "*I don't. I don't want to hear it. I get sick of hearing it.*"

Celebration—positive feedback about what your child or teen is doing well in a given moment—can reduce this shame and build self-esteem. This is not fake praise or insincere positive comments that you dredge up because you know it's good for them to hear. *Celebration* is not cheerleading: it does not consist of superficial compliments or overemphasizing every good thing your child does. *Celebration* is based on observations, authenticity, and sensibility. It entails reframing what is seen as negative into something positive and noticing the small successes that your kids with ADHD may brush aside as unimportant. Ellis, age seventeen, explains how his family's encouragement assisted him:

> They are as patient as they can be. It definitely gets hard, and I'm sure my parents are mad at me a lot, for doing things I didn't intentionally mean to do. But they understand where it's coming from most of the time and just to help me along the best they can. They are never really mad at me, which would turn me off and make me not want to do something. It's always like, "Okay, here's what you did; let's improve it." That way I don't get too mad at myself.

Celebration entails giving positive comments that are direct and precise about something they have done. Dr. Barbara Fredrickson claims that experiencing positive emotions in a 3:1 ratio helps people lead more satisfying, productive lives.[12] Changing the ratio of positive statements to negative ones that you convey will set the foundation for this improved self-worth.

Pay attention to what you say and when. Praise works best when it is used for both efforts and accomplishments and is delivered immediately. Specific details are critical for making it meaningful to kids with ADHD because they often think concretely about things. It's more effective to say, *"You did a good job getting ready for bed tonight. I like that I only gave you two reminders,"* instead of *"Good job going to bed."* The former statement tells your child exactly what they did well and why; the second just tells them you liked what they did. There's no learning for them. Sometimes, just to facilitate that your positive comment is retained in their memory, you can ask them to repeat what they heard you say.

PARENT: "I really want to make sure that you understood what I said. Can you please repeat it?"
CHILD: "Do I have to?"
PARENT: "Yes."
CHILD: "Okay. *[Long sigh.]* You said you appreciated that I hung up my coat when I got home."

This type of exchange helps to build the neural pathways in working memory you are seeking to strengthen while at the same time fostering the parent/child connection. It's a double win.

Celebration also means encouraging your child to follow what interests them and brings them joy. One reason that video games are so appealing to kids with ADHD is that the goals for success are clear and attainable. Your son moves happily from one level to another, knowing what is asked of him and being able to achieve each challenge. Negotiating the ins and outs of school, after-school sports and activities, and jobs can be more convoluted and, at times, less rewarding. Identifying things that they enjoy (no matter how small) is crucial to building their self-esteem. If your fifteen-year-old likes acting, that's easy. If your ten-year-old son only likes Wizard101 online, that's more challenging. Try to find a silver lining in their ideas about what's fun if you don't really like them. For example, does your son want to have his friend over to play Wizard101? If so, this activity may not be your first choice for him but at least he's being social. Maybe you could play Monopoly with him after his hour of screen time is up. Someday your son might create his own computer game. Every child is passionate about something; some just need more assistance expressing it.

The ADHD Parenting Journey

The Five C's parenting approach described in this chapter helps strengthen understanding, personal responsibility, and connection among all family members. It has helped hundreds of families run smoother and get along better. It's a model based on the stories of children and teens who have told me what helps them and what limits them—both at home and beyond. They show how, when one member of a family is in distress, the whole family is affected and often distressed too.

As you read this book, you will learn how to establish a family in which self-regulation, empathy, and rewarding relationships are the norm, not the exception. Using calm, honest, and direct communication, including real listening, you will glean ways of working together to discover lasting solutions that appeal to everyone. Your ability to follow through on what you say and agreements you make, notice when things are going well, and support activities that appeal to kids with ADHD will improve dramatically as you integrate the Five C's model into your daily life.

Chapter 2

....

Understanding the ADHD Brain Makes All the Difference

"I've always heard people say, 'Oh, that person has ADD, they're crazy or whatever,' so I thought, 'Oh God, people are going to think I'm this out-of-control teenager that can't focus on anything.'"   —Emily, age 16

"My parents told me that I needed medication because I was really, really crazy and hyper. I was, like, uncontrollable and did things like yelling, shouting out in the classroom, and moving around a lot. . . . When they told me, I had no clue what the heck they were talking about. I still don't. I think it means something is wrong with me. I was worried if I had to get a shot. . . . I was really happy when I didn't."   —Carter, age 11

"Well, I'm not hyperactive, but I'm kind of always moving a little bit. You know, I'm either playing with something in my hands or shaking my leg or tappin'; more like absent-minded but not so much hyperactive. Even when I'm standin' or sittin' still, I'm swayin' or rockin'. I'm a constant jiggler."   —Henry, age 16

"I have a hard time paying attention. You get very distracted a lot, or you just start to daydream. My parents have to get very loud for me to hear them. Like when I am being reprimanded, I look out the window and see a bird and I comment on that and they get mad 'cause I interrupted them."   —Cara, age 10

What Is ADHD?

It's surprising how many kids with ADHD don't really understand what it is and how it affects them. With lots of myths and hearsay available on the internet or in casual conversations, kids can easily assume ADHD is just about being hyper, never paying attention, or lacking all *self-Control*. Most of the kids I talk to want to understand more about ADHD: how it functions in their bodies, how long it lasts, and what they can do about it. Most parents want the same. Kids usually turn to their parents with their questions even if their pediatricians or therapists have talked to them about things. They rely on you to explain and empathize in ways that make sense to them and guide them. Knowing what ADHD is and how it works makes explaining it to your son or daughter a lot easier. You will also be better prepared to make informed decisions about treatment and interventions.

When you and your child grasp the biology and facts about ADHD, it can be a source of hope, empowerment, and *Collaboration* instead of something mysterious. Connie and Yuan, parents of Ben, age eight, told me: *"A better understanding of how the brain works has helped a lot of times. We can see that what he does isn't as intentional as we thought."* In this chapter, I will give you an overview of the most important things you need to understand about ADHD to be an effective resource for your child or teen so you can advocate for their needs.

ADHD Is a Biologically Based Developmental
Disorder That Exists Around the World

While many people believe that ADHD is a new diagnosis, hyperactivity and impulsivity have been observed in children and adolescents and discussed in medical literature for more than two hundred years.[1] Once thought to be a form of early brain damage, the "hyperactive child syndrome" developed into its own medical category by the 1960s. Ten years later, when Dr. Virginia Douglas identified that children with these symptoms also lacked sustained attention and impulse control, it was renamed Attention Deficit Disorder (ADD) with or without hyperactivity. In 1987, it was changed again to Attention Deficit Hyperactivity Disorder (ADHD)[2] and is currently defined as a "persistent pattern of inattention and/or hyperactivity that interferes with functioning or development."[3] There are three types of ADHD: inattentive, hyperactive, and combined. ADHD is currently understood as a biologically based behavioral condition that impacts the management systems of the brain known as executive functions. It is not solely an American phenomenon; it has been found to exist around the world. Around 5 percent of the global population under eighteen years old[4] is believed to have ADHD, and inattention is the most common type.[5]

Despite global findings about ADHD, in this book, I will talk mostly about patterns and statistics among children and teens in the United States. ADHD affects American youngsters from a wide range of ethnic and socioeconomic groups. Approximately 11 percent of children and adolescents in the United States meet the criteria for ADHD.[6] Boys are diagnosed twice as often as girls, mostly with the hyperactivity/impulsivity type probably because they tend to be more impulsive and their behavior attracts more attention from adults.[7] Girls, though, appear to be diagnosed later. Boys and girls tend to experience similar symptoms and both respond equally well to treatment.[8] As children age, many of them continue to have ADHD, but it changes: hyperactive and impulsive symptoms usually fade away, and inattention remains.[9]

In the past ten years, the number of American children who have been diagnosed has risen steadily—alarming many parents, physicians, and mental health practitioners. This trend might be related to new ways of measuring ADHD, a true increase in the population, or overdiagnosis based on inaccurate conclusions.[10]

There is no single known cause of ADHD, but a number of factors can lead to it. The biggest one is genetic: it is highly inherited.[11] In fact, if you have one child with ADHD, there is a 33 percent chance that another child in your family will have it.[12] Sometimes ADHD can stem from brain injuries, reoccurring trauma, alcohol or drug abuse, or tobacco use during the mother's pregnancy or result from exposure to lead.[13] Despite myths to the contrary, it is *not* caused by diet (including food additives or sugar), too much television, or poor parenting. ADHD brains simply have different structures that make them unique. Let's take a look inside them.

ADHD Brains Are Wired Differently

ADHD shows up in myriad ways in children and teens. Just as no two kids with ADHD are identical, neither are their brains. These differences contribute to what makes each person's experience their own. Here's what some of the boys and girls I spoke to said about what it is like for them to have ADHD.

"It's a struggle. It's craziness going through my brain." —Ramon, age 12

"I have trouble thinking complete thoughts unless I say them out loud a lot of the time." —Brianna, age 17

"I can't remember. It comes into my mind and then it just melts. I can't hold on to it." —Skyler, age 15

"I have to train myself to just focus on one thing and really, really try hard not to focus on the other things going on." —Taylor, age 12

"Well, your hands are looking for something to do and then they start to do whatever they find and then you pay attention to what they find."

—Levi, age 9

"If I'm not really engaged in something, I start nodding off. Really, I can sleep anywhere, and have. Sometimes I fall asleep in school."

—Darren, age 15

Fidgeting, moving body parts, sleep problems, and trouble staying focused are all manifestations of the ADHD brain. Despite individual differences, there are basic patterns that most people with ADHD share and are important for you to know.

The human brain begins growing in utero and reaches its full development in young adulthood. Its regions (called lobes) develop from the back to the front and from the inside out.

REGIONS OF THE BRAIN AND THEIR FUNCTIONS

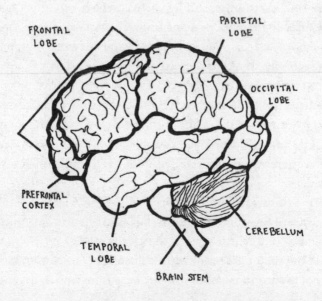

The brain is composed of billions of cells—neurons—that are separated from one another by gaps called synapses. These neurons communicate with each other via chemical messages with electrical charges. When a message arrives at a gap, it cannot move through it to the nearby cell without the help of transport chemicals called neurotransmitters. Imagine that your brain is like New York City a hundred years ago, bustling with activity day and night. Let's say a shoe business in one building wanted to send an urgent message to the hat factory across the street. The shoe clerk (i.e., the sender) would take it outside and meet a messenger at the door, who then would cross the street and hand-deliver the message to a hat clerk (i.e., the receiver). Neurotransmitters are our brain's messengers, and they deliver messages across the streets of our brains—the synaptic gaps—millions of times a day.

Thanks to the advent of recent technologies such as PET and CT scans, MRIs and EEGs, it is now possible to see inside the brain and observe its structure and activity. Researchers have found significant differences in the brains of children and teens with ADHD compared to their non-ADHD peers. First, the size and volume of certain brain areas are smaller, thinner, and less active, which can affect maintaining and directing attention, managing behaviors and emotions, operating memory systems, and communicating between regions of the brain.[14] Secondly, the ADHD brain matures more slowly. There can be a lag of up to three years, especially in an important area of the frontal lobe (right behind the forehead) named the prefrontal cortex. This area is the last part of the brain to fully develop, reaching maturity in non-ADHD brains around age twenty-five. What's important to remember is that over time, ADHD brains catch up in their structural development.

But this is only part of the story of how the ADHD brain works. Let's go back to those messengers in the brain—neurotransmitters. Just like too much or too little salt can drastically affect a recipe, our brains need just the right number of neurotransmitters to run smoothly and effectively. Neurotransmitters called dopamine and norepinephrine are the most influential in ADHD challenges because they directly influence attention, thinking, sleep, moods, and movements.[15] Dopamine affects pleasure, rewards, motivation, and satisfaction; norepinephrine is related to alertness, sleep, and energy. They are the couriers that shuttle messages between the sender for the shoe business and the receiver for the hat business—between one neuron and the next. In ADHD brains, though, the hat receiver is impatient and cannot wait for the message to arrive. She charges into the street, grabs the messenger with the dispatch, and quickly whisks him across the street too soon. The messenger, for several technical reasons I won't explain here, needed that extra time in the street to do his job. In some ADHD brains, there aren't enough couriers in the first place.[16] A similar thing happens with norepinephrine.[17] Either way, ADHD brains wind up with lower amounts of these neurotransmitters than they need. That is why you see kids struggling with paying attention, managing intense feelings, being overly energetic, or not sleeping well.

Everyone with ADHD Has Executive Functioning Challenges

Executive functions are a set of complex brain functions needed to achieve and accomplish goals that exist all over the brain but predominantly in the prefrontal cortex. While they are not specific to one part of the brain, they usually refer to how the prefrontal cortex manages the other systems of the brain. Although there is no single, accepted definition of executive functions, what *is* clear is that you need them to *execute* tasks in the service of *accomplishing* a goal. Let's think of the prefrontal cortex like a director who oversees a major film. She coordinates all aspects of the film to create the version she envisions: the sound, the lighting, the sets, the costumes, the actors, etc. If she needs more volume, she asks for that; if she needs fake rain, she requests it. She makes things happen for a good film. Similarly, humans need executive functions to create, plan, and accomplish tasks; to solve problems; and to handle feelings and behavior. They are the brain director of how you do stuff. Executive functions help you to decide what order to clean the kitchen or what you want to say in a letter: they make things happen by telling the right parts of your brain to get busy.

Let's take a closer look at these executive functioning (EF) skills and how they relate to ADHD. I have synthesized a few approaches into a developmental model to help parents best understand and impart them to their children.[18]

- *Inhibition* (self-regulation and restraint)
- *Emotion* (dealing with frustration and big feelings)
- *Action* (getting started, organizing stuff, estimating time, planning and prioritizing things)
- *Energy* (staying alert, perseverance, speed of processing information)
- *Recall* (being able to hold information in your head and doing something with it—such as remembering a phone number and then dialing it; relating current information with something from the past and applying it to the present or future)
- *Focus* (staying on task, smoothly shifting to new things, setting and accomplishing goals)
- *Self-Evaluation* (self-awareness and self-monitoring)

These skills can be divided into two categories.[19] **Hot skills** are the ones we use consciously in our daily lives—inhibition, emotion, and action—and they tend to be related to behavior.

EXECUTIVE FUNCTIONING "HOT" SKILLS

....

Executive Functioning Skill	How It Looks in Kids
INHIBITION	
Self-regulation	Stops and thinks before doing or saying something; exerts control over body and speech in order to act appropriately in family, social, and school situations.
EMOTION	
Managing feelings	Regulates feelings, especially anger and anxiety; has patience and tolerates frustration; doesn't get upset about little things.
ACTION	
Organization	Keeps bedroom, locker, notebook, etc. clean and neat; finds things when needed and rarely loses items.
Time management	Does things on time and meets deadlines; can correctly estimate how long something will take; doesn't procrastinate a lot.
Planning and prioritizing	Figures out a method for getting things done; knows where to start on big projects and doesn't find them overwhelming; readily decides what is most important when there are multiple things to do.
Initiating	Gets started on chores or homework and finishes them efficiently, often without direction and excessive reminding; motivated to begin a task.

COOL SKILLS ARE more abstract and unconscious—energy, recall, focus, and self-evaluation—and they relate mostly to thinking.

EXECUTIVE FUNCTIONING "COOL" SKILLS

··

Executive Functioning Skill	How It Looks in Kids
ENERGY	
Alertness	Able to stay awake and engaged when doing a boring activity.
Perseverance	Shows consistent efforts when trying to do something routine, new, or challenging.
Processing information	Understands and applies new information efficiently.
RECALL	
Working memory	Holds one piece of information in their head while doing different things; recalls things from the past and applies them to the present or future; remembers and follows steps in a series of directions.
FOCUS	
Sustained attention	Manages attention and resists distractions when faced with a task.
Shift/Flexibility	Able to shift focus onto something else (e.g., stops playing computer games and sits down for dinner); goes with the flow; adjusts to changing situations.
Goal-oriented persistence	Sets a goal, stays focused on it, and returns to the task right after an interruption; sticks with a task over time regardless of its length, and pace of personal processing speed.
SELF-EVALUATION	
Self-awareness	Possesses awareness of how personal behavior impacts other people; responds positively to feedback; shows appropriate judgment; wants to learn from mistakes.

THESE SKILLS OFTEN work in tandem for maximum efficiency and success.

EF skills unfold developmentally as people use them, but not in a linear fashion. In kids with ADHD, this happens more slowly than it does for their peers because of the differences in their brain maturity. That's why they usually have EF challenges such as procrastination, disorganization, forgetfulness, impulsivity, and inattentiveness.[20] Often what occurs to some kids to do without thinking can be harder for your child with ADHD. The director cannot always get her cast and crew to work together as effectively as she would like because they may not all be on the set at the same time. When they finally arrive, she can call, "Action," and, voilà, your son learns how to pour milk into his cereal without spilling. Of course, most kids with ADHD have EF strengths as well as challenges. Your teenage son may keep a messy room but be punctual. Your fifth-grade daughter may forget her lunch but will sit down to do her homework right after school. Learning to rely more on these strengths while strategizing ways to bolster the slower developing skills is an important part of what this book is all about.

The Five C's of ADHD parenting targets EF challenges and offers you clear and effective ways to improve them. *Self-Control* helps with self-regulation, managing feelings, alertness, and resisting distractions. *Compassion* helps everyone deal with big feelings and teaches self-awareness too. *Collaboration* enables you and your child to address EF challenges like organization, planning, or time management by working together to create systems for their improvement. As you do your best to stick with these programs and notice your child's efforts, you use *Consistency* to build goal-directed persistence. *Celebration* increases initiative and self-evaluation through acknowledgment: "*I like how you remember to put your lunch box on the counter when you get home from school now*" or "*You seem to be putting your clothes in your hamper more than you used to.*" You teach the skills and cheer as they become a natural part of daily living.

Without using the terminology we've just discussed, youngsters described to me how well-aware they are of difficulties related to EF skills. As Liam, age nine, talks about how an orchestra rehearsal went, you see his struggles with self-regulation (impulse control), managing feelings (worry), organization (messiness), and self-awareness (how interruptions affect others):

> In orchestra rehearsal, I got in trouble. First, I couldn't find the right music. Then, I stood up to ask when the performance was and Mr. Mitchell said to sit down. But I needed to know. I have a basketball game this weekend, and I wanted to make sure they weren't at the same time. He told me to sit down again or get sent to the principal. I don't know why he wouldn't just answer my question. Then he told my mom and I got in trouble again.

In addition to making others wait for him while he locates the proper music, Liam is nervous that the two things he has to do will conflict and can't wait until after the rehearsal to figure this out. Is he worried about what will happen? Sure. Is he afraid that he won't remember later? Maybe. Does he feel bad about making everyone wait for him? Likely. Later he told me: *"Today was a bad day. . . . Every day that I don't get into trouble is a good day."*

Destiny, age fifteen, has parents who are divorced and share custody. She and her brother, Jack, spend alternate weeks at each house:

> I hate switching places. It's so chaotic. I wish I could just live in one place. I never unpack my clothing or anything. It's literally living out of a suitcase. My backpack is so heavy. I have to take extra stuff to school so I make sure I have it. Half the time one of them [her parents] has to bring things anyway. My brother has a major meltdown if he forgets his Xbox, which he does, like, every time.

Destiny (and her brother, too) have to wrestle daily with moving back and forth from one house to the other. Keeping track of her stuff, thinking ahead to what she will need, remembering where something is and taking it with her, and dealing with the frustration of not having her life in one place is hard for any child with divorced parents. For kids like Destiny and Jack, it can seem impossible.

At first, all parents act as their child's external EF skills. You dress them; you feed them; you bathe them. Quickly, they learn how to follow you around with their eyes and cry for what they want. As they become toddlers and preschoolers, they gain control over their bodies and begin to understand the order of things: putting their pants on one leg at a time followed by their shoes; adding toothpaste on the brush before putting it in their mouth and waiting for the freshly baked cookies to cool before eating them. They develop and use language, move from diapers to toileting, learn to follow basic directions, take turns with peers, and even wait patiently for the Popsicle you are digging out of the freezer. By elementary school, EF skills strengthen as kids begin to create and follow routines, demonstrate greater emotional and physical *self-Control*, stick with tasks until they are finished, and plan for things like birthday parties. Of course, you still provide them with directions, but you don't do everything for them anymore.

The preteen and adolescent years are the period when developing and applying EF skills kicks into a higher gear. In middle school, your preteen now has more independence. Kids navigate a complex schedule with different classes and teachers, shifting peer relationship dynamics, and increased responsibility for homework and outside interests like sports, music, or drama. These can be taxing on their burgeoning EF skills. By high school, homework, activities, sports, part-time jobs, and possibly college applications can be especially stressful on kids' burgeoning EF skills. For parents, it's really tricky to find the right balance between guidance and letting go. Sometimes, your son or daughter will enlist your assistance and appreciate your support. At other times, they reject your help and prefer to go it alone. They may meet with success, or they may not. The scaffolding (support) that you provide along the way is not only essential parenting for *all* children but is especially significant for parenting kids with ADHD. You should expect to support their fledgling director longer than you think as they wind their way toward maturity in their late twenties.

Working closely with teachers and coaches on specific EF skills moves this process along more successfully because your child is getting similar messages in all domains of their life.

It can be very frustrating when your nephew, at ten, makes his bed every morning and comes downstairs for breakfast without being told while your twelve-year-old daughter leaves her bed in a heap, has trouble getting dressed in a timely manner, and needs five reminders (the last one yelled) to come down for her bagel. Take a deep breath and remember that different brains mature and learn EF skills at different paces. Aiding your daughter in mastering the sequence of the morning routine ultimately means you go from telling her what to do to her telling herself what to do. This takes time because internalizing self-talk in youngsters with ADHD takes longer. You may tell your daughter to grab her backpack and stuff for lacrosse and get in the car and hear her talking to herself about what she is going to do. This is a good thing: she is building her EF skills for private speech that will guide her actions. When she arrives at the car with her backpack and lacrosse stick in tow, she is showing you how that self-talk led her there.

> Different brains mature and learn EF skills at different paces.

ADHD Often Brings Company:
Learning Differences and Mental Health Issues

Many kids with ADHD also have other issues. Sometimes they have challenges with reading, writing, or math, commonly referred to as learning disabilities. Perhaps they struggle with anxiety, depression, or disruptive behaviors, often referred to as mental health disorders. Maybe they have some of each. While terms such as "disabilities" and "disorders" are useful from a clinical or educational perspective for identifying a specific problem and obtaining intervention and treatment services, they can sound negative and discouraging to kids and parents. Vince, age fifteen, told me:

> I feel like when people hear the word "disorder," it makes them feel like they're not equal to people. Or you're sick and you're not? Your brain's just different.... "Disability." I don't like that word either. When I hear the word "disability," I think you have an un-ability to do things. Which isn't true. No matter what you have, no matter who you are, you can do things.

These clinical terms don't foster the positive mind-set that helps kids (and adults) with growth and change. For this reason, I prefer using the general terms of "learning differences" and "mental health issues" as much as possible when talking with folks in my office. In this section, you will gain general information about these issues to see if they are present in your son or daughter.

ADHD makes it difficult for kids (and adults) to access and use what they know. They have the information, but they just can't retrieve it or apply it efficiently and effectively. The more severe their EF challenges, the higher the likelihood for learning differences.[21] In the early years of elementary school, a child masters reading first and then reads to learn. She learns to count and then uses numbers for mathematics and problem-solving. She masters the technique of writing and then writes to express herself. As children get older, these fundamental academic areas, which were initially learning goals themselves, now become ways to learn about other subjects like science, social studies, and foreign languages. They are directly influenced by the executive functions discussed in the previous section. Working memory (the ability to hold a piece of information in the brain and do something with it like listen and write notes simultaneously); cognitive processing speed (the rate at which our brains absorb and understand information); and fine motor skills (handwriting and manipulating small objects) are used when learning academic subjects. Time management, planning, prioritizing, goal persistence, and impulse control help a student get through the day and complete projects, papers, and tests. Whether or not your child or teen qualifies for a learning disability, these EF skills—fundamental to the learning process—are already affected by ADHD and require training to fortify them.

Learning disabilities (LD) occur quite commonly in kids with ADHD, anywhere between 45 percent and 71 percent of the time.[22] Struggles with academic skills and processing difficulties are found most often in the areas of reading, math, and written expression, as well as developmental motor coordination. Your daughter may read slowly or skim sentences too quickly without retaining their meaning. Your son may struggle with learning math facts or have difficulty writing down his ideas about a book for a paper. When a student receives an LD diagnosis, it means that they are performing below their intellectual capability in certain areas and not achieving as would be expected for peers of the same age. Like ADHD, learning disabilities are often neurologically based, tend to run in families, and cannot be linked to physical ailments like hearing, vision, or physical problems,[23] although the latter three certainly affect the ability to learn.

Let's look at each one more closely. Reading disabilities, including dyslexia, occur in 33 to 45 percent of kids with ADHD and refer to a child's difficulty in accurate and fluent reading despite having the intelligence and motivation to do so.[24] Specific reading challenges vary from person to person, but they should improve with direct instruction.[25] Mathematics disabilities (dyscalculia) include problems with things like memorizing math facts and recalling them automatically, numerical or spatial math concepts, and math symbols. Math challenges have been found to occur in 20 to 30 percent of children and teens with ADHD, and they also may respond well to accommodations.[26] Developmental motor coordination problems reflect more than clumsiness; they refer to fine and gross motor difficulties seen in handwriting or hand-eye coordination and can improve with occupational therapy.

By far, writing is the most frequent learning difference for these kids, two or more times more common than reading or math.[27] That's because the executive functioning challenges in most ADHD brains make essential writing skills like organization, working memory, attention to detail, perseverance, and planning all the more difficult. Handwriting issues can further complicate tasks. From creative stories to book reports to research papers, our kids are writing all day long, and, if they have a written expression disability, they will significantly benefit from direct instruction, assistance, and accommodations. Kimiko, age sixteen, describes her struggle with organization: *"There's no organization when I start writing. I have to go through it piece by piece."* Logan, age eleven, wrestles with production: *"I sit there for fifteen minutes and not have a single thing on my paper because I'm thinking, I'm thinking. And then when the teacher says, 'Just write something,' I can't get more than three words out. It's bad."* In Chapter 6 you will hear more about what students have to say about reading, math, and writing and explore how the Five C's can help them.

Many children and teens with ADHD also deal with mental health issues, such as depression, anxiety, or disruptive behavior. When things like sadness, irritability, worry, and aggression happen more often and more intensely than is expected for a youngster of a similar age, then please talk to your pediatrician and/or a therapist about your concerns. Almost half of all kids with ADHD (hyperactivity or combined types) have disruptive behavioral issues—atypical patterns of high irritability, negativity, aggression, temper outbursts, and arguing that cause them serious difficulties at home and at school.[28] Carter, age eleven, explains: *"I lose my temper. I get seriously angry. I break stuff, I kick stuff, I throw stuff. I run around screaming."* Martina, age seventeen, shares: *"There are bubbles of big things inside of me. Sometimes, they radiate out and sometimes they explode."*

Angry, out-of-control outbursts like these are upsetting and invariably push people away. They can contribute to the peer rejection that kids with ADHD often experience.[29] Professional assistance can aid everyone in understanding and coping with these intense behaviors.

Mood disorders such as anxiety and depression, while less common statistically, show up at my office just as frequently.[30] Anxiety can increase agitation, distractedness, and impulsivity and make things seem worse than they are. It affects life at home, life at school, and life with friends. With excessive worry, irrational fears, and restlessness, anxious kids with ADHD can seem overly vigilant. Anxiety also worsens common sleep issues for these kids, as Mara, age ten, and her mother, Diane, explain:

> DIANE: "Nighttime is a major challenge for us. Mara wants someone to lay down with her. She is afraid of the dark and being alone. You name it. It takes so long. My rope is short on patience, but I think I stay with her too long."
> MARA: "My friends kinda just go to bed. I wish I could be like them. I need company to go to sleep. I can't do it on my own. My mind is going and going and going."

Mara's fear of not sleeping unfortunately becomes a self-fulfilling prophecy that keeps her up more nights than she, or her parents, would like. Despite her best efforts, she can't soothe herself. She needs help with *self-Control* and *Compassion*: learning to calm herself down so she can get the rest she (and her family) needs.

Depression feeds on negative messages that kids with ADHD give themselves or hear from others. Hopelessness, shame, disappointment, and low self-worth are typical ways that kids signal they are feeling depressed. They can also sleep too much, act irritable or agitated, cry, spend more time alone, or think more slowly than usual. Signs of excessive worry, sleep problems, and depressed moods benefit from professional help. I don't want to frighten you, but the research shows that untreated mood issues (and acting-out behavioral issues) raise the risk for substance abuse among teens with ADHD.[31] Difficulties with managing feelings appropriately, something that is tough for a lot of kids with ADHD because it's an executive functioning skill, can make all these mental health issues more complicated and serious.[32] If this is the case with your child or teen, help is available. Speak to your doctor or a therapist. We'll look at how the Five C's can help with overwhelming feelings and acting-out behaviors in Chapter 10.

A Thorough, Accurate Diagnosis Is Essential

Receiving a professional diagnosis of ADHD and understanding what that means for your child or teen is absolutely critical before making decisions about what you are going to do. Ideally, the person working with you should understand ADHD and learning disabilities, since they go together so frequently. The current scientific literature recommends that kids who are diagnosed with ADHD also be screened for their writing, math, and reading skills and other coexisting conditions.[33] As a first step, it's important to rule out other conditions that can masquerade as ADHD: developmental delays; autistic spectrum disorders; learning disabilities; mental health diagnoses such as anxiety, depression, trauma, or bipolar or obsessive-compulsive disorder; and physical issues such as brain injury, seizures, thyroid disease, or sleep disorders. Screening for some of these medical issues can be done easily with your pediatrician and are worth asking them about. The others should be assessed in a psychological evaluation for ADHD.

Generally, there are three common routes leading to an ADHD diagnosis: through your pediatrician, through a psychotherapist, or by the child's school. Whichever route you choose, make sure the person is very familiar with ADHD and doesn't give a diagnosis without conducting a thorough personal and family history (based on interviews with you and your child) and without giving you some rating scales to fill out. Most parents want clear information that shows their child has ADHD before embarking on a treatment plan (especially one that includes medication), and testing can provide this corroboration.

Testing can also help you understand how your child's brain works in greater depth, how they are performing academically, and what is going on emotionally. It can identify learning differences as well as confirm mental health issues. Only certified school psychologists and licensed psychologists (or neuropsychologists) are trained to do these types of evaluations. One option is to go through your public school system for an evaluation. Or you may decide to see someone in private practice. While this testing can be expensive, some of the costs are often covered by insurance companies. It is important that whoever does the testing includes thorough assessments of EF skills. The Behavior Rating Inventory for Executive Function (BRIEF), Barkley Deficits in Executive Functioning Scales–Children and Adolescents (BDEFS-CA), and the Comprehensive Executive Function Inventory (CEFI) are some of the best tools for assessing many of the executive functioning skills in daily life that standard psychological tests may miss. The Executive Skills Structured Interviews found in *Executive Skills in Children and Adolescents: A Practical Guide for Assessment and Intervention* by Peg Dawson and Richard Guare are also extremely useful. Ask the evaluator to speak to people at your child's school who know them so their input can be reflected in any conclusions as well. The information you gain from these reports, including recommendations or things to do at school and home, can be *tremendously* helpful to everyone—parents, kids, teachers, physicians. Sometimes the reports can seem overly negative because they focus more on weaknesses than strengths. This can be discouraging, but it doesn't have to be. Look at the report as a tool that provides you with new, detailed information about your child or student and how their mind works so you can assist them more effectively.

This chart lays out the three pathways for an ADHD diagnosis:

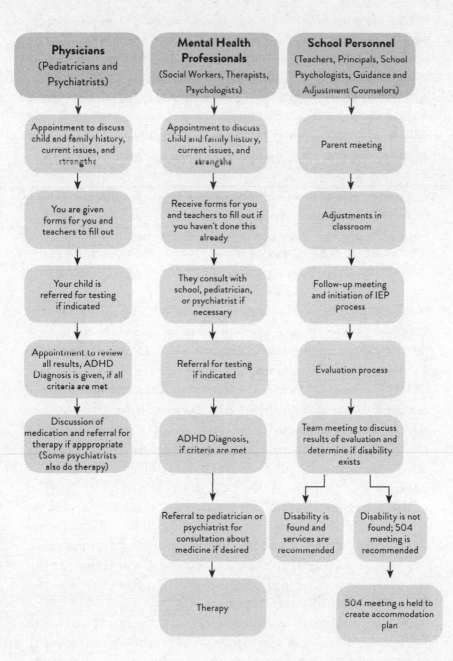

The first path to an accurate diagnosis frequently begins in your pediatrician's office. If you have been noticing that your child is struggling at school and/or at home and you think the problems might be related to attention, you may have already started doing some research on ADHD (books, internet, conversations with friends) to see whether the descriptions fit. If so, you will likely talk with your pediatrician, who often has known your child since infancy and has been giving you sage advice for years. Victoria, the mother of Nona (age nine), remembers:

> We read *Delivered from Distraction* and went to see our pediatrician, Dr. Yvonne. She thought that possibly, given our description, ADHD might be going on. She referred us to someone who could do testing. Dr. Yvonne knew something about ADHD, who to refer us to, and didn't make it sound extraordinary. We didn't feel stupid for asking questions.

Ideally, your pediatrician will be as helpful as Nona's doctor. Like Dr. Yvonne, your physician will talk with you to get a sense of what is going on (including gathering a developmental and family history) and will give you some rating scales for you and the school to fill out. The Vanderbilt, Conners, and Behavior Assessment System for Children scales are commonly used for assessing ADHD. Your pediatrician may also want to speak to someone at your child's school or may recommend a psychological or educational evaluation—in other words, the "testing" I just described. Based on those results and everything else that has been gathered, your pediatrician will then decide on whether to make an ADHD diagnosis. Symptoms and difficulties must occur in at least two settings of a child's life to obtain the diagnosis. The pediatrician will likely discuss with you treatment options such as therapy, medication, coaching, or tutoring. They might also refer you to a psychiatrist or psychiatric nurse specialist to explore further any diagnostic issues and additional questions about medication.

The second route to an accurate diagnosis lies with a mental health professional who may or may not be already providing counseling to you or your child. Perhaps you brought your child to see this therapist because you suspected that your child has ADHD. Perhaps you brought them there to address another concern and he or she is wondering about ADHD. Like your pediatrician, a mental health professional will usually collect a thorough developmental and family history and may give you forms to fill out before making a diagnosis. Often, they will consult with your pediatrician, your child's classroom teachers, or other school personnel. If the therapist or psychiatrist has additional concerns or thinks more data is warranted, they may also recommend testing, especially to rule out any learning issues. Otherwise, they can diagnose ADHD themselves.

The third path to diagnosis is usually with your child's school. Many parents first hear about their child's challenges with concentration and focus with a note or a call from a teacher, typically in the elementary years but sometimes not until middle or high school. Through casual and/or formal meetings with the teacher, principal, or counselor, you may learn that your son or daughter is struggling at school with things like impulse control, focus, remembering things, peer interactions, organization, or emotional meltdowns. These can be hard conversations. Hopefully, they will lead to adjustments in the classroom and in homework to see if these can adequately assist your child. While public schools in the United States are able to identify concerns about attention, concentration, and memory, they cannot legally diagnose ADHD since it is considered a health issue. However, they are mandated under the Individuals with Disabilities Education Act (IDEA) to assess students for possible learning disabilities and to determine if the learning disability is preventing the student from making adequate progress.[34] School assessments frequently include a speech and language evaluation, an evaluation of academic skills and progress, and a psychological evaluation. Similar to private testing, an evaluation through the school can provide you with rich information about your child with the additional benefit of direct contact with their educational environment.

The assessment process is followed by a team meeting to determine the type(s) of special needs your child may have and whether they are eligible for mandated services. If they are, those are outlined in an Individualized Education Plan (IEP); if not, the team may recommend a 504 accommodation plan (named from Section 504 of the Rehabilitation Act of 1973), which will be designed at a later time, or perhaps no services at all.[35] If the team writes a behavior plan for your son or daughter, make sure you are in it. You want to be providing similar reinforcers and cues. As I stated earlier, while ADHD itself cannot be diagnosed by public schools (but can be flagged as a probability), many kids with ADHD also have reading, writing, or math difficulties that qualify as learning differences or disorders. These types of special needs *can be* diagnosed by the school, and if they are blocking academic progress, support services will be provided. The bottom line is, even though ADHD directly affects learning, because it's classified as a health disorder, it must be diagnosed by physicians or mental health professionals, who then send or present their findings to the school.

Medication Can Help, but Pills Don't Teach Skills

Figuring out what you want to do about your child's ADHD is a complicated process. With younger children, parents make decisions themselves about medication, therapy, tutoring, and school interventions. Kids usually go along easily with their parents' choices and are willing to try something and see what happens. Of course, they also have opinions that are important to consider, but by and large you are in charge. Around middle and high school, though, things get trickier. If teens do not buy into whatever treatment program you've created, all your excellent support and thoughtful ways of helping them will be fruitless. Information fuels cooperation and *Collaboration* for adolescents. Sharing what you've learned and having calm, honest conversations about living with ADHD can lead to a successful outcome for everyone.

In 1999, the largest study of treatment options for ADHD kids, the Multimodal Treatment Study (MTA), was conducted to look at which types of services were most effective. It examined four different options:

medication management, family therapy, a combination of these two, and a referral to community resources. Combined treatment of medication and therapy showed distinct advantages over medication alone, but the combination or medication alone were both more effective options than therapy alone.[36] Since then, follow-up studies have confirmed these findings.[37] Unfortunately, many kids with ADHD are given medication but don't go to therapy or coaching.[38] Overprescribing and the misuse of methylphenidate (commonly known as Ritalin, Concerta, Metadate, and Focalin) and amphetamine salts (commonly known as Adderall, Dexedrine, and Vyvanse) happens too often without solid information from a good diagnosis. But, when given appropriately, they work immediately and in carefully calibrated time frames. They also improve how various brain networks communicate with one another and, despite myths to the contrary, have been well researched over the past eighty years. Recent studies looked at the long-term negative effects of ADHD medications on height and weight and did not find anything significant.[39] These medications don't carry over from one day to the next: if you don't take them, then they're not in your body. They can be stopped quickly if any side effects occur. Nonstimulant medications like Strattera, Intuniv, and Wellbutrin take longer to work, remain in your system from day to day, and are similarly well researched.

Medication is a personal decision, and I decided long ago not to tell parents what to do. I send people to their pediatrician or a psychiatrist for medical advice. What I can tell you is that most parents prefer to start with behavioral changes, and if those don't work enough, they will consider medication. Many parents of younger kids tend to be reluctant to use medication, instead hoping therapy will improve things. If it becomes clear that their child really needs medication, especially for school, then they will usually consider it. Parents of adolescents who have been struggling for a while tend to be more willing to do both, particularly if the teen is also frustrated and everybody wants to improve school success.

Therapy works best with specific targets—such as social issues, disruptive behaviors, and distressing emotions—and plans that utilize incentives.[40] Since kids don't grow up in a Petri dish, I recommend family counseling along with individual work to assist parents, especially of younger children, in fostering these changes.[41] While individual therapy can be quite valuable for children and teens with ADHD, without parental participation, kids don't get the scaffolding they need for those all-important EF skills. Henry, age sixteen, says:

> I honestly think the time I've spent doing these kind of life coach therapy things, on my own and when my parents came, has probably been much more important than the medication. I mean, the medication has also helped to an incalculable degree. But I think the time with my therapist and my parents has probably been the most important thing.

In addition to talk therapy, **meditation** has been found to improve focus, attention, and self-regulation.[42] Many therapists are regularly incorporating it into their work and, similarly, schools are now including it in their curriculum. Research on the benefits of exercise has emphasized the importance of **movement** for children and teens with ADHD, while neuro-feedback therapy seems to have limited effects.[43]

If you decide to try medication, with or without therapy, remember that it is not a cure; it's more like eyeglasses. You can see without them, but you see a whole lot better with them on. Rose, age seventeen, explains: *"I don't feel like I've changed. I feel enhanced. It's like getting glasses for my brain. . . . I packed and moved myself with lists and everything, and for the first time ever, I didn't do it last minute."* ADHD medications improve learning disabilities and help with mental health issues because they work on areas of the brain that involve focus, processing speed, working memory, and general efficiency.[44] But keep in mind that pills alone will not teach the EF skills that ADHD kids most need to learn. When medications work, they increase a child's availability to learn those skills, but without direct instruction, those skills simply won't improve on their own. My rule of thumb for parents when considering medication is to gauge how much your child or teen is struggling and being held

Pills alone will not teach the EF skills that ADHD kids most need to learn.

back from reaching their full potential because of ADHD *right now*. Thinking about whether your son or daughter will be taking medication five or ten years down the line isn't helpful. Stick with the present and near future and what can make a difference now. That's enough.

Speaking with kids about the topic of ADHD medications revealed the mixed opinions you would expect. It helps some of them and not others. Side effects such as poor appetite, headaches, and trouble falling asleep really bothered some kids, while others were willing to make any possible trade-offs for better concentration in school. Some of them didn't know what the medication was for or what it did in their bodies. Some of them disliked swallowing pills and how it made them feel. Others are grateful for the positive ways the medication helped.

"I have the ADHD. I was told I needed to take a pill, and I really didn't want to take it. I started to like it, and I sort of stopped being a bit hyper but not all hyper. It made me not get in trouble anymore, slow down and calm down and relax more often. I like that."   —Christian, age 9

"I remember when I first took it, it was a big change, because I physically got sick from it. Just my attention span and everything was a lot better. But I could barely eat anything that day. I was hungry inside, in my stomach, but nothing looked good. . . . It made it hard to work, but I still got a lot done. I decided I wanted to get off it, because I didn't feel natural."

—Carlos, age 15

"It works really well for me. The static goes out of my brain. Like, I can complete a thought without interrupting myself. Growing up I was never really the best at anything. Then this year, I am getting straight A's my freshman year of high school. That's cool."   —Ana, age 14

"I guess it makes me pay attention more, and stop fidgeting, and listen, and be able to take tests at school. It keeps me calmer then I remember things better. I don't like taking it because I don't like swallowing things without chewing them. I even chew water which is weird."   —Tiana, age 9

"Some days I don't take it. I just want to be myself. People tell me, 'Did you take your medication today? Because you seem a little hyper and a little wired,' and I'm like, 'No, I didn't.' If I forget, it's kind of embarrassing, but some days I just want to be free and think about everything."

—Emily, age 16

GIVEN THESE UPS and downs of taking medication, talking openly about this decision with your kids, your pediatrician, and/or a therapist keeps everyone on the same page and helps kids feel as though they know more about what is going on.

Moving Forward

What does all this information mean for you and your son or daughter? The goal of this chapter has been to arm you with science, facts, and hope. Dispelling myths about ADHD based on real information leads to understanding what it is and what it causes. You become a resource for your child and for your family. You are better able to empathize with what is going on in your child's brain and body and explain it to them so that they don't feel "crazy" like Carter told us at the beginning of this chapter. This builds *self-Control* and *Compassion*. As your child watches you advocate for them with more confidence and knowledge, they can begin to do the same: speaking matter-of-factly about their unique ways of thinking, learning, and feeling with their teachers, other caring adults, and even their friends. Together you discuss the possible interventions (with you having the final say) and then *Collaborate* to help them succeed. This nurtures *Consistency*. When the choices you've made and the help you've sought bring about improvements, you'll notice that your child is happier: *Celebration*. The Five C's assists you every step of the way.

Chapter 3

·············

Accepting the ADHD Brain You Have

MEET MAYA, AGE 13: *"Having ADHD is like a thorn in my butt, but I laugh anyway."*

Mom told me in second grade I had ADHD. It actually made me feel kind of special. I was like, "OOOH, I have ADHD; now I'm cooler than everyone else." I made up a nickname for it: "bullet brain," because of skiing.

It was my first time at Lone Mountain, and Mom decided to put me on a steep run called Freedom Trail. I didn't know how to ski and went straight down because I didn't know I was supposed to turn. Somehow I got to the bottom without falling or crashing, and when I stood up, I realized that was one of the funnest things I ever did. Mom skied up, her face dead white, all "Oh my God, what did I just do?" I hollered, "That was totally awesome!" Ever since then, she's called me her "little bullet." So that's where "bullet brain" came from, because I go fast and am always one step ahead of my thoughts.

Now that I'm thirteen, I think of ADHD as kind of a thorn in my butt. It's not special anymore. It makes me look like I'm stupid sometimes or socially awkward, which I don't really think I am. It's *annoying that I super focus on things. I can lock into something and do it with all my heart but when I get jolted out of that, it's really hard for me to go back. Or I get so sidetracked that I forget something really important. Sometimes it's like walking out of a house without your pants but having everything else on.*

I guess what has helped me accept my "bullet brain" is my meds, my therapy, and my parents. They are so good about reminding me, and the meds help with focusing. My therapist helped me understand and accept it. I know I have it, and I can't do anything about that. The best thing I do now is to laugh at myself. Because I make so many mistakes, I have to have a good sense of humor. I've trained myself to smile at my mistakes. What I've noticed is it's kicked in so much that when I'm thinking about something I did that I regret so bad, I find myself grinning. I'm like, "Wait, am I smiling? Yes, I'm smiling! I don't mind this anymore. This is water under the bridge." I'm laughing with myself, and that makes me feel better.

Maya's story reflects a journey of acceptance that I wish more kids shared. Initially, she started off thinking ADHD made her special, but over time, she grew to see it as annoying. Now, several years later, Maya has tools to handle her memory lapses and can laugh at herself, foibles and all. How does a child or teen embark on a similar exploration to accept their ADHD? This chapter will focus on what you can do to help them along the rocky road to that destination.

I Am What I Am, and That's *Okay!*

Kids and parents cope with ADHD much more easily when they come to a place of acceptance. The tools that will take you there are the Five C's of ADHD parenting. You've had your testing and evaluations. The cards are on the table. Your child has ADHD, and you need to acknowledge and adapt to it. This process of acceptance can be broken down into three phases.

1. **Phase one** focuses on family reactions to the ADHD diagnosis. *Self-Control* helps manage the range of feelings and thoughts everybody in the family will have to this new diagnosis. *Compassion* is crucial in understanding what ADHD looks like for your son or daughter, how it shows up in daily life, and how it affects the entire family.

2. **Phase two** revolves around using *Collaboration* to brainstorm ways of living better with ADHD. Together, you find and develop new alternatives to challenging behaviors.

3. **Phase three** focuses on *Consistency* and *Celebration*. You, along with teachers, coaches, or other caring adults, practice *Consistency* by supporting your child in trying to make improvements. If they hit a bump, you tweak things so they move forward again. Along the way, you practice *Celebration* by expressing pleasure and pride in whatever changes they're making.

Let's look at them in detail.

Phase One of Acceptance: self-Control

Acknowledging that you have a child with ADHD starts with reflecting on the diagnosis and your reaction to it. *You, as the parent*, need to figure out what having an ADHD child means to you. You can't offer genuine or effective support if you haven't explored your own feelings. They will inevitably leak out in interactions with your son or daughter, often in unhelpful ways.

Ask yourself if some of their struggles are familiar to you personally, and if they are, how did you deal with them when you were younger? How do you address them now? If their struggles are foreign to you, consider how you feel about having a child who is different from you and has challenges with attention, focus, and emotional intensity. It is perfectly normal for your feelings to run the gamut from uncertainty to relief, anxiety, anger, worry, or sadness. This process embodies *self-Control*: you unravel the threads of your own response to the diagnosis in a thorough and reflective manner.

Parental Responses to an ADHD Diagnosis

Parents whose children are diagnosed with ADHD fall on a spectrum: relieved at one end and distressed at the other. Most parents are a mix of both. Relieved parents, while often sad that their child has a diagnosis at all, are primarily soothed that they have something to hold on to. The diagnosis is like a life raft after years of confusion, worry, and frustration in an often stormy sea. They are comforted knowing that their child's perplexing behaviors have a name; that there are medical, therapeutic, and academic options for treatment; and that there are many other parents dealing with similar situations. They move into action, seeking out resources and embracing personal and family changes that show support for their ADHD child. Sometimes they have ADHD themselves so they are not surprised that their son or daughter has it too. Other relieved parents look at their own issues with concentration, memory, or emotional outbursts and realize they may have ADHD, too, and seek professional help or medication for themselves.

Distressed parents, on the other hand, struggle with the diagnosis and protest its arrival on the family scene. They may neither believe it nor understand it. They may think that ADHD is overdiagnosed or the school is biased. Or, they may say something like, *"That explains why my child has been so difficult to raise."* Regardless, they are often angry at all the ways that they have bent over backward for their child or teen throughout the years. They haven't been rewarded with the successes or accomplishments they have seen in their friends' or relatives' families, not to mention not receiving some gratitude from their child. Distressed parents can see the ADHD diagnosis as confirmation that their already challenging child will be impaired forever and, while they may feel some sadness like the relieved parents, they usually feel predominantly scared about their child's welfare and future success. Despite saying they will do whatever it takes to help their child, they might resist advice from professionals, ignore what they contribute either genetically or behaviorally to the family ADHD dynamic, and dwell mostly on changing their child.

Obviously, there are many parents who fall in the middle of these two groups. They likely feel comfort at having a name for some of the challenges that they and their child have faced. They are motivated to help their son or daughter but remain skeptical about the usefulness of interventions such as therapy, medication, or special-needs accommodations at school. They may be embarrassed as well. Likely, they harbor some sadness for their child and their family about the diagnosis. These parents especially tend to benefit from information about ADHD—books, podcasts, articles, and websites—because they feel reassured that ADHD is very common, "normal," and manageable. They want their child to succeed and are willing to participate in this process by examining how everyone can change for the better to make this happen.

Kids' Responses to Getting an ADHD Diagnosis

For the children and teens I have seen in my practice, in school consultations, and in social situations, receiving a diagnosis of ADHD is often a mixed bag. For some, it is a huge relief to get a name for what they knew was different about them. For others, it indicates that something is *wrong* with them. Some kids feel a combination of relief and shame. With all the myths and misinformation about ADHD in the world, it can be confusing for both kids and parents. Despite any comfort that accompanies the diagnosis, it usually involves a trip to a doctor or to several specialists. These visits often do not convey the message that ADHD is "normal" to a child or teen. After all, most of us go to the doctor when we are sick and something isn't right—a fever or a rash or a cough that won't go away. Nobody goes when they are doing well and everything is running smoothly.

Frequently when kids receive a diagnosis of ADHD, they see this complicated name as meaning something is wrong with them (i.e., they're flawed). They may know that they have trouble concentrating and be relieved that their challenges have a name. Later on, like Maya, they may come to feel proud of the idiosyncratic ways their brains work and enjoy their learning differences. But initially, what child, teen, or even adult wants to have a *diagnosis*? Not too many. While it can be useful with getting extra help at school or medication that addresses the symptoms or therapy to build coping skills, being labeled with having a "disorder" is not something most children long for.

For some of the kids who speak to me, ADHD is a negative label. For others, it's a liberating one. For all of them, it means adjusting to how they see themselves.

"It was last year in first grade. I didn't like sitting at a table. I was kind of running around. I don't really like reading; it's hard for me. I think my teacher talked to my mom, and I had to do some testing thing. I don't like everything about it. I wish it would go away."   —Chang, age 8

"I found out I had ADHD in kindergarten. My teachers were saying I was really hyper with everything. I had a really hard time paying attention. They wanted us to get it checked out. I didn't exactly know what it was, and I thought something was wrong with me."   —Kyle, age 12

"I was failing, not failing but I had D's and C's. I was fourteen, and it was like describing a loser in my mind, and I was like, 'What the hell?' I was nowhere near ready to put that label on myself of having ADHD because of what is said about it when you look it up. I don't throw tantrums and stuff. I got diagnosed, and I realized I wasn't stupid. That was the only cool part."   —Jasmine, age 17

"My mom told me, and I know it was true because I am hyper. I'm pumped of energy. When I take my pill, I'm calmer. I like that because it makes me happy."   —Hector, age 6

WHILE THEIR INITIAL reactions range from anger to misunderstanding to relief, these kids explicitly show that it takes time—*a lot of time*—to understand what having ADHD means. First, they have to accept the name and relate it to themselves and their lives. Most of them needed help to do this—from siblings, friends, or parents; other people in their lives who have ADHD; kind teachers; encouraging coaches; knowledgeable physicians and therapists. Some of them, like Maya, create names for ADHD that they feel fit their experiences of having it and feel better to them to use:

> "I like 'fast brain,' not ADHD. Sometimes my teacher calls it being a mover."
>
> —Liam, age 9

> "I call it 'bully brain' because it can be like a bully and get me off topic."
>
> —Darryl, age 10

> "I make a joke of it. I call it 'ADLS': Attention Deficit— Oh Look There's a Squirrel, because I am distracted by squirrels all day long. See a tree, see a squirrel running up. 'Squirrel.'"
>
> —Anthony, age 16

> "I live in the moment. It's like a 'this minute only' brain."   —Jade, age 12

> "It's a brain that just keeps going. It's an idea brain."   —Bree, age 11

> "I call it 'hyper boy' because I'm usually always hyper. . . . I just run all around the house and places. I like it."
>
> —Omar, age 7

IN MY OFFICE, I call ADHD "attention wandering" or "fast brain" like Liam. I also like how Dr. Edward Hallowell, a leading international expert on ADHD, tells his patients that they have "a race car brain with bicycle brakes."[1] The importance of any of these names is the positive perspective behind them. Instead of using a medical term that can feel foreign, scary, or diseased to some kids, you reduce the stress of the ADHD label by focusing on what is personal about it for them. Your son or daughter may not need this and may be totally comfortable with the medical term. That's fine too. The goal here is to follow your child's lead in the first stage of acceptance: acknowledging that ADHD is real for them and figuring out what they understand it to be.

Compassion: Understanding What ADHD Means to Your Child

Phase one of the acceptance process also relies on *Compassion. Compassion* depends on empathy to foster understanding. How can you appreciate what the experience of having ADHD means for your child or teen so you can support and assist them in ways that really help? Start by observing and asking your son or daughter: *"How does this news affect you?"* Listen to their words, what they say to you and to their friends, watch what they do. Imagine what it is like to spend a day in their shoes, and notice the particulars of how ADHD manifests in them. Reflect on their strengths, and identify their challenges. I encourage you to get a notebook in which you can write your responses to the exercises like the following that occur throughout the book as well as other notes you may want to make.

> ### EXERCISE 2:
> #### Your Child's Strengths And Challenges
>
> What do you really like about your child?
> What do they do well? (Include special talents, interests, and hobbies.)
> What do you do for fun together?
> What challenges or limitations does your child face?
> What do they do when frustrated?
> How do you show them that you are upset but you still love them?
> How do you give them feedback?

When you remember what you love about your son or daughter, it's easier to see challenging behaviors as signs of their frustration instead of personal weakness. When you look at your own ways of expressing your annoyance with them, it's easier to remember that you two are doing a dance together. You are intertwined. They need you to be on their side, even when they are doing everything they can to push you away. You treasure times when they make you laugh, when they give you a hug, when they say thanks. Holding on to these moments of connection reminds you of your love and nurtures the *Compassion* you need to get through the rougher times. Regardless of what lies ahead, the ways you attempt to comprehend their experience of having ADHD shows them that you are interested and care about *them*—diagnosis or not.

Identifying the "good parts" of having ADHD is just as important, if not more so, as naming the challenging ones. They make up all the strengths that your son or daughter relies on for self-esteem, competence, and self-confidence. As Sofia, age sixteen, told me: *"I want to spend more time on the parts of me that I like; I already have to spend too much time on the parts of me that I don't like."* When you appreciate what makes your kid special, you promote those qualities, interests, and talents. It's like putting plant food in the soil of your rosebush: you give it that extra oomph to nourish its blooms. Yes, you need to know what is problematic (in your view and theirs) to intervene successfully and build new skills. But, to move in a positive direction, you also need to know what is working and what they like about themselves. This is the baseline from which future changes will come.

Here's what a few kids with ADHD told me they liked about themselves.

"I'm good with my imagination. Sometimes I think of something, and then I think of something else and something else, and then I am way away from the first thing I was thinking about. The fun part is that I can think of weird things and creative ways to fix problems. I find stupid stuff really amusing."   —Chloe, age 10

"I notice different things, like patterns. Say there's a leaf on the ground. Some people will just glance at it, but I stare at it, looking for patterns. Also rhythms. Sometimes I'll drum and experiment. I find different ways to remember things and pay attention. It's definitely easy to entertain me because things are interesting."   —James, age 12

"I'm very in the moment. I am very good at forgetting, which is honestly one of my favorite qualities. Because I don't hold on to things for very long, so if something bad happens, it doesn't stay for that long. I mean, it depends on what it is, but small things don't bother me a lot."

—Ella, age 16

"I like the energy. I can do more than one thing at a time. I can change the conversation really fast and switch it to something else. I really enjoy and appreciate that. If I like something a lot, I'll hyperfocus into it. Like a book or writing poetry or watching a movie. I think it adds creativity to me."

—Henry, age 16

ENERGY, IMAGINATION, LIVING in the moment, thinking differently, creativity, being fun—these are great personal traits. These characteristics make kids with ADHD feel good about themselves, and naming them also counteracts the negativity bias in our brains as well.

ADHD is an everyday part of life for these kids. Maya says: *"ADHD's always been this big thing that's kind of looming on the horizon for me, like a part of my sky. Even though I didn't always know about it and try not to think about it, it's still there."* For her, like so many kids, it's not just a condition named by medical jargon. It's who they are and who they know themselves to be. Your patient listening allows you to see their point of view about having ADHD and helps create a shared perspective. While it can be harder for younger kids to articulate their likes and dislikes because the capacity for self-reflection is not as well-developed, they still have ideas about what is going well for them and what isn't, just like teenagers. Most kids with ADHD like certain things about having it. You, too, may like these same parts along with other wonderful qualities.

Unfortunately, the challenges of having ADHD or having a child with ADHD can tip things off-balance and make accepting it tough. For some kids, the list of what is troublesome about having ADHD, especially during the school years, can be a long one. They likely have been hearing from teachers, parents, and other adults about their deficits for years. You may also be keenly aware of your child's limitations and, despite your frustrations, saddened to see them struggle. Sometimes you have been successful in reducing their pain, in teaching them skills they need to learn, in offering advice that they accept. At other moments, they rebuff you. They don't share your agenda, they don't like your ideas, and they feel criticized instead of supported.

To chart your course toward new behaviors together, start by listening to what kids with ADHD feel is frustrating

"Sometimes I don't hear exactly all the stuff people say. Then I get in trouble because I missed something. I'll blank out on what people are saying, like, if they're talking for more than a minute. I'll be like, 'Yeah. Yeah.' They're like, 'What? I didn't ask a yes-or-no question. I didn't even ask a question.'"
—Nona, age 10

"Organizing. It's the hardest thing for me. I don't think that's ever going to stop. I think I'm going to have to keep trying to improve that. Managing different things at once is multitasking, and I can't do it, even if I think I can."
—Oscar, age 15

"My number one thing that I hate about having ADHD is my being late everywhere. I suck at thinking about how long things will take. The second thing I hate is that I lose *everything*. In the past four years, I have lost more than thirty water bottles, four or five lunch boxes, clothes at school, my iPod or iPhone at least eight times, which is a huge deal for me because I live around my phone and I'm always listening to music."
—Dustin, age 16

"I dislike everything. It's just super inconvenient. Sometimes I don't feel as smart as my friends. We take the same AP classes, but they just do better. I also hate the anxiety part of it. Sometimes I feel like there's a cinder block sitting on my brain that's stopping me from doing something. That's the worst part. That cinder-block feeling and then the anxiety and insecurity that comes with that."
—Brianna, age 17

"Not being able to focus when you want to. Really, I get distracted easily. People talking, one. Two, I just daydream off, forget everything I was
doing. Or I see it start snowing and look at snowflakes. Anything that
catches my attention."   —Tyrone, age 14

TROUBLE STAYING FOCUSED, distractedness, missing what people are saying, losing things, chronic lateness, forgetfulness, disorganization, stress,
anxiety—these issues are the flip side of the energy, creativity, and spon-
taneity that kids with ADHD like about themselves. Even though many
of them may minimize the effects of having ADHD publicly—in school
or with friends—when asked privately, they admit to struggles that are
burdensome. The emotional and cognitive executive functioning skills
needed to address many of their problems haven't developed in their
brains yet. As their parents, you have seen and heard these private
revelations—sometimes in heart-to-heart conversations, sometimes in
bouts of tears and shame, and sometimes in fits of rage. Regardless of
how they express it, your ADHD child is showing you how they feel
about having a "disorder" and how they are challenged by it.

Acknowledging the ways they are unique and talking about their
struggles with you and/or others signals that your son or daughter is
accepting their ADHD. They are developing the capacity to notice and
admit both positive and challenging things about themselves. This
self-reflection is the precursor to any future changes in behavior.
When you can listen to them, keep your reactions in check and be
sympathetic; you, too, are accepting their ADHD. You have shown
them you care about their experience and want to understand it.

Phase Two of Acceptance: Collaboration

Coming up with interventions that are helpful, imaginative, and effective means strategizing together. At this point, your son or daughter
knows that they have ADHD; they have some comprehension of
what it is, and they feel as though you understand part of it too. The

Collaboration stage of acceptance relies on your partnership with them in identifying what is going well and what needs some improvement. In conversations about all aspects of their lives (home, school, sports, activities, jobs, friends), you encourage them to brainstorm with you about what they would like to be different and why. You assist them in reframing their failures as challenges and point out the crew of folks in their lives who are available to help them and want to see them succeed. Then, you co-create plans that foster any desired changes and show them that you are on their side for the long haul.

Coming up with Solutions to Dreaded Tasks Together

Let's look at how Taylor, age twelve, and her mother, Natalie, collaborated to stop battling about what Taylor is supposed to do around the house each day.

> NATALIE: "Our conflict is mostly around communal space and respect for others. Taylor comes home from school, drops her stuff in the middle of the kitchen floor. Then she grabs her iPod, checks for messages, plops on the couch with her snack, and watches television. I tell her, 'Move your stuff or we'll trip on it.' She says, 'Wait one sec,' but never moves. Meanwhile, I'll go out and when I come home an hour later, neither Taylor nor the stuff has moved."
>
> TAYLOR: "I forgot. I did it when you got home and told me to. You yell at me so much, when I leave clothes in the bathroom or forget my house responsibilities. You're always saying you have to remind me a million times. If I say, 'Wait one sec,' maybe you'll stop yelling at me."
>
> NATALIE: "Usually I don't start by yelling. I try not to, but there is intensity in my voice. Yelling means anger—I'm mad, I've had it. Sometimes I use reprimands. Reprimands are daily mom-isms like 'Hang up your coat, please.'"
>
> TAYLOR: "It sounds the same to me. Why can't you just come over to me and talk to me like a normal person?"

NATALIE: "I guess I could. I'm usually just too stressed out and rushing around."

Everyone agrees that this frustrating pattern isn't working: Taylor isn't doing what she needs to do, and she doesn't like how much her mom yells at her. Natalie is a reminder-machine who also dislikes the yelling. To foster a collaborative solution, I ask what the ideal situation would look like:

NATALIE: "I want to say what I expect, maybe give *one* reminder, and have Taylor do it. I don't want to hear 'Wait one sec' and have it never happen. 'Wait one sec' is a filler. I'm a single mom. We all have to chip in."

TAYLOR: "There is too much stuff for me to remember. I already get myself up for school and put myself to bed. I make my own breakfast, lunch, and my bed. I fold my laundry and put it away. All my friends' moms do everything. They have a few chores and get rewards. I want money. *Brilliant idea alert*: Get a whiteboard and make a list of what I need to do. Then pay me. And stop yelling."

Both positions are valid. If a small allowance is something that her mother, Natalie, is open to and the chores for Taylor are clear and mutually agreed upon, then, in my experience, kids like Taylor will follow through. She'll buy into the program because she's helped to create it and she'll be getting the money she desires. The next step is to make that list on a whiteboard to guide her through her chores without Natalie's reminders. The likelihood for success increases if the list includes some things that she already does as well as new chores. This way, she won't be overwhelmed by a bunch of stuff that she hasn't mastered yet. Natalie gains something too: she gets Taylor to complete chores that matter to *her*. This type of evenhandedness makes *Collaboration* appealing to everyone.

Taylor wants to make her own checks on the board. She gets a check (or point) for each completed task. Since improved participation, not perfection, is the goal, they agree that out of forty possible points, Natalie would accept thirty as the basis for the five-dollar weekly allowance. This allowed for those days when things aren't accomplished as planned. Taylor asks her mom for one reminder to use the whiteboard if she needs it, and Natalie agrees to do this. Their chart looks like this:

TASKS	M	T	W	T	Fr	Sat	Sun
Make bed							
Put away clothes or clean laundry							
Put backpack on the counter after school						N/A	N/A
Empty lunch box and hang up coat						N/A	N/A
Put dishes in sink or dishwasher after eating							
Put away food from snacks							
TOTAL:							

NOW COMES ONE of the most challenging questions I am often asked: should Natalie take away allowance money if Taylor doesn't have a good attitude, needs reminders, or does the tasks poorly? After all, she hasn't earned it, right? My answer is no. If she does the tasks and gets the points, she should have the money. She may very well need some coaching about how to do them better, but taking away things from your ADHD child or teen that you said you would give them won't accomplish your goals for improving your family situation. This is an incentive-based program, and the incentive—something Taylor came up with—is what will motivate her. Punishing her will only increase tension and alienation.

Instead, when the system doesn't work, I suggest a conversation in which Natalie calmly states her disappointment and frustration with whatever is going on, reminding Taylor of her commitment to this plan (without a lecture) and asking her daughter what needs to happen for a different outcome next time. The last part is crucial. *Ask* your child what they need to change things; don't *tell* them. This shift toward their cooperation will likely take time and extra patience—not always easy to do. If, after a few weeks, Taylor is still not cooperating, then renegotiate the plan. Maybe change the incentive. There is no point in using an incentive if it isn't working, and remember: kids with ADHD can get bored quickly with them as well.

The biggest obstacle parents face in the *Collaboration* phase is they want their kids with ADHD to shift too many things too fast. Most kids, especially those with ADHD, really can't alter more than one thing about themselves at a time. Most adults, including myself, can't really do this either. But ADHD youth frequently get overwhelmed by the number of things they are told they need to "fix" about themselves. Ashamed, embarrassed, frustrated, or mad, they shut down and reject help. When this happens, negotiations fail and *Collaboration* doesn't occur.

Here's why several kids with ADHD told me they reject help:

"I don't want to ask for help. I want to prove that I can do it by myself, because I have people to look up to like my mom, my dad, and my brother. I just want to be like everyone else."   —Carlos, age 15

"I'm proud. I just won't go to seek help from teachers, I'd be like, 'I don't need their help, I can deal with this on my own.' Yeah, I get a little cocky. I should figure it out on my own."   —Feng, age 12

"It was hard to ask for help. I was embarrassed that I had a disability."   —Ella, age 16

"I hate asking for help. My friends get mad because I have to ask them to repeat things. Sometimes they just yell at me, 'Pay attention.' I'm trying, but there's too much going on. I hear them, but I can't figure out what they're saying. Then they yell at me that I'm stupid and ask if I took my medication. It's awful. I'm doing the best I can. That's why I don't ask for help."   —Kia, age 12

INFORMATION OVERLOAD AND not wanting extra help is when the *Collaboration* phase can flop, especially in the beginning. Most of these kids want to be independent and see asking for help as a sign of weakness. Giving them a long list of what to do differently implies that a lot is "wrong" with them. The *Collaboration* phase works best when parents and kids focus on *one thing* that is already going well while simultaneously focusing on *another thing* that needs improvement. When Taylor and her mother made their whiteboard chart, it included tasks that she already felt good about while simultaneously having ones that were challenging for her. Natalie facilitated this process by listening and adapting to what mattered to Taylor while including what mattered to her. You build on the "good stuff" that your child already does easily to create new desired changes in behavior.

Phase Three of Acceptance: Consistency and Celebration

This final phase of accepting the ADHD brain involves taking your collaborative plan, putting it into action, and making it stick. Implementing alternative approaches to old problems requires *Consistency* and *Celebration*, which in turn depend on *efforting*. *Efforting* happens when you and your ADHD child practice and integrate these new solutions. It requires a big dose of persistence and resiliency because there will surely be unforeseen setbacks. When you hit these bumps, you make adjustments. Sammy, an eight-year-old girl with ADHD, summarized this idea when she told me "practice makes progress," echoing the philosophy of the local Montessori preschool that she attended a few years earlier. Hanging in there with your child not only teaches them about grit but it also shows them how much you care.

Being consistent is easier when things are going well and according to plan, but that's not always the case. Your thirteen-year-old daughter has a messy room and you've agreed that she has to clean it up weekly on Saturday before she can go out that night. If things are not cleaned up by 5:00, she stays home. You agree to give one reminder on Friday and one on Saturday morning when she wakes up. She thinks this is fair because you won't be nagging her and she has to do it only once a week. It's a win-win, and *it works*. After she missed one Saturday and you held your ground based on the agreement, she has been steadily following the plan. You showed her what it means to stay the course. The next day, she admits to you that she likes when she can see the floor of her room and find her clothes. She is *efforting*: learning and practicing follow-through, cooperation, organization, and cleanliness. You have facilitated this process of trial-and-error learning instead of focusing more on perfection. The result: less conflict and more appropriate behaviors.

Persistence in the face of challenges, while crucial for all kids, is particularly important for kids with ADHD. Most of them have difficulty envisioning how things can be different, given the frequent negative feedback they receive. Like all kids, they struggle to accurately perceive the future. When things are hard, they quickly become upset, angry, or defeated. But when they see you struggling to hold on to your shared goals in the face of unpleasantness, when you hit an obstacle and regroup instead of quitting, when you continue to exert yourself despite being tired and discouraged, then they learn that they can do it too. Obviously, you can't do this all the time. The goal for you is to do it more often than not—to make agreements that you can manage. Your modeling is essential—both for effective *Consistency* and persistent *efforting*.

How Defeats Offer Learning Opportunities

Nathan, the father of Davis, age nine, came into my office very discouraged. Davis, diagnosed six months earlier with ADHD, struggled with working-memory deficits, emotional upsets, and impulse control.

Nathan and his wife were highly frustrated and not able to stick with most plans. Davis admitted that he had "big feelings" and "big melt-downs" at least once a day and sometimes more often. Although these "meltdowns" usually occurred at home, they also happened in the car, at family gatherings, during errands, and sometimes at school. His teacher reported that Davis often spoke when other students were talking, and he walked spontaneously around the classroom several times a day. Davis told me:

> I have trouble sitting still. Sometimes my brain goes fast, and sometimes I miss directions. People tell me to "be still" and to "pay attention." The problem, for me, well, I just get mad, really mad. Like when my brother does something and I get blamed for it. Then I get into more trouble.

Davis, his parents, and his teacher agreed that his "getting mad" was the first thing they wanted to work on. They created a plan that would be similar both at home and school to maximize helping him with *self-Control*. Davis loved to read. They all decided that when he was upset, his teacher or his parents would encourage him to go to his own quiet space or to his room to read for ten to fifteen minutes. If he was un-able to do this, Davis agreed to empty the trash in both places—something he didn't like doing. He thought this deal was fair.

After three weeks, this plan was not working. More days than not, Davis argued about going to his quiet place, and neither his parents nor his teacher followed through with the trash task. When he re-fused at home, his parents yelled at him and he ended up crying. When Davis refused to go to the quiet corner, his teacher sent him to the principal's office. His parents were losing their patience. They started taking away chunks or all of his beloved hour of computer time as a consequence for his meltdowns. This made him even an-grier. Nathan, his father, was fed up:

> Our family is intense, but at the center of it has always been great joy. I'm not enjoying parenthood right now. I feel incredibly disempowered; I have

to work so hard to follow our plan. Sometimes it just feels like punishment for me. I know it's what I should do, but some days I just want to quit.

Nathan expresses what I have heard from many parents of ADHD youth who visit my office: "*I can't do this anymore. I can't hold on in the face of repeated defeats.*"

I believe that these defeats are not failures but critical pieces of information. When a co-created plan intensifies problem behaviors, then obviously it needs to be modified. These adjustments mean you have to examine the cycle of what is happening step by step with your plan, noticing the functional parts and the dysfunctional ones. When I spoke with Davis and his parents about the "failed" plan, we uncovered that the breakdown was occurring in three places: 1) Davis disliked how his parents yelled at him to go to his room or how his teacher raised her voice and sent him to the quiet corner; 2) he felt lonely and ashamed of being there; and 3) there was no follow-through by the adults if he didn't go. The plan lacked *Consistency*, and the incentive—avoiding doing the trash—was ineffective.

After Davis tearfully told me how the plan had "failed" and how "nothing helps," he put his head on his mother's lap. I watched him slowly calm down as she stroked his hair. He settled, and we regrouped. We devised a new plan: when Davis was upset, a parent or his teacher would take him aside (reduce his stimulation), make a connection with him (listen to what he was saying), and ask if he wanted time apart (to read in a quiet space) or time together (sharing a book, doing a task, getting a hug, playing a game). The adult would then follow through immediately. These activities helped soothe Davis, by his own report, and felt comforting to him. If he was still unable to settle down, he asked if he could go to the main office or go to his room for fifteen minutes. His daily electronic playing time was reduced to forty-five minutes, and when he used the plan effectively, he would earn fifteen extra minutes of electronic playing time the next day, putting him back up at one hour. This incentive worked for Davis because it mattered to him: video games and watching television were some of his favorite things to do. Everyone, including his teacher, decided to try this out.

For Davis, these interventions emphasized *connection not punishment, correction not shaming*. This time, the adults followed through regularly. Within three weeks, there was already an improvement: Davis was still getting upset, but he was managing those moments with more skill and calming down with more ease. He told me with pride how many days the previous week he had earned his fifteen minutes of screen time. While acknowledging the family still had "a lot of work to do," Davis's father, Nathan, felt more hopeful. This back-and-forth, the shaping and molding of *Collaborative* plans until they run smoothly, is what facilitates *Consistency* in the process of change.

Why Your Encouragement Really Matters

New solutions to any kind of problem have to include *Celebration*. When you don't notice that things are improving, it is difficult to keep up the momentum for these changes to settle in. Most kids and adults, whether or not they have ADHD, like positive feedback. When anyone tries hard to alter something about themselves—losing weight, being on time, staying organized—encouragement and good results keep them going. Kids with ADHD, who already receive so many negative messages, especially benefit from enthusiasm when they attempt to do things differently. When parents and teachers recognize how hard these kids work to get by each day, doing tasks or behaviors that don't come naturally to them and sticking with agreed-upon plans, you communicate that success means staying in the game as much as getting things right. It's the learning and growing that matters, not a perfect outcome. *Celebration* makes this happen.

I am not talking about false praise or fake excitement. When your thirteen-year-old son miraculously puts his wet towel on the hook on the door after a shower, he doesn't need a trophy. A casual "Nice job hanging up your towel" will suffice. When your seventeen-year-old daughter comes home by her curfew, she doesn't need a cake. A sincere "Thanks for cooperating" is enough. Your opinions and support really matter to them. When you notice their *efforting*, they thrive: you are their ally and their witness. This is *Celebration*. Regardless of how your ADHD son or daughter may act—defiant, grateful, disagreeable, appreciative, rejecting, or cooperative, children and teens repeatedly emphasize how important their parents have been to them in accepting their ADHD and learning to live successfully with it.

> "I think my family has been my support; they've made my life better. They gave me love, food, and patience, a lot of patience."
>
> —Chang, age 8

> "My dad reminds me about things. Like, we had to write something after a field trip, and I was really excited. Then we left school. I ate a snack and completely forgot about it until Dad was like, 'Did you do your homework?' I was like . . . 'Oh yeah.' I mean, I don't like when he does this, but it helps me get my work done."
>
> —Layla, age 9

> "My mom did a lot. She would help me get everywhere I needed to go. She helped me remember what homework I had. She asked if I had any questions, she would see if she could help, or she would get me a tutor. I rejected her help for a long time because I didn't want to be seen as someone that needed extra help. But it eventually became very handy."
>
> —Kimiko, age 16

> "I'm sure my mom is the reason why I'm still in school because she noticed my ADHD first. She would make sure that I was staying on top of my things and staying organized, even reminding me a thousand times to do something. That's super helpful because my brain doesn't remember stuff. Yeah, sure, it gets hard. I'm sure my parents are mad at me a lot, for doing things I don't mean to do. But they are super patient. It's always, 'Okay, here's what you did, let's improve it.'"
>
> —Tyler, age 17

PAYING ATTENTION; SHOWING support; reminding them about chores, work or errands; listening to their stories—all of these reflect the caring, quality parenting that help ADHD kids thrive. These are the traits of true *Celebration*. When you pay attention to your ADHD child's efforts to do things differently, you make them feel seen, heard, and valued. Instead of mostly pointing out what they should do differently, you do the opposite: let them know what they have done well. Not so easy to do, right? Especially since it's easy to focus on flaws and inadequacies in our perfectionistic and achievement-oriented society. Nonetheless, parents, not just ADHD parents, have to do this to raise kids who feel good about themselves and competent in the world. Using the Five C's, your son or daughter can end up like Maya: aware of her strengths, managing her challenges satisfactorily, and enjoying the idiosyncrasies that make her unique. Isn't this what you want for your child?

PART TWO

Life at School

Chapter 4

Overcoming
the Hurdles of School

MEET JOSÉ, age eleven, a fifth grader, and Oscar, age fifteen, a ninth grader, as they talk about school. These brothers share the diagnosis of ADHD but have different types: Jose has combined hyperactive/inattentive, and Oscar is primarily inattentive.

OSCAR: "School's always been hard for me—learning and interacting with people. But not reading. I love to read fantasy fiction. I couldn't concentrate well before I was diagnosed and got medication. Even now, in high school, I can't put different ideas together like some people can. I'm kind of like waving around, not knowing what to do."

JOSÉ: "I'm good at math, much better than you, but my writing is bad. I'm a really slow reader, so I have to be extra patient. I have a special reading tutor to help me. The best part of school is my friends, math, and gym. The worst part is everything else. School is just not that fun. I can't wait for the summer."

OSCAR: "Being the first one in our family to get diagnosed, I didn't exactly know what it was, and I thought something was wrong with me. I was kind of alone. Then, I realized that I wasn't alone and that it was just a different way of living."

José: *"Really?* I didn't know that. I felt alone because mine was different than yours. I found out I had ADHD when I was seven. My mind would wander off and think about the most recent movie I saw or something. My teacher would know I wasn't listening because my head would be looking away. I liked to run around the classroom during free choice. If it's really bad, you have to repeat a grade like I did. They just said it was a mistake, but I know it was because of my ADHD."

Oscar: "You missed your friends so bad you cried for a week. Dad said that you ran on batteries. For me, in high school, ADHD is confusing. I can write poetry, songs, and stories, but I can't do analytical stuff. I like learning and school and all my friends, but I'm just not that good at it. My writing tutor and the medication help, but it's embarrassing. Sometimes I forget to turn in homework without a teacher asking. School is harder for me than other kids. That's the truth."

For these brothers, like most kids with ADHD, school is a complicated journey. Both boys name some of their intellectual interests and talents as well as their trouble spots. Oscar, who loves reading and mostly enjoys learning, struggles with writing, concentrating, and remembering to turn in his assignments. José, on the other hand, generally dislikes school but similarly wrestles with writing and staying focused. Both boys accept help from others and are aware of their different social styles: the elder brother, shy, and the younger one, outgoing. Clearly, their understanding of themselves as learners and the assistance they receive from their parents, teachers, and tutors helps them navigate academics with more confidence and success.

This conversation between Oscar and José reflects their fortitude: how much strength and courage it takes to get up, go to school, study challenging things, behave appropriately, and then come home and do more of what you don't like to do in the first place—schoolwork. How do they muster up the energy and resilience to do this day after day? While many adults may have to do this for work, usually they manage because they can think about the future and what would happen if they don't do it. They also value the money they are earning. The mature director in their brains can perceive the benefits of doing something unpleasant but necessary, while kids with ADHD often cannot. If it's not fun to do now and the consequence lies in some intangible moment in the future, it often won't be completed. How do these brothers and other kids do it?

Clinical experience and consultation work with kids and schools have shown me that the answers lie in creating a strong, supportive network involving children, teens, *and* caring adults. a network that provides resources, offers positive approaches, and respects what kids with ADHD think and say about themselves as learners. One that acknowledges school as typically the most challenging area for kids with ADHD because it requires them to rely on the parts of their brains most affected by their executive functioning deficits. They need a team that is facilitated and coordinated by caring adults who practice the Five C's of ADHD parenting.

Creating and Managing the Network Team

You undoubtedly lived through highs and lows, criticism and encouragement, successes and failures as you journeyed through the educational system. You bring along these conscious and unconscious memories as you enter the maze of educating your child, especially when you meet with their teachers, principals, and other school officials.[1] Lugging this invisible backpack of memories, parents do their best to address their youngster's attitudes about school and homework separate from their own history. But it can be tough to balance constructive involvement that improves your child's learning experience with corrective involvement that seeks to right whatever wrongs you were dealt through your child's current situation.

EXERCISE 3:
Your Reflections About School

Take a minute now and reflect on your own education, on the relationships of people who helped or hindered you. Jot down your recollections in your notebook.

What was school like for you?
What did you like about it?
What was hard?
Who helped you?
What did they do?

A BALANCED APPROACH mimics the role of the manager on a baseball team. Since I live in an area with many Red Sox fanatics, most kids and parents I work with can relate to this analogy. In professional baseball, each team has a manager plus a number of specific coaches (first base, batting, pitching, etc). The manager (a man in Major League Baseball but not necessarily in our scenarios) has the overall responsibility for running the team day to day. During games, you'll see him sitting on the bench, deciding which players will play, when to make substitutions, and whether to argue with an umpire about a call. The coaches deal with issues related to their specialties. The manager and the coaches work together for the best outcome of the team. For our purposes, you have been the manager of the team named [Your Child] since their birth, concerned about what is best for their welfare and survival. Your pediatrician, extended family members, preschool teachers, etc. have been early coaches on your team. They have likely given you advice about stomach bugs, potty training, and books to read. Appropriately, your child's input on these things during that time was limited. But now your child is older, school age and beyond, and has received a diagnosis that indicates they have some biological and behavioral challenges that impact how and what they learn at school. While you are still the manager, the dynamics on the team have changed. Even as young as kindergarten, your child has accumulated experience and opinions about themselves, how they play this game of baseball we call Life, and what they think might help get the team a "win."

One of your primary jobs as manager, both on the field and off, is to ask specific questions about school and elicit information from your son or daughter. Armed with this knowledge and any results from psychological and educational evaluations, you venture into assisting them to obtain the necessary academic and even social skills they need. Most likely, you will need help. Enlisting the participation of "coaches" such as reading, math, or writing specialists; homework tutors; therapists; professional ADHD coaches; after-school instructors; and leaders for sports, art, or music activities facilitates the learning your child needs. Schools (and, more specifically, guidance counselors) can advise you where to find these resources for low or no cost and, if they are mandated by an education plan, will provide some of them. In my town, high school honors students who need volunteer hours have been especially helpful with tutoring younger kids with ADHD free of charge. Figuring out what best meets your child's needs within your budget and according to their IDEA rights is your mission and, honestly, sometimes you have to be relentless in pursuing it.

The most important thing you can do as a good manager is to recognize that school is often the hardest area of functioning for kids with ADHD. It requires them to use their weaker executive functioning skills such as planning, organization, persistence, and impulse control that are characteristic of having ADHD. Solid academic achievement can be a tougher goal to attain than most kids would like, and all too often, they underperform.[2] Sometimes they thrive with less direction and you watch the game from the bench. At other times you are more actively engaged. When there are issues that involve safety, health, and justice, obviously you jump in. Research has shown that when parents and teachers cooperated on improving academic skills, the child's rate of academic success improved.³ If your eight-year-old daughter is angry and depressed due to repeated academic defeats and insufficient classroom support, you must act immediately. When the principal calls you because your son is stuffing paper towels down the toilet in a locked bathroom stall, you also must act right away.

Generally, though, your parenting goals about your child's education should revolve around developing their autonomy and competence.⁴ When your twelve-year-old son doesn't understand the math homework and you don't either, arguing about the right way to solve the problems is likely fruitless. Let him talk about it

Errors mean lessons.

with his teacher while you step back. If he fumbles around a bit, it's okay. Errors mean lessons. Professor and author Brené Brown thinks courage is the flip side of defeat. Your job is to cultivate courage in your ADHD son or daughter by sometimes biting your lip when they experience *small* defeats and the disappointment that accompanies them. This is how kids learn the essential life skill of bouncing back. Your words or interventions cannot teach this. You probably remember similarly challenging times when you gained such lessons. Young people build both resilience and confidence from such *efforting*.

What the Team Metaphor Looks Like in Action: José, Oscar, and Their Parents

José and his family illustrate the value of using the team metaphor. His father, Diego, born and raised in Mexico, was diagnosed with ADHD shortly after Oscar. He recognized that he had some of the same challenges and went to his physician for an assessment. Diego understood the academic struggles of both his sons. As a student, he had loved learning but struggled with doing work in a timely fashion and remembering to turn in assignments. José's mother, Juanita, was born in New York and had been a stellar student for whom school was interesting and fun. Although she did not have attention issues, she was very supportive of her sons and husband. Both high school educators, they saw doing well in school as the key to future success. They were concerned about how often José forgot homework assignments or didn't turn them in when he actually remembered to do them. For the past two years, they had worked with his teachers to instruct him on writing down his daily homework, but he hadn't been able to do it consistently. Often, when José wrote a thing down, like many kids with ADHD, he would miss something in the transition from looking at the words on the board to writing them down.

Concerned that José's grades showed he was falling behind, his parents, in their joint role as manager, had searched at a local college and hired, at a bargain price, a graduate student in education as a tutor to supplement the school reading support José received. They mentioned their concerns to her, and she offered an inventive suggestion. At first, they were skeptical because it relied on technology, and they preferred that he write things down, like they did. But they were concerned enough to give her method a try. José explained his tutor's method to me:

> She told me to use my iPad to take pictures of my homework. At first everyone was worried that it would be bad for me not to write it down. But then I started doing better, so they let me keep doing it. When I go to middle school, I won't have to do it because everything is online already. I think that will be a lot easier, but it's also kind of bad because if I miss an assignment I don't have an excuse like "I took it at a bad angle."

José's tutor turned out to be, metaphorically speaking, a great first base coach. She brilliantly had him use technology (something he loves) for something he struggled with. Then, his parents "sat on the bench" and watched what unfurled. It turned out the tutor's strategy was successful, and things started improving at school for José. While his parents wanted him to physically write down homework assignments like they had and were worried about him not learning to, they ultimately chose to trust her because their way hadn't been working.

Just like a good manager has faith in his first base coach, they gave the tutor's plan a chance, and it worked.

Sometimes this happens, and sometimes it doesn't. If it hadn't worked, they would have needed to take a pause in the action, conference on the mound, and come up with a new strategy or maybe even another tutor. By monitoring the game without micromanaging the situation, by setting aside their experiences as students as the standard for José, and by trusting the tutor's ideas, they managed to be involved but not overbearing. Together they boosted José's director. Unless your child is in a dangerous situation, you can do this too. You observe, listen, assess what's happening, and create a network of competent, caring experts (your version of specific coaches) to assist and encourage them.

We have now looked at how reflecting on your own educational experience and taking a team approach can positively influence your child's education like it did for José. Let's listen to what kids with ADHD have to say about school and how the Five C's can help you address common obstacles like homework and learning challenges that families often face.

Chapter 5

....

Don't Freak Out

Using and Teaching self-Control

TAKING A DEEP breath when dealing with *anything* related to your child is always the first best step, but where school issues are concerned, it's a crucial one. I try to use one of the breathing techniques (outlined on page 15) when my daughter tells me about some injustice with a teacher or coach. When you are a bit calmer, take time to reflect on the issue at hand. Remember that the goal is not just gaining skills and knowledge about various academic subjects but also building a lifelong foundation of learning that fosters curiosity, confidence, and autonomy. Consider if there are any similarities between your own educational history and your child's current situation. Then do the same thing with differences. Notice how you turned out okay. Be reassured that your child will, too, because they have *you*—a caring, committed adult who is on their side.

It is difficult to have perspective when you are in the thick of turmoil. Your child may or may not love school, but they still have to go there every day and spend their time and energy studying. For kids who don't like school, this attitude may not shift over the years. What then? While you want your kids to learn, grow, and enjoy scholastics, the fact is that many people succeed in life by depending on nonacademic skills. They find themselves and their careers in their twenties or beyond. This path may not be the most common one, but it exists and has been fruitful for lots of folks. Maybe even for you. Often, kids with ADHD need more time to get through school and/or benefit from a break after high school by volunteering, working, or traveling.

Yuting was a very smart, artistic young woman with severe ADHD who barely finished high school and had no interest in college. After graduation, she worked as a salesclerk and waitress for three years, making art and volunteering at local artists' openings. Now, at twenty-one, she has a job as a gallery assistant, supplementing her income with waitressing. She's happy; she has state health insurance, an apartment, and friends. She even manages to save some money each month.

Adrian, age twenty-six, is finally and proudly graduating from college after six years and three different universities. After dropping out the third time because he failed several classes and smoked too much pot, he was depressed when he came to see me. His parents were extremely worried about him. Adrian started working at Target, cut back on his smoking, and started looking at his ADHD brain. He realized that he could attend school only part-time. Otherwise, he felt too disorganized, overwhelmed, and anxious. His parents met with me and, using the team metaphor, figured out what type of managers they wanted to be. They chose sticking by him, offering emotional support and confidence in his capabilities even when he lacked it. Using *self-Control*, they stopped judging him for being different and focused on what he was doing well. They accepted that he would have menial jobs for a while and that his educational path would be longer than they had hoped. Their support and Adrian's personal revelations were the keys to his diploma and future success. Now he runs an after-school program for inner-city youth and is applying to part-time graduate programs in education so he can help others. His parents are beaming with pride (and relief).

Taming the Homework Monster:
Applying *Self-Control* to School Issues at Home

Overseeing homework is where many families (ADHD kids or not) really struggle. If I had a dollar for every time I hear complaints about homework, I could retire today. While kids' homework is their own to complete and turn in, handling the homework hassle starts with you. Avoidance, aggression, conflict, tears, resistance: facing the "homework monster," as Davis, age nine, called it, can be infuriating and exasperating for everyone. Many parents have told me their woes about homework. Rachel, the mother of Chloe, age ten, thinks homework is unnecessary. She told me: *"I would like to boycott weekend homework in fifth grade. I mean, do we really need homework on Halloween? Chloe's writing assignment had her in a puddle when I came home."* Paul, the father of Kyle, age twelve, doesn't know how to motivate his teenager to do homework instead of playing computer games: *"I moved his computer to the kitchen table so I could supervise his homework, but he lied about it to play Dota. I want to trust him, but I get daily emails from his teachers about missed assignments. What am I supposed to do?"* Paul, fed up and worried like many caring parents, has run out of ideas. John loses his temper when his son, Shawn, age ten, yells and throws things in a rage about homework: *"Shawn can't practice his math facts with me for ten minutes without yelling, 'Shut up! You're such a jerk.' Once he shoved a chair at me. That really hurt! We try to work through it, but it's hard. I usually yell too much."* These

> **Handling the homework hassle starts with you.**

parents feel lost, frustrated, and hopeless. They want to help their kids but often don't know how.

Before we tackle this cycle of frustration and defeat, let's talk about technology. Cell phones, Facebook, and other social media are not useful during study periods. Of course, kids may need to contact peers about homework questions. This fosters important cooperation skills. That's not the problem. It's the myth of multitasking that is detrimental to effective studying. Every beep or swish of a cell phone or computer steers your child's delicate concentration away from what they are doing and slows their productivity. Multitasking means switching from one thing that is occupying your memory system to something else. It can take anywhere from ten to fifteen minutes to regain full focus from these regular disruptions.[1] For this reason, help your kids avoid the lure of multitasking by taking it out of the equation. *Keep access to cell phones and social media limited during study periods and their computer in a place where you can see it.* Your teen will probably balk at this, but explain how the brain functions and why you are doing it. Remember, the manager doesn't allow cell phones on the field. Why should you?

Parents usually have more contact with a child's teachers while they are in elementary school. In middle school and high school, with more teachers and changing classes, this connection is more detached. For teens with ADHD, the homework situation becomes more complicated not only because of increased workload but also because their parents may not know or understand what the homework is. In addition, teens are tougher to monitor, and pushback is a normal part of any adolescent-adult dynamic. Andrea, the mother of Ella, age sixteen, explains:

As soon as she gets home from school, she eats and gets on her phone. The last thing she wants to do is sit and work. I let her chill out for a while, but then I nudge her to study. She slowly takes out her books. Then she gets a drink. Then she starts to work and her phone goes off. She answers the text. I remind her to get back to work, and she yells, "Stay out of my life!" She'll study until another text interrupts her. Then she goes on Facebook to ask how to do something for her homework, or she gets up for a snack. It goes on like this for two, maybe three hours. I can't stand it. We end up having a fight because nothing much gets done.

When adolescents like Ella outwardly reject the help that they so clearly need and see their parents as annoying interferences, it's hard for adults to know what to do or where to draw the line. Whether your fourth-grade child is having a meltdown about writing a book report or your teen is avoiding studying the American Revolution for a history test, your first task is to take those calming yoga breaths and ask yourself what matters most right now. That answer should involve connecting positively with your child and reining in your aggravation. Your solution and plan for dealing with *anything* will come after this.

When the final bell rings in the afternoon and school is over for kids with ADHD, most of them need a break from studying, such as playing outside, doing sports, participating in an after-school program, listening to music, or being with friends. Their brains need to do something different. Your job is to support this break in whatever way you can. The key to successfully beating back the homework monster is to make sure that your child knows this break is time-limited *and* that homework lies on the other side of it. Just like the manager knows when his players need a water break, tells them to take five, and calls them back to the field when it is over, you can similarly give your children and teens some nonacademic, time-limited brain breaks. These academic "time-offs" will help them later when they have to settle down to work. You can help make that transition easier by letting your son or daughter know the parameters of the break. If your child takes a long-acting stimulant medication, it usually wears off by 5:00 p.m.— the time when many kids *start* their homework. This challenge further complicates how parents can give their kids with ADHD needed downtime.

Richard, the father of Alexis, age eight, was confused about how to deal with this exact puzzle.

The homework pushback is harder now that Alexis is in third grade. Her ability to focus is right when she gets off the bus, but that's her least favorite time to work. After dinner, there's no meds left and she has meltdowns. I walk away so I don't lose it, but I am discouraged and depressed about the whole thing.

Richard told me that he was especially sad because school had been unpleasant for him and he hated to see Alexis embark on a similar route. He felt that nothing was working. I asked him if he was open to trying something different. Initially uncertain, he ultimately put his hopelessness aside and said, "Okay, let's give it a go."

First, we consulted with her pediatrician and talked about taking her pills later in the day. She would start at 7:30 a.m. after breakfast instead of 6:45 a.m. before she ate and at 12:30 after lunch instead of 11:30. This way, she would still have some "medicine juice," as Richard called it, in her brain to take a break after school *and* do her homework, since her short-acting Ritalin lasted about four hours. She rarely had problems going to sleep, so it was worth a try. (This may not be a solution for your child or fit with your values about medication, and that's fine too. Using the structured plan outlined in the next chapter can be quite useful on its own.)

With Alexis we also created a homework plan. Normally, she does the easiest thing first and then slogs through the tougher stuff, when she is most tired and has the least amount of medication left in her brain. What about reversing that? Alexis liked that idea: *"If I have reading and spelling, I do spelling first so I can have more time to read. Do the thing I don't like first and get it over with."* Alexis also said that she didn't want to yell at her dad. She agreed with us that if she had a break after school with a timer before doing her homework, then she wouldn't be so angry with him. *"It has to be the kind with the numbers that count down so I can see how much free time I have left."* Richard said he would purchase one on the way home.

If she raised her voice at him during homework time, instead of yelling back, he would try *self-Control* and immediately do some breathing exercises. Then he will ask if he can help, if she needs a short break, or if she wants a hug. Alexis liked this because she really didn't like to study alone and she could do something other than get mad when she was stuck. By dealing with his own frustration successfully, Richard was able to create an alternative to the unhappy homework routine they had despite his initial reservations.

When parents follow Richard's example, calming themselves first so they can deal more effectively with their son or daughter, it's like following the instructions about oxygen masks on airplanes. You put yours on and then one on your child. This *self-Control* gives you the perspective and clarity of mind to tame the homework monster.

Chapter 6

Walking Through School in Their Shoes

Three Steps to Building Compassion

Step 1: Listening to Voices
About School: Good, Bad, and Indifferent

Despite differing ages, types of ADHD diagnoses, and academic skills, there are common threads that weave through the stories about school that the kids with ADHD tell me. Threads of honesty, adaptability, strength, and struggle; of frustration, shame, persistence, and triumph.

> "I like school. Reading, recess, and lunch are my favorites. At school I need brain breaks, like recess. I wish we had more. We have to sit more in second grade, and we go to the rug only two times the whole day. I have to control myself, and then the energy goes right out of my belly. There's none left. That's why I need flippy floppy time when I get home."   —Terrell, age 8

> "I've always been excited about school. I love it and do lots of things. Sometimes my lunchtime block is triple-booked! I got straight A's until Calculus this year. That is why my dad doesn't want me to have ADHD. To him, I am brilliant, organized, and perfect. It doesn't fit with his image

of me or mine either. But I forget things, and my mom brings me stuff like three times a week."   —Kayla, age 17

"When I was younger, keeping my focus on whatever the teacher was talking about and finishing projects was always really hard. When they said, 'Write a five-paragraph essay,' I struggled terribly. I couldn't think. Kids were talking and I'd look out the window. Even with Adderall, it's still tough. I expect myself to succeed, but it's like a constant state of my head being just above the water. I can't get my work done in one sitting, maybe in five sittings."   —Alex, age 13

"Starting in first or second grade, I compared myself to others and came out on the bottom. I couldn't do stuff that other kids could. I remember struggling with times tables and reading the clock. It still flusters me. Thank God for digital. I didn't feel inspired until last summer, when I discovered rock climbing and backpacking. It totally changed my perspective on school. Now I'm psyched to make being outdoors my career path."   —Ella, age 16

THESE HEARTFELT CONFESSIONS contribute to nurturing *Compassion* for your child or teen by giving you, the manager of the team, insights into some of their daily experiences. Jump-start your family's conversation by gathering information that may go beyond simple likes and dislikes. For instance, your son may be good at spelling but not that interested in it. He might dismiss it because it is easy for him. This is good for you to know. In order for you to create a supportive, lasting network that your son or daughter embraces, you have to start with understanding what their daily life at school is like. Do this exericise first on your own; then repeat it with your child or teen.

EXERCISE 4: SCHOOL REFLECTIONS

What are your child's academic likes and dislikes? Why?

What are your child's nonacademic interests and capabilities? What do they really like to do?

Do any of these occur at school or translate into academic material? If so, how? (e.g., If they like building things, could they collect and reshelve books in the classroom? Make a diorama for a social studies project?)

Have you, a teacher, or your child noticed if they understand certain types of information differently? Fast with math concepts but slow with math facts? Quick with puzzles but lagging with reading?

Step 2: Esme and Her Parents:
Honest Conversation Leads to Change

Here's one way this dialogue can unfold in your family. While it happened in my office, using the Five C's approach, you can absolutely do this at home and will learn how at the end of this section.

Esme, a biracial fifteen-year-old ninth grader with heavy eyeliner and a kick-butt attitude, was referred to me for therapy by her high school. She had been involved in numerous "dramas" with peers, frequently cut classes, and could be argumentative and "fresh" with teachers. She smoked marijuana most days after school ("just a bowl") and on the weekends. She told me:

I've been suspended twice for "stirring the pot," whatever that means, and I've had a bunch of detentions. I don't care. The last one was for going after Tiffany and pulling her hair at lunch when she called me a b*tch for talking to her ex-boyfriend. I mean, they're not even together anymore! School sucks. I failed Bio last semester and got D's in everything else.

Esme and her parents were fighting most of the time, so conversations about school were practically impossible. Her father, Reuben, said: *"She has my bad temper. When she gets mad, she has a really terrible attitude."* Her mother, Danielle, was very worried about Esme and didn't understand why she was having so many problems at school: *"I try to talk to her and sometimes she will cry about how much she hates school, but I don't get much information."* Reuben said they wanted her to *"Make better choices, be less angry, and not get in so much trouble at school."* Esme said she didn't like being suspended and wanted her parents to back off.

In my office, Esme and her parents discussed, for the first time, her academic challenges and their own. Both Reuben and Danielle had finished high school but hadn't much liked it. They were both born in the United States, but Reuben's parents were born in Puerto Rico. They spoke English at home, with some Spanish mixed in. Her father works as a plumber, and her mother is a certified nursing assistant. Reuben shared about having dyslexia and his preference for watching sports on television over reading. Danielle admitted: *"I am lousy with numbers and barely passed Trig."* Esme felt that they had unfair standards for her given their own distaste for school. She resented their expectations for her to bring home good grades without any academic assistance. With some gentle guidance from me, they considered her point. They discussed how they want more for her than they were able to achieve scholastically and their dismay about not being to help her do this. Then they asked her about her interests, what she saw as her strengths and weaknesses, and what type of help she wanted from them. They listened to her responses.

Esme began having academic difficulties in fourth grade. She was tested but did not receive any services. In middle school, when her grades dropped to D's and F's and she was having numerous behavioral problems, no one recommended testing even though Esme told people *"that reading was hard for me."* Her mother wondered if Esme had a learning disability but was unable to get an evaluation for her daughter: *"I was told to call one person, who sent me to someone else, and then they didn't know anything. I gave up.*" Both Danielle and Reuben shared their frustrations with the school system and their regrets about not being more persistent. They talked about how Esme had been fighting with them and getting high: they felt pushed away. Esme admitted to spending more time with friends, where she didn't feel like a disappointment.

Esme, her parents, and I agreed that the first step would be investigating whether Esme had a learning disability. In order to do this, though, Esme had to stop smoking marijuana after school so the testing could show her true cognitive functioning. We spoke candidly about whether she would cut back on her substance use so the evaluation would give us a useful baseline of what was happening in her brain. She grudgingly agreed, and later, in private, the two of us explored how she could do this. Danielle and Reuben thought that testing through the high school was the best approach and wanted guidance in initiating that process. Until then, Esme and I talked about what she could do right now before getting any test results. We agreed she could start by trying in classes she liked (Math and Biology). Esme agreed that "trying" meant going to class daily and staying for after-school help once a week. It also meant talking to her teachers, telling them that she was attempting to improve her grades, and asking for their input.

Three months later, Esme had reduced her smoking substantially to limited weekend use, and her testing was completed. It indicated that she had ADHD and dyslexia. In fact, she was reading at a fifth-grade level. She was immediately placed on an IEP, enrolled in an academic support class, and started receiving reading instruction. She was still very unhappy in school:

> I had to take all these stupid tests that you recommended and now I find out that I have ADHD and dyslexia, which means that I can't read, so really, Dr. Sharon, why should I bother? I can never catch up. When I am sixteen, I can drop out and get my GED. No one cares anyway except you and maybe my mom.

When I asked her if that was really, deep down, what she wanted to do, she became very quiet and teared up. *"No. Only losers drop out. I would like to graduate high school with everyone else. I just don't know how."* We talked about how the academic support class, "trying" in classes, and getting extra advice from her guidance counselor about problems with teachers were great ways to start. For the most part, she stuck with this plan. She let Danielle check in with her Learning Strategies teacher each week by email so she was informed about her progress without Esme telling her. This relieved some of the pressure that Esme was feeling at home and reduced family arguments.

Three months after that session, she proudly showed me her progress report: A's in her Learning Strategies class and C's in her Math, Biology, and English classes. Reuben and Danielle were very pleased and shared their happiness and relief with Esme. Their fighting had diminished somewhat, and Reuben was pleased that she was hanging out now *"with kids who want to do good in school."* She had stopped smoking marijuana completely, telling me, *"It's not helping me get anywhere."* While school continued to be taxing for her and she still got a few in-school detentions (one for being late to class and one for screaming in the hallway at her ex-boyfriend's new girlfriend), she was not suspended. She and her parents saw her as being on a more positive track. Esme happily shared with me: *"I don't have to drop out anymore. I know that I will walk across that stage with everyone else in three years."* Though loathe to admit it, Esme wanted more for herself, just like her parents did. She didn't know what, but it wasn't dropping out. Ultimately, she graduated high school with her class and now works as a manager of a clothing store.

Tips for Having Honest Conversations About School

1. Make a plan to sit down together to talk about school at a time and place that works for everyone.
2. Start with your curiosity. Ask your child or teen for their opinion about how things are going. What are they good at? Where do

they struggle? Be neutral and show genuine interest to counteract any possible defensiveness.

3. Repeat exactly what you heard them say. "*I heard you say*_____. *Is that right?*" Make an empathic statement that shows caring. "*It sounds like*_____." Ask who, if anyone, understands them at school. Perhaps share a challenging school experience of your own (from Exercise 3) and how you got through.

4. Ask your child about their own goals for school. These should be specific, such as "*I want to take art classes*" or "*I want to have good enough grades so that I can play football.*" Discuss how you or someone else could assist them in making those goals a reality.

5. Create an action plan in which each person has a particular task. Set a follow-up meeting time for the following week.

6. Appreciate your son or daughter for being honest and talking with you. You may receive gratitude from them; you may not. It doesn't mean that they don't feel it.

Step 3: Facing Daily Academic Challenges

Building *Compassion* about school also entails asking and listening to what kids with ADHD have to say about reading, mathematics, and writing—their most common trouble spots. Children and teens regularly reveal to me their awareness of their academic competencies and challenges with surprising insightfulness. The following are some of what they've shared by subject area, with extra comments about writing since it is often so challenging for these young people.

Reading Challenges

"I'm interested in a lot of books, but I don't have the patience to read them. I skip, like, seven hundred pages and just go to the end. . . . I love when my dad reads to me, but not lame books like *Pat Sat on Mat*. Harry Potter and Percy Jackson are my favorites." —Jayden, age 8

"Things with words are way easier for me. I get very distracted very easily except when I am reading, which I love. I eat faster when I read. Dad doesn't think so. Yesterday, he took my book away and it took me like an hour to eat a little bit. I eat faster because I am thinking about the book. But if I'm not, I'm like, 'Oooh, I wanna break this little grain in half and see what happens.'" —Tiana, age 9

"I was raised speaking Spanish until I was about four, and then I had to switch to English. I was getting confused, so I had to just do English because it would've affected my schooling. English is where I struggled, and that's where my second disorder is, my reading and writing disorder. I already had trouble sitting down and focusing. I loved when my mother read to me, but I never really enjoyed sitting down myself with a book until last year." —Xavier, age 15

"You know I don't like reading out loud, right? I'm a slow reader, it's hard for me, and I don't want to do it in front of everyone. Last week, Mr. Brady kicked me out of class because I refused to read out loud. I feel bad holding up the class and when I don't know a couple of words. Sounding out words makes me look dumb." —Destiny, age 15

WHETHER IT'S OVERFOCUSING on a story or avoiding reading as much as possible, hearing what these kids say about reading improves your understanding of their experiences. Just like the manager probes his pitcher's reasons for wanting to stay in the game, you can wonder about reading by considering things related to it: engaging content, English as a Second Language, dyslexia, or slower verbal processing speed. These issues are researched, and effective interventions are available through your school or private tutoring. The first, most important step is making sure your child has been properly assessed for any reading disabilities and determining with the school if they are receiving appropriate instruction and accommodations. If they qualify for a reading, speech, or language disability, they will need special interventions to help them improve their skills and support to accept their learning differences. These interventions will occur at school but may also require supplemental help. Even without a diagnosis, though, reading can be unpleasant for kids with ADHD, especially if the material is not inherently interesting.[1]

Finding creative ways to practice and enjoy reading can be a can of worms. You've probably tried a hundred different ways to make this happen. The goal here is reading *anything* (except pornography or violent material) that is engaging and interesting *enough* for them to do it. They may or may not like it. The manager makes sure the team players are in good physical condition so they can play baseball strong and hard. They may or may not like fitness exercises, but they do them in service of the larger goal of being in shape to play well. Your goal is to make sure your child knows how to read proficiently. Then, hopefully, reading will be less arduous and more pleasurable in the future, but who knows? Not everyone likes reading, and your child can still be successful in the world without it being a passion or even a hobby. You have to focus on the now first. Minecraft books; joke books; graphic novels; two-minute mysteries; magazines about sports, music, fashion, or other interests; the daily newspaper—time spent perusing any of these should qualify in your home as reading.

Reading at school can be especially difficult, and you may want to use alternative approaches. Perhaps your son is more of an auditory learner and likes to hear books on tape. You could supplement visual reading with listening to a text. Maybe your daughter needs shorter reading assignments that better match her attention span and processing speed with a wider range of topics to make them more appealing. As the manager, step in and discuss these options with your child and their teachers, advocating for a way to make reading accessible and tolerable. One boy I know loves nonfiction but dislikes fiction. His sixth-grade teacher wanted the students to read a novel for their book report. He and his parents had been arguing about this assignment because he *"couldn't find anything good."* We talked about finding a novel that read like nonfiction: something historical or a fictional biography. His teacher helped him find one, and everyone was pleased. Don't give up—problem-solve.

Mathematics

"Math is definitely my least favorite subject because I am not good with dividing or subtracting numbers. Or fractions. Fractions take a long time, and I get bored." —Jade, age 12

"Math is hard for me, and asking a friend would be embarrassing. When I have math for homework, it's really bad. My parents can't help. None of us get it. If I don't do my math, I don't get to go to recess because I have to redo it while Ms. Luu shows me how." —Sanjay, age 10

"I do well in math. Math is usually cake for me. It's how my brain works. I got good scores on math and reading comprehension on my PSATs, but it doesn't really matter because I always feel stupid because I can't write." —Anthony, age 16

JUST LIKE READING challenges, math struggles are best approached with inquiry first. Instead of focusing on resistance to doing math, incomplete problem worksheets, poor memorization of math facts, or failing geometry test scores, you and the school should look at what will improve your child's understanding and performance. Auditory and visual processing difficulties or challenges with spatial relationships can make math very difficult for some kids with ADHD. Again, a good assessment of your child's math skills and achievement levels is crucial.

Furthermore, if you do not understand your child's or teen's math homework, do not try to help them. It can lead to frustration for everyone. Instead, look for math tutoring. Most schools have after-school homework support sessions with teachers; older students, including National Honor Society students, will often tutor for free or at low cost; homework clubs offer a supervising teacher and potentially helpful peers. It's just like when the manager calls in the batting coach to help a player who isn't hitting up to their potential. You don't have to play every necessary role on the coaching staff—but you'll need to find someone who can.

Writing

"Writing is like I am trapped inside the page and there are no words. I have a good idea and I write some of it down, but then my brain wanders off."

—Jack, age 8

"I stammer sometimes because I don't know what to say. It's easier with writing. I love writing stories. When you're writing, your hand decides if there's, like, two words or two sentences. Then it goes ahead and chooses whatever it feels like writing. My fingers cramp up when I write. Typing I can do, but I hate it because it's not handwritten." —Kia, age 12

"I like writing. Yesterday, I did a story in school really fast called 'When the Teacher Didn't Come to School.' I used the alphabet. Al erased arithmetic, Bob barfed, Calvin choked, Dan died, Emmett went to the emergency room. It was very funny. Like Pam pooped and Oscar spilled the olive oil. It was great." —Liam, age 9

"I go to the writing center at my school for help. They revise your papers and give you tips. What I like is they don't do it for you. They help you and kind of hint you toward it. They teach you how to do it, so later on, when you're more, what's the word, inept? No, hah, I mean adept."

—Oscar, age 15.

"It's much easier for me to speak than it is to write. The words come a lot easier. Writing seems more permanent. I can go back and analyze and see exactly what I've done wrong. I think fear has something to do with it. I am constantly thinking, 'Oh, does this person understand this?'"

—Anthony, age 16

"When I draw, it makes me write more. I get my drawing book and start to draw for, like, twenty-five minutes. I just sit there and think. I draw, and it's just like, 'Oh, what can I say, what can I write to make this fit?' and then I stop, and I go write something. It's just a back-and-forth process."

—Ivan, age 17

WHILE SOME KIDS with ADHD like writing because it is a venue for expressing their many ideas quickly and creatively, others despise it. Getting even a few words on the page is torturous. Sometimes the physical act of writing is hard and penmanship can be tough to decipher. Organizing thoughts in their heads and translating them into coherent essays requires that several key executive functioning skills run simultaneously, like clockwork. Skills like deciding what you want to say and what is important to write about (prioritizing), remembering what you have read or learned about a topic (retrieval of information), making an outline for how to say things (planning, sequencing, organizing), managing data and ideas (more prioritizing, organizing, and planning), and using your time productively and sticking with things until they are finished (time management and goal persistence). These skills, typically weaker in people with ADHD, synthesize writing into a well-formed essay.

Writing can often be a source of tension in families. Just as asking your son or daughter neutral, probing questions about reading and math leads to improvement in those areas, discussing their individual and idiosyncratic process of writing can help too. In a calm moment, grab a pen and paper and try a conversation like this:

1. Together, identify something that is easy or *not that difficult* about writing. Maybe it's getting an idea, researching a topic, or even the typing. Find something and jot it down.

2. Next, help your son or daughter use a rating scale from 1 to 10 to assess writing: 1 = THE EASIEST PARTS and 10 = THE VERY HARDEST PARTS. Use this list of basic skills needed for writing to help you:

   a. Come up with ideas about a topic that are relevant and doable.
   b. Apply known information about the topic to focus ideas.
   c. Use a graphic organizer that makes sense to your child or teen.
   d. Outline your project, which combines research with your own thoughts.
   e. Estimate the amount of time it takes to do the writing.
   f. Talk out ideas prior to writing them down.
   g. Create a work schedule that realistically leads you to completion.

3. Here's a sample conversation:

   ADULT: "What number would you give coming up with an idea?"
   TEEN: "I have lots of ideas. I just don't know which ones to go with. They are all important."
   ADULT: "So that would be a low number, like what?"
   TEEN: "This is stupid."
   ADULT: "Let's just try."
   TEEN: "Fine. Ideas, two. Choosing the best one to write about, ten."
   ADULT: "Got it. How about researching a topic?"
   TEEN: "That's not too bad. I like learning new stuff. Maybe a five."

4. Brainstorm alternatives to areas that your son or daughter identifies as THE VERY HARDEST PARTS. These ideas can include

getting writing support at school from teachers, going to a writing center at school, working with a friend, or finding a writing tutor.

5. Break writing assignments into smaller, achievable parts. Obtain clear guidelines from teachers to increase your child's comfort and skills with writing.

6. Don't proofread if you two already argue about writing. Let the teachers or other specific coaches do this so you can maintain your role as manager.

Kids with ADHD are cognizant of what they love, what they do well, and what is challenging about school. Their insights show that they know enough about themselves to join you in creating effective and lasting interventions.

Chapter 7

Creating School Solutions That Stick

Collaboration *Is Key!*

Family-School Collaboration

You have an eight-year-old daughter, Amelia, who has a diagnosis of ADHD along with a language-processing disorder. She has already been identified as needing reading support and receives specialized assistance outside the classroom twice a week as part of her IEP. You have been getting emails from her second-grade teacher, Mr. R, that she is behaving inappropriately in class and he would like to speak with you. Instead of meeting alone with him to discuss Amelia's challenges in the classroom, you arrange two meetings: one with adults (certainly the teacher and reading specialist but also maybe the principal or school counselor) and one that includes your daughter and Mr. R.

The first meeting allows you, her teacher, and others to discuss what is going on in the classroom and at home. This is not a formal team meeting; it's a time to ask questions and share information. Mr. R says he really likes Amelia: she is spunky, artistic, and funny. She has some good friends too. He also tells you that, in spite of his efforts to redirect her, she often spaces out, fiddles at her desk, puts her head down, or talks to other kids during reading time. She has trouble focusing during morning meetings, even though she sits right next to him. Sometimes, Amelia cries when academic tasks are too hard for her. You, Mr. R, and the reading specialist agree that classroom reading, both silent and aloud, are her most challenging times. You explore interventions that might help Amelia, including temporarily reducing her workload to strengthen her reading stamina and build her confidence.

The second meeting provides you with an opportunity to explore Amelia's ideas about school. It goes something like this:

MOM: "We're meeting with Mr. R today, not because you're in trouble but because we want to make school better for you. Tell us what you like best about school."

AMELIA: "Recess. I get to play with my friends and no one tells me what to do."

MOM: "Is there anything in the classroom that you like?"

AMELIA: "I like when there is free choice time. I get to draw or do puzzles. Sometimes I like math."

MR. R: "You are good at drawing, and I've hung two of your pictures by the window. You're also quick with numbers and help other students when they are stuck, which is great."

MOM: "What don't you like so much?"

AMELIA: "Do I have to say? Okay, I don't like morning meeting or writing that much. Reading is boring and hard."

MR. R: "I've noticed this. If you had to choose one to go better, which would it be?"

AMELIA: "Reading. I mean, it's okay but too long. And there are no books that I like."

MR. R: "What would be a good book?"

AMELIA: "I don't know. They're just boring."

MOM: "Maybe Mr. R can help you find more interesting books."

MR. R: "Sure, but I wonder if it would be better if you read for eight minutes instead of fifteen. Maybe you could quietly draw for the other time or do some math problems. If that goes well for a few weeks, then we can try ten minutes. What do you think?"

AMELIA: "I guess. How will I know when the time is up?"

MR. R: "I'll quietly tap your desk. Let's start tomorrow and check in Friday."

MOM: "This sounds like a good plan. Thanks, Mr. R., and you, too, Amelia."

You and Mr. R have asked Amelia about her likes and dislikes and her strengths and challenges related to school. In real life, just as in this conversation, there will be overlaps between what the adults see as primary challenges and what your child or teen thinks. This overlap is your golden ticket to co-creating alternatives. Homeschool *Collaboration* has been found to be "particularly important for students" with ADHD and learning disabilities to promote educational success.[1]

Collaboration at Home: Creating Plans That Actually Work!

When a task is fundamentally unrewarding or uninteresting (the way that kids with ADHD often perceive homework—or an adult might perceive sorting through a little-used closet), no one feels excited to do it. Your child's ADHD brain especially needs for things to be engaging to accomplish them. The executive functioning skills of motivation (why you do something) and initiation (getting started on it) are simply developing more slowly than for kids without ADHD. It is common for kids with ADHD to face challenges in these areas, and finding your own reason to do something and deriving satisfaction from doing it doesn't consistently emerge until late adolescence. There are two types of motivation. **Extrinsic motivation** refers to an outside request, reward, or responsibility that depends on achieving a goal. You turn in your sports permission form by the due date or you can't play on the basketball team. **Intrinsic motivation** means striving toward a goal for personal satisfaction or accomplishment. You attempt to break your record on a favorite computer game. When a child or teen with ADHD can't see any immediate satisfaction from a task or grasp any long-term benefit (especially tough for their "now/not now" brains), they will struggle with doing it.

Incentives help kids with ADHD who struggle with motivation and starting things. They build extrinsic motivation toward a desired goal, which, when achieved, nurtures the positive feelings for internal motivation later on. For instance, you might link completion of a dreaded book report to an extra thirty minutes of playing Wii. *Incentives that motivate are incentives that matter to kids, not what you think would be good for them.* You link something unsavory that needs to get done with something they want. It's a win-win for everyone. You may balk at the idea of using incentives for stuff that simply has to get done, but these external carrots train your ADHD son or daughter to internalize the concept that effort leads to satisfying accomplishment.

Consider something from your own life. Let's say that the garbage needs to go out but you would rather watch your favorite television show. You don't really like taking out the trash because it is smelly and gross. So you make a deal with yourself: you can get cozy on the couch with your favorite show *after* you empty the trash. You are using the pleasure of vegging out as your motivator to complete the chore. This is how incentives work, and they absolutely promote success. People often confuse incentives with bribes. The difference is that a bribe gives the reward before the desired action ("Hey, kid, here's five bucks to take this bag across the street" versus "Hey, kid, if you take this bag across the street, I will give you five bucks"). The incentive provides the reward afterward. Effective incentives should change periodically to keep them appealing.

Another issue related to getting started with unpleasant tasks is procrastination. Procrastination is directly related to the size of a task. Something that may seem small to us, like doing a math worksheet, can feel enormous to a student with ADHD. They often think: *"Why start something that seems impossible to finish? Why even bother? If I don't try, I can't fail."* They freeze and unwittingly become masters of avoidance.

The best solution to feeling overwhelmed by a project, task, or chore is to break it down into smaller pieces. This process can be tough for the growing ADHD brain because it also involves understanding a sequence of events. When the task of reading a chapter of a book seems daunting, tackling five pages at time is likely more manageable.

Before putting these concepts into action, consider a few things and write them down:

1. **What does your child** *love* **to do?** No activity is too unimportant to consider. Whether it's additional time playing outside, using electronics or social media, or going out for a special ice cream, these are privileges that your child can earn. All children need nourishment, security, and love to thrive; they do not "need" access to Instagram. These beloved activities or treats can act as motivators for doing homework.

2. **What type and size of homework assignments do they manage successfully?** You likely have noticed how much and what kind of studying your child can do easily and what is harder. Breaking things down helps them accomplish *something*. Since no step is too small, reflect on the quantity of work that they manage.

3. **How long can your son or daughter focus on homework before getting distracted or bored?** For kids under ten with ADHD, this period can vary from five to twenty minutes. For kids between eleven and fourteen, it's usually twenty to forty-five minutes, and for teens between fifteen and eighteen, it's likely anywhere from thirty to sixty minutes. With hyperfocusing, these can be longer, and times vary with individual kids. Generally, you want to stop the work period before boredom and negativity set in.

You are now ready to sit down with your child or teen at a predetermined time (i.e., not in the middle of an argument) to talk about homework. Start by asking *them* the same questions you asked yourself and write down their answers. This not only helps you remember exactly what they said but it also shows them you are taking their opinions seriously. Then, discuss what is going well with homework and what isn't. Ask what differences they would like to see and share your opinions too. Together, pick one issue that you both have identified as problematic. Is it getting started? Is it staying focused on the assignments? Is it remembering to turn in the work? Write down what you decide in your notebook for future reference or even post it in the kitchen.

Most kids ask for incentives that involve technology: more computer, television, or gaming time. You can do this, but you can also offer your time with them as an additional incentive. Regardless of what they say or do to the contrary, you matter a great deal to them. Kids want to feel that they are your priority and that you share a connection. For elementary school kids, playing a game, building LEGOs, kicking the soccer ball, or reading together can be something to eagerly anticipate. It's a bit tougher with middle school and high school kids since what they often want is space away from you and with their friends: whether it's going online, or to the mall, parties, or sleepovers. But they might opt for watching a television show with you (one that they really like even if you don't), cooking something together, or cyber shopping. If you offer this, you *must specify beforehand* the guidelines about together time. A parent recently asked me if she should take away time with her adolescent son if he didn't fulfill his part of the bargain. My answer was no. I advised her to set up a dual-option program. If he does his part of the agreement, you both relax and watch his favorite show (Option One). If he doesn't, you will work together to clean his room (Option Two). Either way, you are spending time together. After two sessions of tidying his room, her son's cooperation improved. Soon they had watched three seasons of *Game of Thrones*.

Let's set up the details of the plan that you *both* can agree on. This includes establishing the total length of the desired study time and shorter work periods. These blocks are then broken up by *timed* breaks of no longer than ten minutes. Depending on your child's or teen's age, interest, and your house rules, breaks can include snacks, a game of cards, a phone call, walking around, playing with a pet, texting, Instagram, etc. At the end of the entire homework period, your child has hopefully earned their incentive by doing the agreed-upon work. If the work is not completed, then the reward doesn't occur. If the agreement is that your daughter gets thirty minutes of iPad time and a game of UNO with you once all her homework is completed (Option One) or no electronics and loading the dishwasher if she doesn't (Option Two), that's what has to happen. Do not renegotiate the terms of your program if your son or daughter doesn't meet them. *Collaboration rarely happens under pressure.*

Initially, you may have to work alongside your child or teen to make sure that studying is occurring during this period and to answer any academic questions that arise. You can call this "family work time" and use the opportunity to catch up on your things (like balancing the checkbook, answering emails, reading an article of interest). Just as the manager reviews the plays before the game, it's good to go over the various homework assignments before starting. This allows you to help them prioritize, decide how long of a study time is needed, and, if necessary, double-check that all homework is completed. Make a photocopy of the following form to assist you and your child or teen with this process. Teachers, parents, and students (despite any protests) have found them helpful in cultivating executive functioning skills that contribute to academic success.

ASK YOUR SON or daughter if they prefer to start the homework period by tackling the hardest assignment first when their brain is the freshest, followed by something easy, and then medium. Some kids prefer to do something easy first to feel a sense of progress. Otherwise, the easy and medium tasks offer a break from the demands of the tougher ones. This progression builds stamina and persistence. When your child wants your assistance, help them out. If you are working simultaneously, you are right there to notice if they wander off into YouTube or Twitter and then calmly steer them back on course. Do your best to keep your comments about how they could do things differently and more efficiently (i.e., better) to yourself.

HOMEWORK FORM

Today's Date: _____

Teacher Signature (to make sure information is correct) _____

Parent Signature (to acknowledge you have seen this) _____

(Signatures needed for elementary school students)

Subject	Assignment	Materials Needed	Due Date	Rank Of Difficulty (Easy, Medium, Hard)	How Much Time Should It Take?	Incentive
EX. 5th grade Social Studies	Fill in the names of the states on the map of the U.S.A.	Worksheet, geography book, and pencil	Friday	Medium	One hour	A game of UNO
EX. 9th grade English	Read 30 pages of *To Kill a Mockingbird*	The book	Friday; in 3 days	Medium	One hour: 30 mins today and 30 mins tomorrow	10 mins extra phone time

Notes:

Later you can casually offer a suggestion about improving their study habits: *"I noticed last night that you have all your class papers in one file and it took a while to find what you needed. What if we separate them into files for each class to save time?"* This way they won't feel criticized or monitored when they are trying to do their own thing during family work time. Reviewing their work itself is tricky: sometimes with its focus on "errors," your child can feel bad about what's been done instead of good about completing it. Let their teachers correct any mistakes so you don't get into that hornets' nest.

Figuring out how much you should be involved in your child's homework can be complicated. Many parents struggle with knowing when to step in and when to hold back. If you are unsure about what to do, start by checking in with teachers or guidance counselors who know your child best about academic performance or possible concerns. Then talk with your child or teen about their own impressions about their academic work and goals for school. Share your thoughts without diminishing theirs. Many parents and kids agree about general academic goals but not about how to achieve them. Sho-li, age fourteen, unhappily showed her first-quarter report card of *B*'s, *C*'s, and a *D* to her parents. She agreed with them that she could do better, and she wanted to get more *A*'s than *B*'s as much as they wanted her to (the internal motivator). Her mom spoke to her guidance counselor and learned that Sho-li's biggest problem was missed assignments. Sho-li had stopped using her planner: *"This year no one checks it, and there's nothing to write down anyway. I can remember everything."* Her parents disagreed, and her low grades showed otherwise.

We set up a plan where her dad would meet with her nightly to review her planner and homework, and afterward, she could have extra phone time (the external motivator). No meeting with Dad, no phone bonus. Sho-li groaned and complained about being treated "like a baby" but went along. Everyone agreed that if her grades improved by the end of the semester, she and her dad could cut back to twice a week (an external motivator for any teen—less parental involvement). Sho-li brought up her grades, and her dad pulled back as promised. Collaborating like this results in effective, successful homework plans.

Chapter 8

Keeping It Going

Fostering Consistency *About School*

Routines and More Routines

Consistency means doing what you say you will do without putting pressure on yourself to be perfect. All kids, even those without ADHD, really benefit from dependable routines. School starts and ends at specific times with defined breaks and choices. Homework should be similar: the same daily workspace, doable time limits, and breaks with timers. These routines help the director develop by fostering all-important executive functioning skills like prioritizing, planning, and persistence for school success.

Most adults like some predictability in their lives. It helps us orient ourselves, whether it's the nine-to-five schedule of our workdays, our to-do list of errands on a Saturday, or our plan to spend the day at the beach. Children and teens, who naturally have less control over their schedules, are not that different. They need us to help them remember, organize, and follow through on what is happening when. If you have your own organizational challenges, don't berate yourself. Everyone has strengths and limitations. Get some support from friends, technology (alerts and calendars are great aids), or a therapist or coach if you need it. You will benefit, and your kids with ADHD will too.

The Importance of Persistence

Routines nourish persistence—how you get things done. They provide

Routines nourish persistence.

essential structure for doing things. Kids with ADHD depend on them to organize their lives so they don't have to. Persistence also relies on *efforting* and resiliency. When school is challenging for young people with ADHD, they have to figure out how to approach and continue with unpleasant academic tasks and recover when their attempts don't work out. They need to get through classes and homework long enough to make a decent effort and feel good just for trying. Successes boost them. But, as highlighted earlier, if the studying seems boring, overwhelming, or unachievable, discouragement sets in and kids will likely lack motivation. Often they give up or avoid *efforting* to eliminate any possible failure. Knowing that if they apply themselves today to boring science questions the unit test next week will be easier doesn't really matter that much because the experience *now* is so intolerable. Persistence flies out the window.

So what keeps them going? Here are some of their comments about persevering with schoolwork:

> "I have really hard homework, but I do it. I don't give up. Mom helps me stick with it. She keeps saying, 'Do your homework. Come on, come on.'"   —Jack, age 8

> "My other counselor would tell things I can do, like having music on when I study. Because if I'm listening to music, I'll start singing along with it. I'll get my homework done faster."   —Taylor, age 12

"I just tell myself, 'Hopefully this works'. If not, I'm going to have to find a new way. I'm like, 'Okay, I'll just try harder next time,' and I move on."   —Darren, age 15

"If my friends are available, I'll go and study with them because I'm less likely to spend time on Facebook or looking at videos on YouTube if they are working across from me. One time my friend Evan and I, we both had to write the same paper for a class. We were both having serious mental blocks, so we decided to do it together. I ended up pacing back and forth in my living room and dictating to him while he wrote. Then he did the same thing with his paper. It sure helped."   —Lila, age 17

WHETHER IT'S PARENTAL or peer support, music or self-talk, these kids show us about persistence. Even if their work is incomplete or incorrect, if they have really tried to do something, then it's hard for anyone to accuse them of being lazy, uncooperative, or unsuccessful. Encouragement from you and teachers nurtures their efforts and eases their struggles. Their director brushes herself off from a stumble and takes another go at the task, showing us her burgeoning resiliency. Trying and making mistakes, not perfection, is how all of us learn and what most parents want for their kids.

Parents and caregivers who practice *Consistency* about school can sometimes appear like those vans that follow cyclists on the road. You chug behind your son or daughter, providing necessary support, guidance, and sustenance without taking over the direction of the route. You help them keep home and school routines reliable while staying as calm as possible in the face of any obstacles. You forgive yourself when this doesn't happen and try again. Remember that you are the manager of this team, and your ultimate goal for success is building strength and skills. This is persistence at its best.

Chapter 9

Celebration

More Than Saying "Good Job!"

Encouragement from Outside and Inside

Celebration about school starts with noticing and, yes, congratulating your kids when they achieve academic successes. Whether or not they show you, your belief in their abilities matters to them. It feels good for everyone, ADHD or not, to hear an enthusiastic "Way to go!" Of course, it is equally important to affirm when you and your daughter have a successful homework period by pointing out what you observed that went well: *"I liked how you stopped doing your math at break time but then went right back to it"* or *"I see how hard you are working on that science project, and I am proud of you."* These encouraging comments go a long way toward building self-confidence and emphasizing the positive efforts that your kids with ADHD are making.

But these words do more than offer praise: they also model the language that kids can use for themselves. Children and teens internalize our voices. If adults tell children repeatedly how their efforts aren't good enough or how they can do better, those negative words remain louder

> Children and teens internalize our voices.

than the positive ones. *Celebration* about school is about noticing what is working and saying it aloud to your son or daughter *many times*. Then, this voice becomes more ingrained than the others.

Celebration is also more than praise or encouragement. *Celebration* occurs when your son or daughter accepts their ADHD brain to the point where they can start to advocate for themselves. When they can talk with composure (and little shame) about having ADHD with teachers or even peers, when they show responsibility for their studies, and when they cooperate more than they avoid, they go beyond acceptance to celebrating who they are. They are not hiding having ADHD and a brain that learns differently. Instead, they are able to talk about these differences and ask for what they need to achieve academic success.

Self-Advocacy: The Pinnacle of School *Celebration*

Just as important as nurturing a positive inner voice in their heads is speaking up appropriately for themselves at school. This is an essential part of being a successful learner. Feeling capable and competent flows naturally as a follow-up to consistent *efforting* and persistence. Your kids with ADHD may have needed accommodations, interventions, and support to participate and succeed in the classroom and accomplish their homework. Over time, they realize what works for them in achieving their school goals. They see the benefits in any assistance they have received (from you or their teachers, therapists, counselors, or tutors). You want your kids *not* to be silenced by shame, embarrassment, or dislike of ADHD. Self-advocacy demonstrates *Celebration* because it fuses an understanding of their strengths and limitations with speaking up. Youth with ADHD have ideas about what makes sense to them in school, and they need encouragement from the adults in their lives to ask for it appropriately. Taking this step on their own behalf expresses their growing confidence while simultaneously empowering them.

Kids from kindergarten to high school can talk about what works for them at school and with homework. This ability becomes increasingly important they grow older because adults become less involved in the intricacies of their lives. Here's what some of them shared with me:

> When I finish a math problem, I know what I've done. I want my mom to tell me how many problems I have to finish before my break, not the time I have left or how long it took me. Minutes don't mean anything.
>
> —Desiree, age 9

> I like to use a timer. My dad sets it for fifteen minutes, and when it goes off, I take a five-minute break. I can do some LEGOs or run around or get a snack. When the timer goes off again, I go back to homework. My teacher says I don't have to work longer than forty-five minutes, so if I can't do it all, that's okay."
>
> —Jared, age 10

> I've learned that I'm a read-and-write learner. I'll see the teacher write it on the board or in a book, and if I write it down, or if I type it, it sticks with me, versus just hearing it. I'm not a good audible learner. I need to take notes. If I miss a class, then I'll read the section or look at the notes that they covered in class and write some of my own because it helps me better.
>
> —Oscar, age 14

Self-advocacy marches alongside these examples of blossoming self-understanding and helps kids with ADHD grow into self-sufficient adults. When our children are young, and even as they age, you are their primary advocates, but you are not with your kids every moment of every day. While you can make sure the structures are in place to best assist them in the learning process (or elsewhere), ultimately your sons and daughters have to learn to do this for themselves, whether or not they have ADHD. Knowing themselves as learners and having both the confidence to ask for help and the willingness to receive it are the greatest tools you can nourish in your child.

Self-Advocacy in Action: Emily's Success

Self-advocacy doesn't mean being demanding, entitled, or hostile. It's knowing what you need and how to ask for it strongly and respectfully. Emily, a shy ninth-grader who liked to please just about everyone and hated making waves, struggled with ADHD and a language-based learning disability. Although she tried hard in school, her grades weren't always what she wanted and homework sometimes brought her to tears. She was easily discouraged and felt embarrassed about asking for the help she needed at school. Her parents regularly told her that they saw how hard she was working and that they appreciated her efforts, but they worried about her low self-esteem and the way she avoided talking with her teachers. Her mother wanted Emily to *"figure out her own ways to advocate for herself. I can't step in all the time. I work full-time. She has to learn to do this."* With parental encouragement, meetings with her guidance counselor, and six months of therapy, Emily eventually learned how to speak up for herself:

> *I have a very extensive 504 plan. I don't have an IEP, but I probably should. I like school, and I want to do well. I want to play lacrosse in college. Usually I get A's and B's and sometimes a C in math. Right from the start, Ms. Jefferson, the new English teacher, gave us vocab and spelling tests every week. In my accommodations it said that I didn't need to take spelling tests, and she was like, 'No, that's stupid. Everyone has to take them, including you.' I kept failing them because I can't do spelling and vocab. That's why I have a 504, duh. My grade was like a C–.*
>
> *I complained to my parents, who thought it would be better if I could take care of it instead of them calling. So I just tried harder to pass those stupid tests, but I couldn't, and I was scared about getting a D in a class that I like and want to do well in. I talked about it with you because you're my therapist, you showed me my 504 plan, and we talked about my rights and how I learn. You agreed with my parents*

about me talking to my guidance counselor. Which I did even though I was dead scared.

Then there was a big meeting at school and everyone, except Ms. Jefferson, decided I didn't need to take them. I was nervous, but I said to her, 'If a person has glasses and it allows them to see better, are they cheating? If a person has a learning disability and they have accommodations to put them on the same playing level as everyone else, is that cheating? No!' and that kind of made her say, 'Okay, you're actually right.' I stood up for myself.

Emily conquered her fears, followed the appropriate channels at school, and was able to get her needs met. Without understanding the intricacies of why spelling was hard, she knew that it was challenging and that she wasn't supposed to take spelling tests. She accepted this part of her brain and fought against what she knew was wrong. This was a turning point for her.

Like many kids with ADHD, Emily wants to be successful. She needs the right tools, the right environment, and the right support for this to happen. She knew that having accommodations would move her in this direction. Emily's parental encouragement and adult supports assisted her in gathering enough determination to speak up for herself. Emily shows us how the self-advocacy part of *Celebration* can look at school: insightful, brave, and articulate.

PART THREE

Life at Home and Beyond

Chapter 10

Managing Big Feelings

MEET MALIK, AGE 12, and his parents, Robert and Chantelle, who came to my office recently.

MALIK: "You know my music teacher, Mr. Burke? The mean one? He picks on me. I got in trouble because of him and can't use computers at school."

ROBERT: "Now that's not the whole truth."

SS: "Malik, why don't you start at the beginning and tell me what happened?"

MALIK: "So I was in his class. I wasn't even talking. I was sitting down, said hi to my cousin, and gave him a hug, and Mr. Burke says, 'Can you shut up?' Why can't he use a different word? Like, 'Malik, can you be quiet,' or 'Malik, stop talking.' But to just come out with 'Shut up'? Nah. He is disrespecting me. So I looked at my friend, and I was thinking maybe Mr. Burke was talking to him 'cause I wasn't talking. I was like, 'Yo, Thomas, he's talking to you, bro.' And Mr. Burke says, 'No, Malik, I'm talking to you, shut up and sit down.' And I was like, 'Why are you telling me to shut up?' And he goes, 'Because you're talking.' He made me so mad. I left the class and went to the office like I'm supposed to. Then I go to Social Studies. We are studying colonial America, and I write my essay on the computer about my colonial school and my bad colonial music teacher. I say somethin' like, 'He bullies me and if all goes well, he'll hang tomorrow.' It's funny, right?"

ROBERT: "Well, his Social Studies teacher didn't think so, and she showed it to the principal, and the next thing we know is Chantelle and I have to go into school and meet with him because Malik has threatened a teacher. He got a detention and lost computer privileges for two months."

MALIK: "Yeah, now I do nothing in computers, my favorite class. I'm good at it. I help other kids."

CHANTELLE: "When we told him, he had a fit. Kicked a chair, cussed, and yelled about how it wasn't fair. We sent him to his room. On his way, he stopped in Corinne's room, pulled out all his sister's drawers, and dumped everything on her floor. I agree that it's not fair, but there's nothing we can do, and why go in Corinne's room? It's just mean."

What's Going on Here?

Malik, a spirited middle schooler, feels wrongly targeted by a teacher he knows dislikes him. He follows the plan we have worked out with the school: when he gets really upset and thinks he might lose it, he goes to the main office and waits until the next class. Then he channeled his upset creatively into an essay that was then interpreted as a threat to his teacher, whom he had no intention of harming. As far as he is concerned, he did nothing wrong and was punished anyway. It seems unfair to him and, quite frankly, I think we could all agree that the teacher's use of "shut up" was inappropriate. With no assistance from the administration, Malik and Mr. Burke lack an opportunity to clear the air for Malik to make amends. When his parents tell him the school's decision, he can no longer contain his anger and explodes, taking it out on them and his older sister. Later, he told me: *"I hold it together at school because I know if I don't, I will get in big trouble, I will get expelled. I can't get expelled from home."* But now he has two problems: one at school and one at home.

These types of situations can occur for all kids, but unfortunately, they happen all too often for kids with ADHD. The intensity of their feelings—positive or negative—flood their developing capacities to gauge the consequences of their behaviors. Their overtaxed executive functioning skills often cannot cope with effectively managing and responding to this rush of emotions. Kids told me about how they get overwhelmed: sometimes by excitement or passion (which they saw as positive feelings), but more often they mentioned anger, worry, and disappointment (which they perceived as negative ones). At times they monitored themselves, but at others they could not. Some of them readily acknowledged how their big emotions affected those around them. In this chapter we will look at how to deal with the so-called negative emotions when they become too intense.

Emotions Make Things Happen

Emotions create action: they get things started and keep them going. When kids—any kids—are flooded by feelings, they struggle to access those parts of themselves that know what good choices are. The big emotions push aside any sensible information about how to deal appropriately with what is happening right now. With ADHD kids, their executive functions are simply not developed enough to do this as adeptly as a peer or an adult would. Of course, everybody gets flooded. You may lose your temper, say or do things you regret, and then struggle with guilt and shame. It all boils down to what Daniel Goleman in his book *Emotional Intelligence* calls the "amygdala hijack."[1]

In Chapter 2, you learned about the biology of the ADHD brain, and here, in discussing how to manage emotions, the importance of neurobiology reemerges. Deep in the middle of the brain, inside its emotional center (the limbic system) lies the amygdala. It sets off the flight-or-fight response. When the amygdala senses danger, real or imagined, it jumps into action and charges up the brain to tell the body to run from danger or fight it. That's when you feel a rush of adrenaline, a faster heartbeat, and quick breathing. The amygdala works incredibly fast. While it can take someone around three hundred milliseconds to become consciously aware of a disturbance, the amygdala reacts within twenty milliseconds: this is typically called a "knee-jerk response."[2] Remember the prefrontal cortex—aka the director—from Chapter 2? When the amygdala becomes fired up and takes over, the director goes offline, and feelings rule the day. As the director matures, she helps the amygdala calm down by engaging language to name the elevated emotions and think about the situation.

Another big part of managing feelings lies in our working memory. Working memory is the gateway to long-term memory. As we discussed in Chapter 2, working memory has three principle parts: it holds one piece of information in your mind while you do different things (such as remembering a phone number long enough to write it down); it calls up something from the past and applies it to the present or future (such as remembering that the last time you pushed someone you were sent to the principal's office); and it recalls and follows steps in a series of given directions (such as "hang up my coat and put my backpack on the table"). Dr. Thomas Brown calls working memory "the brain's search engine."[3] We use it to elicit memories that have emotional impact and help us to arrive at thoughtful decisions about what to do when our desires and feelings are bumping into one another.

Research has linked working memory to controlling and expressing emotions. One study found that people with strong working memory are less reactive to events and more capable of assessing emotional situations than those with weaker working memory.[4] Working memory also helps us see the big picture: the forest through the trees. When you consider that working memory is one of the executive functioning skills frequently impacted by ADHD, you can start to understand how your son or daughter can be triggered faster and flooded with big feelings more easily than their peers. It can be tough for them to overcome the effects of an amygdala hijack and recall things they know they should do.

The Flip Sides

Everything that happens in our lives involves emotional reactions. When a driver cuts in front of us, we feel angry. When we find out that a loved one is ill, we feel sad. When we have to prepare for a big presentation, we get nervous. The associations between things that happen and how they make us feel stay with us. When feelings like anger, sadness, or anxiety bubble up inside, we get disturbing internal signals. Nobody likes to feel distressed. Yet, barring traumatic situations, I am suggesting that something positive and useful can be gleaned from these uncomfortable feelings, and there is value in considering their flip sides. This resembles what Dr. Edward Hallowell calls mirror traits: "The mirror traits are simply the positive side of the negative symptoms associated with ADD [and ADHD]."[5] For example, he describes distractibility as "turbocharged curiosity," creativity as "impulsivity gone right," and energy as an alternative to hyperactivity.[6] I am by no means minimizing the seriousness of negative feelings or the effect they wield on daily living. I am simply reframing how to view them to connect more to your whole child rather than their challenging parts.

Let's take a look at alternative ways of viewing outbursts. Anger is a strong feeling of annoyance, displeasure, or hostility and shows up as anything from mild irritation to frustration to seething rage.[7] Sometimes it masks fear and vulnerability. It is often expressed as yelling, irritability, meanness, withdrawal, or aggression (hitting, kicking, biting, slamming doors, or throwing things). Underneath this description of anger may reside some desirable aspects: energy, passion, and sensitivity. Anger is often empowering: tantrums and explosive outbursts require much excitability and strength. Or consider anxiety, typically defined as excessive worry or fear about a possible event in the future. While the concerns may or may not be justified, the reaction is usually disproportionate to the event itself. On the flip side, you can look at anxious children and adults as having good imaginations. They think about what could happen and try to plan for that. While it may be misdirected toward uncertain negative outcomes, this creative, future-oriented planning actually uses important executive functioning skills.

Most kids with ADHD talk to me more about disappointment or regret rather than depression. Their disappointment often reflects discouragement or defeat related to unfulfilled hopes, intentions, or desires. They frequently feel sad about things they said or did and wish they could try again. Experiencing disappointment, though very painful, actually indicates something positive: the existence of goals you had hoped to meet and the motivation to accomplish them. Regret shows their conscience and their ability to ponder their words or deeds. Of course, these emotions don't exist in distinct categories inside of anyone and are usually intertwined. This is particularly true for kids with ADHD whose minds naturally move rapidly from one thought or emotion to another.

Overwhelmed by Big Feelings

Whether the topic is anger, anxiety, or disappointment, children and teens with ADHD describe being overwhelmed by the intensity of these feelings and how they cope:

"I smile when I get mad. If I don't, I kick the wall or slam the door or I mess up my room somehow. Like if my sister gets away with stuff and I don't. Or when I get blamed."   —Deng, age 10

"I haven't been succeeding at school and life, and I expect myself to succeed. . . . I just get so overwhelmed. I worry all the time about stuff I forget. It's a constant state of my head being just above the water."

—Henry, age 16

"Even when I go to sleep I think about stuff I could do. I worry about being wrong; it's not efficient. I get lost in my thoughts and it's not fun. . . . I don't like being by myself. When no one's there it's too quiet. Being quiet is annoying and creepy." —Carly, age 12

NONE OF US can stop big emotions from occurring, but you can help kids with ADHD refrain from criticizing themselves because of how they do or do not manage them. Your son may lose his cool and lash out like Deng, or your daughter might worry and catastrophize like Henry. They may or may not verbally regret how they acted in those moments, but inside they often run a different conversation—one that puts themselves down. These responses make everything more complicated. Now they have two sets of intense feelings to contend with. Brianna, age seventeen, explained: *"I'll flake out on something or double book and then get mad at my friend when she calls me on it. . . . I feel like crap about myself after."* Ethan, age seventeen, talks about his "crazy thinking": *"I speak positive, but what comes to mind is negative stuff first. It may not bother me, but it happens. I don't know why. I'm not a negative person. I just think like that."* When I suggested to him that he could change the words "crazy thinking" to "racing thoughts" to more accurately reflect the pressure and nervousness he felt inside regarding his new job, he smiled. *"I've never thought of it that way. Yeah, that's what happens. My thoughts are racing around like crazy, but I'm not crazy."* It's ultimately more helpful and less damaging to their self-concept if they can separate their *feelings*—anger, anxiety, or disappointment—from the *self-criticism* they pile on top of themselves.

The Pitfalls of Negative Thinking

While eliminating negative thinking is unrealistic for anyone, given the high frequency of criticism that kids with ADHD receive, reducing it is crucial for fostering self-esteem and resiliency. Malik's parents knew he felt bad about his sister's room once he saw how upset she was. They all agreed that he needed to clean up the mess, and while he was doing so, they heard him mumble, *"I suck. I'm a bad brother. I don't do anything right."* This really upset them because they know that he does plenty of good things. You want to assist kids like Malik to change their relationship to the negative voice: to point out that there is a difference between events in their lives and the stories they tell themselves. These interpretations directly influence how someone makes meaning from whatever occurred. Your child may interpret things more harshly than the situation calls for. Brianna gets mad at her friend but then judges herself unkindly for doing it. Ethan feels terrible about having anxiety. Too often, these kids label themselves as "flawed" because of what they do.

Kids with ADHD need help from caring adults to stop playing in the traffic of negative thinking. They have to put negativity outside of themselves and treat it as a separate entity to reduce feeling bad. It's almost as if they need a crossing guard in their heads to protect them by saying: *"This road is now filled with speeding, critical cars that make you hate yourself. Do not enter the crosswalk, or you will be plowed down with their negativity. Remain on the sidewalk until the coast is clear."*[8] When young people with ADHD create such a crossing guard, they learn to slow down or refrain from attacking themselves and deal with their big feelings directly instead.

While it is normal to have some critical feedback loops in our minds, you want to avoid being ruled by them. All too often, kids with ADHD leap from grasping the "wrongness" of their actions to seeing themselves as "deficient." When you ask what the negative voice says to them and then brainstorm together ways to talk back to it (like the crossing guard), you assist your child in learning how to avoid believing everything that voice says. Some of Malik's guilt and regret were appropriate given how he damaged his sister's room. But negative thinking added an emergency broadcast about his worthlessness as a person and his failure as a brother. Malik needed the crossing guard in his mind to say:

Dangerous put down traffic in the road. Turn around. You made a mistake, apologized to your sister, and cleaned everything up. You are not bad.

Externalizing negative thinking takes *a lot* of practice and strong support from you. It may seem awkward at first, but learning to control the volume on that negative voice is a life skill that sustains crucial resiliency and self-esteem. You can help them create positive self-stories.

I ask kids directly about what they tell themselves when they make a mistake or do something they regret. Some speak about judgment and shame; others speak of resilience and acceptance. A few skillfully talk back to the negative voices in their heads:

"When I get bad a grade, I just feel bad. I don't want anyone to see the score. I put it in my desk right away. I say, 'I'm bad,' and 'I don't like myself.' It's pretty harsh. I regret it the next day."   —Deng, age 10

"It seems like no matter how hard I try, I have this pessimistic view of everything, which causes me to worry. I really wish that wasn't the case. If I don't do well on something, I get mad at myself, saying, 'I should have done better.' I get down on myself with soccer too. I really, really hate to lose, because then it's like, 'Oh, man, what did I do to make that happen?'"

—Willow, age 17

"I try to look at why I made a mistake, and if I find out why I'd just probably redo it. If the whole class is knowing how to do something and I don't know how to do it, I just shut down. 'Cause then I feel like I'm the dumb one. I don't want to ask a question, 'cause then I'll feel like it's going to make me look stupid. I do kinda feel ashamed. I say, 'Wow, I'm really slacking.' But I try to keep myself up and not let it get to me. Whatever happens at the end, it's meant to happen for a reason."

—Tyrone, age 14

"I always wanted to do things perfect. I didn't like when people brought things up because I didn't want to be wrong. When I made a mistake, it was like, man, I did something wrong. Before, it was like a punch-the-wall type of feel. Just hit something. Junior year, I started growing up more. When you make mistakes, you gotta learn from that. You can't let it always break you down."

—Ivan, age 17

EVEN THOUGH NEGATIVE thinking has affected each of these young people in some way, I am impressed with the strength and spirit they have to bounce back. Mistakes are opportunities to transform the errors, as Ivan describes. You can assist your child in learning to do this. When you use *Compassion* to empathize with them, *Collaboration* to talk about what's happened and brainstorm alternatives, *Consistency* to present a more positive story, and *Celebration* to notice their efforts, you succeed at teaching them how to separate the noise of the negative traffic voices from the person they really are. That is what builds the resilience they need in life.

Stop, Think, Act
....

When your son or daughter feels overpowered by big feelings, the first step toward regaining balance is getting their director back in charge by activating thinking and working memory skills. Teaching kids to consciously *Stop, Think, Act* helps tremendously. When most people experience intense feelings, they tend to act first, stop second, and think last. Instead, you want to switch this order around: stop and

> Teaching kids to consciously *Stop, Think, Act* helps tremendously.

breathe first, next reflect on what's happening and your options, and then act. The goal is instructing your children to manage their big emotions by engaging the thinking brain. I've had kids tell me that they say this over and over in their heads when things get heated so they can remember to follow it. Just by repeating the words *Stop, Think, Act*, your youngster's speech *will* kick-start their thinking process and activate the director. You may want to practice this yourself as well.

Darryl, age ten, and his father, Sam, describe a situation over the weekend that called for *Stop, Think, Act*. In the first hour of a three-hour drive to visit his grandparents, Darryl started acting up.

> SAM: "He's yellin' at his sisters and singin' loudly. It gets overwhelming for me as the driver. I say, 'I need you to stop what you're doing,' but he keeps doing it and things ratchet up. He won't stop until I turn around and grab him or throw whatever's next to me to get his attention."
>
> DARRYL: "It never works. It just makes me mad. I just didn't want to stop. It was funny, and my sisters liked it. But I went too far."
>
> SAM: "It's dangerous to drive with this going on. I can't focus. I can't do Stop, Think, Act and be all calm and businesslike. I don't want an accident."

At times like this, pausing and reflecting seem impossible, but the conscious effort of *Stop, Think, Act* is exactly what Darryl's father,

Sam, needs to do. It isn't easy for anyone to press the pause button when they are triggered, and we explored his options. Yelling at Darryl, grabbing him, or throwing something were neither working nor something Sam felt good about. It became clear that the best option was either to stop the car or get off the road as soon as possible. Then he and Darryl can get out, take some deep breaths, and break the cycle of escalation. Darryl liked this idea and thought it might help him calm down better. He added: *"That's good. Can I have a hug? A hug would help."* Sam sighed. *"I don't know if I can do that. I'm too frustrated."* He looked at his son. *"I guess the hug will literally pull him together. I'll try."* Sam is aware that he has a problem in the car, but in that moment of his own amygdala hijack, he is too flooded to intervene effectively with Darryl. He needs to use **Stop, Think, Act** himself to harness his own *self-Control* as best he can and then assist his son in doing the same.

For a child with ADHD, whose brain is wired differently and whose executive functions are not fully developed, it's a big challenge to use **Stop, Think, Act**. For a teen, whose hormonal and physiological changes in their minds and bodies make them emotionally volatile and extra-reactive, pausing in the midst of an emotional storm is an even greater feat. But neither is impossible. Just as you teach your kids to say please and thank you, they can learn to practice saying this to themselves. When Malik left his music class and went to the school office, he was exhibiting the behavior he had learned: to stop, realize he was mad, and go somewhere to cool down. He told me that he didn't want to get in trouble by staying in his class and knew he had to leave. Learning to do this took considerable practice and support from the adults in his life.

How do you help kids with ADHD to Stop, Think, Act when they most need it? Call in the Five C's. First comes *self-Control*, self-discipline, and mindfulness. When there is an amygdala hijack, you need enough awareness to keep it from steering you into a tailspin so you can take back the wheel and right yourself. This awareness comes from noticing what is happening inside your body when you are

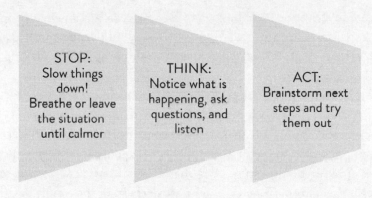

"Stop, Think, Act" Cue Cards

provoked as well as what is happening around you. Maybe your heart starts beating faster and you feel revved up. Maybe you start talking louder and faster. Maybe the people around you are looking distressed or raising their voices. These are clues that emotions are heating up, and a **Stop** may be in order. As we were wrapping up her therapy of eighteen months, Sonya, age seventeen, shared how she learned to do this:

> I'll say, "You know what, we're going a little crazy here," and then I'll just excuse myself, or I'll say, "I need to take a minute," and think about what I'm doing. How I need to focus more and let my brain cool off for a minute.

Sonya figured out how to use self-awareness to let her "brain cool off." You can teach your child to do this too. First, take a minute and think about yourself. What is your pattern when you have big feelings? Now reflect on what happens to your son or daughter when they experience emotional flooding? It's important to set aside some time to talk with them about this when things are calm and their thinking brain is available to learn, not in the midst of a meltdown. Identifying triggers is the beginning of learning how to respond to them. What do they notice about what sets them off? What do you notice sets you off about them? These are important questions to ask and answer together to reduce conflict and build effective coping skills. Take a minute to share the basic biology of an amygdala hijack when people get upset. Explain how the feeling part of the brain gets puffed up with strong emotion and takes over the thinking brain, making it hard to calm down.

Stop, Think, Act is your ticket to getting the thinking brain back in charge, and it takes much practice. Reassure them that some days, people catch themselves; at other times, the feelings may be too powerful or you don't care and let it all out. This helps normalize their experiences. You can do the "stupid Dr. Sharon breathing exercises," (as Malik calls them) from Chapter 1: use nostril, chest, or the candle breaths to strengthen the pause muscle. For some, time apart by going outside or leaving the room reduces agitation. Perhaps creating a special calm space with favorite toys, books, or music helps them cool their inner fire. For others, like Darryl, a simple hug will suffice. Together, name ways to slow things down and then make note of them. Post this list in the kitchen where everybody can see it when needed. Repeatedly direct their attention and body language away from the tidal wave of emotion inside to those ideas or other things happening around them. The adrenaline rush will subside, and a relaxation response emerges.

Once the storm has moved offshore, you help them make connections between emotions and behavior by noticing—**Think**. This is not the time to strategize about emotional and behavioral patterns; that comes later, when things have rebalanced and you have some time after the event. This is a moment to use curiosity in place of any type of judgment. Instead of *"You are over-reacting"* or *"Stop driving me crazy,"* you ask non-blaming questions such as *"What happened that you got so angry?"* or *"How did things become so heated up?"* You make nonjudgmental, observational statements about what is upsetting them. *"It seems like when Tommy beat you at basketball, you started getting upset"* or *"I noticed when it got too late to finish your homework you became scared about school tomorrow."* You are like Sherlock Holmes: you investigate what is going in the mystery of the amygdala hijack and collect the facts about what set it off. Curiosity not only spurs your child's thinking but it also nurtures your *Compassion*. As you share your observations, you simultaneously offer your empathy. These tactics will help you later when you strategize about how to deal with this situation—*Act*. Here is where you both brainstorm ideas and use problem-solving techniques, working as a team but knowing that you, as the responsible adult, have the final word.

With practice, as their director matures, your child or teen will learn to do this for themselves. Outbursts, while usually unpleasant, are the best times for learning this skill. As things become clearer, you both figure out the next steps, perhaps referring to previous collaborative agreements or similar experiences. When you link the present to the past, you not only ignite working memory but you also demonstrate *Consistency*. Once you are able to have a calm conversation, you know the thinking brain is back in control. Together, decide what's next. Acknowledge them for calming down and (eventually) talking with you. This gives them the positive reinforcement that helps new patterns like *Stop, Think, Act* stick.

Blowing Up: Energy, Passion, and Sensitivity Disguised as Anger

Every child or teen who meets with me brings up anger. Whether they share what makes them "mad," why they argue, what frustrates them, or how they lose it, everybody has an anecdote or comment. Generally, they see anger as a part of themselves they don't like very much—mostly because they can't control it and they regret their actions afterward. Many of them also offer insights about what sets them off.

> "I just don't like authority at all. Authority likes to belittle people. There are certain teachers who act like they have ultimate power over you. It makes you feel less than you are. Like, Mr. Tully's normally rude to kids and disrespecting them. I'm not taking it. . . . Yeah, I back talk."
>
> —Marlon, age 15

> "I like to tell my story. but sometimes my parents interrupt me and tell me to stop because I talk too long. It makes me mad. I slam my door or

fight with my mom. . . . I don't want ADHD no more. I keep getting angry a little too much."   —Layla, age 9

"In elementary school, like fourth grade, I had a worse temper. If a teacher said something to me, I'd just get mad. Like, 'Leave me alone, get away from me,' and I would smack something, or push the chair out the way. I used to try to show teachers up and make them look dumb. They were like, 'Oh, I don't want to deal with you, so I am kicking you out.' That would get me mad."   —Pablo, age 15

"Last week, my mom told me that my basketball game was canceled because the other team's coach was sick and I would miss the makeup game. I was furious. I stormed up to my room, slammed the door, and face-planted on my bed for a while. Then my brother came up asked me to shoot in our driveway. We played, and my anger went away."
                                                                          —Sanjay, age 10

DISRESPECT, CONTROL, UNFAIR treatment, things not working out: these events can lead to aggressive expressions of anger displayed in explosions and tantrums. These are the times to pull out *Stop, Think, Act.*

Kids with ADHD tend to have a strong sense of justice, sensitivity, and, of course, energy. When they feel wronged, disempowered, or unheard, they can become quite mad. When their expectations about what is supposed to happen and what actually occurs differ, they often struggle to adjust and can explode. They may also lack the skills to express their feelings appropriately and explain what is going on for them. Kids without ADHD struggle with this too. It's just that for ADHD kids, the switch gets flipped faster and the flooding comes sooner. Chantelle described such an incident during one of our parent consultations:

On Sunday morning, I decided to make a nice family breakfast. Eggs, bacon, pancakes, toast—the whole nine yards. When everyone sat down and started to eat, Malik noticed that there's a hair in his eggs. One of my hairs. Not a big deal, right? I can't help that. Just pull it out and move on. Well, he had a complete meltdown. He screamed bloody murder about being grossed out. I told him to calm down, that I would take the hair out, but he grabbed his eggs and smashed them on the table. He couldn't come up with any other solutions. Robert yelled at him to sit down, but he just got angrier. His sister tried not to cry. It was a mess. I wiped up the eggs and apologized again. Malik stormed off, and we ate without him. When he came back later, he was sorry and hungry, so I made him a frozen waffle like he asked. I didn't want another outburst.

It's tough for any parent in a heated situation like this one to know what to do. *Collaboration* on house rules designed to create an atmosphere of safety and respect is as important as not taking your child's tantrum personally. Chantelle can't help that her hair accidentally fell into the eggs, and Malik can't help that he felt grossed out. But his reaction, typical of many kids with ADHD, was disproportionate to the situation. He couldn't stop even when Robert asked him to. Although Chantelle attempted to solve the problem by removing the hair, nothing seemed to work.

In hindsight, Chantelle realized that she could have reminded everybody about **Stop, Think, Act.** *"Maybe I should have called a 'Dr. Sharon moment' like we do sometimes. 'Hey, it's time to do Stop, Think, and Act.' We usually laugh about it but do it anyway."* We agreed that a family pause would have slowed things down, permitted folks to reflect aloud on the situation, and come up with a mutual solution. While it was clear that the hair in the eggs caused Malik's reaction, his intensity grew when no one at the table acknowledged its unpleasantness or how it might spoil his breakfast. Instead, Chantelle and Robert tried what many parents do—make the problem go away. Chantelle reflected: *"I could have said something like, 'Having a hair in your food is icky. What should we do?' He would have been upset but not off the wall."* Robert recognized that yelling at Malik only made him angrier and didn't address his son's frustration. We all agreed that throwing eggs was unacceptable, and ideally, he should have cleaned them up or helped his mother do it. That would have been a reasonable consequence. I suggested that Malik help with the cooking for next Sunday's breakfast as a way to make amends. He could contribute and hopefully ensure that no hair fell in his food. Plus he could participate in something he loves: food. They followed through, and he was excited to make pancakes with strawberries on top. The following week, the family reported having a pleasant meal.

Believe it or not, outbursts are opportunities to guide kids with ADHD in alternative directions to deal with strong feelings. When things are out of control, many parents are inclined to punish their children for their inappropriate behavior either by taking things away or sending them to their rooms. Research has shown that punishments don't work because they fail to address emotions or thinking. They leave kids feeling wronged or bad; they do not teach empathy, making amends, or what appropriate choices would have looked like. This goes for time-outs too. Time-outs do not work when people use them to control a child rather than teaching *self-Control*.[9] These types of *"Sit on the stairs for ten minutes and do not talk"* or *"Go to your room for an hour"* are shame-based interventions, and while better than hitting kids, they do not guide them toward improved *self-Control* and better choices. Certainly, logical consequences that are related to problem behaviors or poor decisions *are* useful tools for instruction. If your daughter gets angry, slams her door, and it cracks, then it makes sense that she goes with you to get a new one and helps to pay too. This teaches her that there is a cause and effect to her actions that she'll see every time she closes that new door.

How can you teach your son or daughter with ADHD to accept their feelings, curb inappropriate behaviors, and handle emotions more adeptly? In addition to *Stop, Think, Act,* call for a time-apart with a specific time to reconvene (*"Let's take a time-apart to cool down and meet back in the kitchen in thirty minutes"*). This indicates that you see a separation is needed but you are not using it as a punishment. Instead, when you come back together, the listening, caring, and teaching begins. Your child will absorb lessons about what to do or not do when you are very specific and clear about behaviors you need to see. What is obvious to you may not be obvious to them. Keep your examples short, and break things down. Instead of saying, "*You have a bad attitude about doing the chores and, if I don't yell, you don't do them. I'm sick of this,*" you could try, "*I want you to understand that we all have to chip in to make this family run smoothly. I know it's hard to remember chores, so let's figure out a different system without yelling that works better for both of us.*" It's a more precise way to communicate. Likewise, incentives are much more productive than taking things away. Studies have found that incentives based on time with you are the most effective ways of motivating kids with ADHD.[10]

Worried and Watchful:
Creativity and Planning Masked as Anxiety

While anger demonstrates an energetic and passionate overreaction to a past or present event, anxiety reflects an excessive, intense fear about something in the future. Anxious kids want certainty and comfort: they like to know what's going on, what will happen, and how to feel safe. It is common for all kids and teens to experience anxiety. In these moments, it's typical for them to retreat from the source of their concerns (and the discomfort they feel) and rely on parents or friends for reassurance until they feel more confident. Usually these concerns go away when a child has mastered the tasks associated with the new situation. For kids with ADHD whose executive functioning challenges may delay mastery and confidence, this anxiety can stick around longer. In addition, the constant stream of corrections directed toward them can increase their insecurity about whether they can manage what comes along.

Our job as parents is to teach them how to tolerate and cope with uncertainty in their lives and realistically evaluate the safety of a given situation on their own. Reassurance, however tempting, does not provide a lasting solution because it teaches kids to rely on other people making things "okay." The content of a worry actually matters less than the pattern of when and where it occurs and how to deal with it.[11] Most people want to avoid anxiety and what provokes it; they try to push it aside. Moving away from worry only makes it stronger. Instead, when you move *toward* what is concerning, you weaken the (irrational) fear and resist being controlled by it. You probably got to where you are today by tolerating discomfort and overcoming fear at various points. The goal is for your child or teen to do the same.

How do you maintain your support without relying on reassurance? You tap into *Compassion* and teach your youngster to talk back to worry, just like you did with negative thinking. In fact, much of anxiety *is* negative thinking colored by apprehension. Anxious kids with ADHD, and their big feelings, want reassurance intensely. Of course, your six-year-old needs comfort after falling off his bike. Your twelve-year-old needs assistance managing her nervousness about starting middle school. The learning process happens developmentally and incrementally by reminding them of the ways that they have succeeded in the past—in spite of worry. Anxiety is very talented at erasing memories of courage and triumph. You could try one of these:

It sure is scary to fall off your bike, and I understand why you don't want to ride again. Remember when we went to the park last week and you rode over the bump without falling? How did you do that? What did you say to yourself? Let's try that again now.

Or:

It's really rough not to know many people in your new school and to feel worried about making friends. That sounds pretty normal. I am wondering how you got to know your buddy Sophie from camp this summer? Sometimes worry can block our memory of how we have done hard things before, and we need to remind it.

When you can separate the worry from the person, listen to what it says, figure out how it tries to protect you, and talk it down, you slow down the panic alarms from the amygdala hijack and empower the thinking brain.

Afterward, later that day or the following one, sit down with your son or daughter and walk through what happened. Identify the cycle of anxiety, contemplate alternative responses, and make a plan for what to do if a similar event occurs. You will likely have to be the memory for this until they build the skills to do it themselves. Just like with anger, the first step is your *self-Control*: you manage your natural concern when your child is anxious, so you can think clearly about what is happening. This can be really tough, because no parent wants to see their child fretful and panicked. Similar to angry outbursts, anxiety attacks present you with opportunities for assisting your youngster to practice their developing coping skills.

Worry can be productive or poisonous. Productive worry is worry about doing things: homework, getting to work on time, or remembering to charge your phone. These traits contribute to the helpful, planning side of anxiety. Poisonous worry is worry about things you can't control: thunderstorms, whether people will like you or if the plane will crash. The first can be motivating; the second, debilitating. Just like anger, when worry takes over, we want to engage the thinking brain. Trying a worse-case scenario exercise can bring it back online: *"Let's say you get on the school bus and you don't know anyone. Then what? And what happens after that? Then what?"* When you follow the worry to its irrational end, logic (and often humor) kick in, bringing back the director and calm along the way.

In my conversations with boys and girls with ADHD, they worry about a variety of issues, such as social skirmishes with friends, new situations, sleeplessness, or remembering and getting things done.

"Ever since I was little, I would have really irrational fears of bad things happening, or things not working out. Just really pessimistic views of everything, and that would make me nervous about reality, I guess. Changes in my life would also make me nervous, to the point that I would be physically sick, or I would just shut down. New schools, a new team."

—Ellis, age 17

"My worries start as a hair clip in my stomach and then become a swirling in my head. Sometimes when I am nervous, like in school if I don't know the answer, I chew on my shirt. Sometimes they say, 'You're not going to be able to sleep. What if you can't sleep?' and that makes me not sleep. . . . It's hard to stop my brain. It goes neh neh neh. I think maybe you can turn a worry enemy into a friend or tell it to back off, but that doesn't always do it."   —Maisie, age 10

"My mom may worry about things that she has no control over, like the weather, but I worry about things I have to do and forgetting them. I totally feel panicky because there's something I think I need to be doing but I can't remember what. Hopefully me thinking about it and keeping it in my head makes me do it. Otherwise, if it's not in my head, it doesn't exist."
                                                              —Dustin, age 16

WHILE SOME OF these kids recognize the irrationality of their fears and not being able to stop them, many others talk about their efforts to be perfect and the discomfort that causes them. Perfectionism is an attempt to limit mistakes and reduce future shame. Many kids with ADHD struggle with this as a way to prevent criticism from others and even themselves. Sometimes it can be debilitating: kids can't start or finish things. Other times, perfectionism motivates them into action or creating order.

"Sometimes I have a fit if things aren't right. I want to do everything right. Like with the trumpet. I want it to sound good, really good, but it gets too hard. I like to play rock songs, but those are harder. I'll try, quit, try again, get more annoyed, and then I give up."   —Cara, age 10

"When I go to bed on a school night, I have to do something in a certain order or I feel like my whole night's messed up. I have to do my work, I have to put my do-rag on, then do my chores, then go to bed. If I put my do-rag on first, everything is messed up. Then I'm either going to play

on my phone too long, or I'm not going to go to sleep on time. That's
how I stay focused."   —Marlon, age 15

WHILE MARLON'S ROUTINE probably seems rigid to you, he told me
that it helps him feel less overwhelmed and distracted during the hec-
tic school week. He manages his anxiety about all the things he has to
do by creating an order for them that he can remember. Ideally, as he
builds confidence and strengthens his memory skills, he can intro-
duce more flexibility into his evenings.

Let's look specifically at how the Five C's of ADHD parenting can
assist you in effectively addressing anxiety in your son or daughter.

- *self-Control*: When kids are anxious, they often are not breathing.
  Interrupt anxious thinking with breathing techniques. This
  slows down the amygdala hijack. Some kids like to draw or listen
  to music too. Stay calm yourself, and avoid simple reassurance or
  dismissing concerns as irrational.
- *Compassion*: Think about the situation or the fear from your
  child's perspective. If you don't understand what that is, ask for
  clarification. Maintain your support in the face of your child's
  irritating or frustrating behaviors: these are outward demonstra-
  tions of their limited skills and ineffective attempts to create security.
- *Collaboration*: Work together on finding solutions that reduce the
  power of their worry. Brainstorm things they can say when anxiety rears its ugly head. Talk about logical ways to deal with scary
  things instead of avoiding them. Redirect their creative imaginations to draw pictures, write stories, or use humor as tactics to
  address worries differently. If appropriate, create an incentive
  program.
- *Consistency*: Encourage regular routines in sleeping, eating, and
  exercising. These offer your child predictability (along with security) about aspects of their daily life in the face of so many other

uncertain events. If you are using incentives, really try to follow through on them.

- *Celebration*: Acknowledge courageous behavior and talk it up in the family. Remind your child of their past bravery when new challenges emerge.

Bummed and Blue:
Expectation and Goals Cloaked in Disappointment

While ADHD kids will often express aloud their feelings of anger or anxiety, disappointment is a more internal emotion. It usually lies below the surface of anger or anxiety, hidden when your son or daughter is yelling at you for something completely unrelated. Because you see the outburst and not the disappointment, it's harder for you to grasp what is really going on. That's why waiting to talk until after a blow-up or a panic attack has passed makes such sense. When you discover the irritants and dig beneath the meltdowns, you may very well find discouragement or sadness. I regularly ask kids about what disappoints them and how they cope when other people are disappointed in them. They speak about every area of their lives—school, home, friends, and work.

"My teachers tell me that I have this potential: 'You're so smart, you just need more discipline. You don't give it all you got.' For them to say that just makes me really sad, because it's like, 'Well, how?' I get overwhelmed. I have other things to think about. I feel bad because I don't like to let people down, but I do it all the time."   —Kelly, age 16

"My classmates at my table share their scores on tests. I just pretend that I am happy about my score. I'm pretty good at that, holding it in that I feel bad. . . . After I show my parents and I'm alone, I let it out, but I don't cry. I wish I could make it better."   —Nolan, age 11

"I think what really disappoints people and hurts people is that I am late so often because they take it personally. Me losing things disappoints people. I bottle it up and get really frustrated with myself about what is going on. I never like to think about it, so I just avoid it."   —Darren, age 15

SHUTTING DOWN, ISOLATION, avoidance, giving up—this is how disappointment often looks in kids with ADHD.

Tolerating disappointment can be rough for any of us, and it's a muscle that best develops over time. While caring adults cannot make disappointment vanish from children's lives, we can teach youngsters how to live with it. Kelly, Nolan, and Darren, while sad and frustrated, also reveal their longing to do the "right thing." This is the flip side of disappointment. Despite how this desire fuels motivation, young people with ADHD frequently report how their executive functioning challenges thwart their intentions. You can assist them in achieving the success they aim for by collaborating on ways to build those skills. Encourage breathing or an activity that quiets them; review something that's happened; empathize with their frustration or shame; assist them in considering options; appreciate their efforts to accomplish things and urge them to keep trying; and offer praise and enthusiasm when something goes well. Your support can make feeling disappointed a lot less painful.

Encouraging Themselves

I am constantly impressed and inspired by how kids with ADHD combat negative thinking, shame, anger, worry, outbursts, and disappointment. They have many ways of rebounding and keeping their spirits up. Hobbies, music, sports, television, computers, and friends are often mentioned, but most children and teens have something encouraging they say to themselves:

"Sometimes I make the wrong choices. No one's perfect. It's one of my songs. 'No one's perfect, and that's okay. I'm not perfect, I like me anyways.'"   —Camilla, age 10

"If you ask yourself questions during the day, like, 'What am I doing right now? What can I do to make this situation a little better?' Not beating myself up. Just do better."   —Hunter, age 17

"I like dancing and cheerleading. I love my family. I love my friends. There are things that are good about me. I don't let those bad thoughts get in the way anymore. I'm like, 'Okay, I'll just try harder next time,' and I move on. 'Live and learn,' like Mami says."   —Ana, age 15

". . . that I should try fixing that mistake and try not doing that ever again. It works good."   —Christian, age 9

"Hopefully this works. If not, I'm going to have to find a new way to get it done. It's hard sometimes, but there's always a way to pick yourself up."
                                                                     —Jade, age 12

THESE YOUNG PEOPLE show us the resilience parents work so hard to cultivate. They are learning to accept their big feelings and find the good in themselves. They are starting to recognize that everyone makes mistakes. They are experimenting with different strategies to get back on track when they veer off. Using information about how intense emotions affect the ADHD brain, the impact of negative thinking, and the benefits of pausing to regroup, you apply tools from the Five C's to give them skills to manage their feelings more successfully. Together, you examine difficult times, discover the triggers, talk about what could go differently, and support trying something new. Just like Chantelle and Robert did with the breakfast fiasco, you reboot. As Ana mentions, it's all about living and learning.

Chapter 11

....

Getting Stuff Done

MEET AYESHA, AGE 14, sitting at the kitchen table in her family's apartment as she and I talk:

> AYESHA: "My room is neat to me. It might be messy to others, but I see it as . . . a sophisticated mess. I know where everything is at. It might look messy to you, but to me, everything has its place, not perfect but a certain place. Clothes in one pile or another and on my bed. And to you, it might be like, 'Why's there clothes around the room?' but to me, this is where one thing goes, this is where the other thing goes, this is where something else goes. . . . You asking about cleaning it? I do it myself. I don't want her touching my stuff and I'm old enough to do it. Besides, the last time she cleaned, I lost it. I had no idea where anything was after she moved everything. I was so mad."
>
> TONYA, HER MOTHER, COMMENTS FROM THE ADJACENT LIVING ROOM WHERE SHE IS WATCHING TELEVISION: "I don't know what your problem was. Your room was a pigpen with junk everywhere—empty chip bags, dirty plates and glasses, clothes all over the floor. I was afraid we would get mice or something so I cleaned it when you were in school. Did I get a thanks? No, you hollered about me being a

'b*tch.' I told her if she wants me out of her room, she has to clean it herself when I tell her and we went over, one more time, how I like it. Now it's not half bad."

AYESHA SMILES. "Yeah, that's cool 'cause now, if she sees my room's dirty, she'll write on a sticky note: 'Clean your room before I get home,' and she'll leave it on my door so I know and clean my room up for her real quick. Then we don't fight so much. Sometimes, she'll come in and we do something big together like cleaning out my closet."

AYESHA LEANS OVER AND WHISPERS TO ME: "You want the truth about how I clean? I'll take what's big, what you can actually see, and I move it to one corner. Then I sweep up, I take other stuff move it to another corner. Then I look at it and I'll be like, 'Does it still look dirty? Can she see the floor? Let me fix it a little bit more.' So I'll take everything else and move it somewhere else until it looks better than it did before. I leave it like that. If she tells me it's still dirty, I'll be like, 'All right, let me move a little something over here.' I just move stuff in more sophisticated spots."

This situation has probably played out in your house. Your son or daughter with ADHD prefers a messier room than you are comfortable with. A tiring battle ensues as you struggle with them to get their room into a semblance of what you consider clean enough. Perhaps their idea of cleaning is picking up a few toys from the floor and then playing with them. Maybe they shove unfolded, clean laundry into their closet to remove it from sight. For all you know, they are moving piles around just like Ayesha without picking up anything at all.

Yet, just as telling kids how to do their math homework or how to study for their social studies test brings more conflict than success, insisting on your methods for organization and productivity without *Collaboration* also has limited effectiveness. Tonya has spent years conveying the basics of tidying up until *something* finally clicked. As part of their truce, Ayesha moves around the piles until her room looks better than it did before, though it may not be her mother's ideal standard. While this arrangement is not perfect, both of them appreciate that it is a step toward a less stressful, co-created solution.

Kids with ADHD have their own ideas about order, cleanliness, and planning that make perfect sense to them. They want their ideas—however simplistic or silly they seem—to be heard, considered, and hopefully integrated into whatever organizational routine you can establish. Their input increases their participation. It's *Collaboration* in action! You set the standards, negotiate what is achievable, incorporate some of their ideas, and teach them the skills to make it all happen. It's neither "my way or the highway" nor "their way or no way" but rather "our agreed-upon way." When kids are younger, working in concert on the task at hand, helping them to learn the necessary steps, and offering your assistance is essential. As they mature and their director develops, you slowly step back. Believe it or not, your influence eventually takes root. Kelly explains:

> My parents always say, "Oh, Kelly was here. There's a trail of junk leading to where she's going." They would say, "Look back. Look behind you at the trail you're leaving," because, like, I'll cook something and think I'll clean it up later but forget. It really doesn't even cross my mind. But then I started babysitting for this family and I had to clean up after the kids and I found myself saying, "Look back at the trail you're leaving." I showed them how to turn around and look back. It was strange.

Kelly, without thinking about it, has taken her parents' teachings and, much to her surprise, incorporated them into her own life. In this chapter, you will see how the Five C's are a blueprint for assisting your child to organize better and procrastinate less.

Work Together to Understand
Family Executive Functioning Skills

Arguments as you rush to get to school and work in the morning, tripping over a forgotten shoe left in the middle of the hall, or finding a container of spoiled milk left on the kitchen counter in the morning—incidents like these can drive you crazy as a parent. It may seem like no matter how many times you remind your youngster, the same problems keep coming back. As frustrating as that can be, you have to remember that no film director starts off with a big-budget movie: it takes practice, experience, and time to build the necessary credentials. Similarly, your child's director requires trial-and-error learning.

Whether or not you also have ADHD, you likely have some executive functioning strengths and challenges as part of the genetic material and behavior patterns you have passed on to your son or daughter. Realizing that, like your fifteen-year-old son, you may have trouble finishing what you set out to do, gives you more *Compassion* and patience. Remember those gutters you never got around to cleaning out last month? It may not be that far from those gutters to an unfinished history paper about the Middle Ages or the remnants of a snack left in the den. Kids love to discover similarities with their parents and compare their differences as well. When Vince, who has trouble remembering to turn in his homework, heard that his father, Tony, struggles with his memory, he laughed: *"Oh yeah, Dad, you forget stuff, like my basketball game last week. Ha!"* Tony smiled: *"You're right. That's why I put things in my phone, but I sure missed that one. I set an alert to make sure I'm at the next one."* Vince and his dad not only bonded over their shared struggles with recalling things but his father also modeled how to cope with it.

Even if your child has had testing, discovering where you both may share some characteristics was not part of that process. Taking time to examine your executive functioning skills while they think about their own can start all kinds of useful conversations. This exercise will assist you in this process.[1] Make sure each person has their own copy of the form below to complete.

EXERCISE 5: UNDERSTANDING YOUR FAMILY'S BRAINS

Executive Functioning "Hot" Skill in Real Life	How often do you . . . ? 0 = Rarely 1 = Occasionally 2 = Sometimes 3 = Usually	Executive Functioning "Cold" Skill in Real Life	How often do you . . . ? 0 = Rarely 1 = Occasionally 2 = Sometimes 3 = Usually
Self-regulation: Stop and think before saying or doing something		Alertness: Stay awake and involved in a boring activity	
Managing feelings: Tolerate frustration, worries, or disappointment without yelling, anger, or fighting		Perseverance: Keep trying something new, even if it's hard	
Organization: Keep room, notebook, desk, etc. neat; find things when you need them		Processing information: Understand and practice new concepts quickly.	
Time management: Do things on time and correctly estimate how long they take		Working memory: Remember to do or turn in things; follow directions with several steps	
Planning and prioritizing: Figure out how to do things, where to start and what's most important about them		Sustained attention: Stay focused and resist distractions	

Executive Functioning "Hot" Skill in Real Life	How often do you...? 0 = Rarely 1 = Occasionally 2 = Sometimes 3 = Usually	Executive Functioning "Cold" Skill in Real Life	How often do you...? 0 = Rarely 1 = Occasionally 2 = Sometimes 3 = Usually
Initiating: Begin chores, homework, or projects without procrastination or many reminders		Shift/Flexibility: Adjust to changes in schedule or plans easily	
		Goal-oriented persistence: Set a goal, stay focused, and return to task after interruptions	
		Self-evaluation: Be aware of how your behavior affects others; be open to feedback and learning from mistakes	

ONCE EVERYONE IS finished, take a look at your answers. Where are people alike, and where are they different? Discuss what each person does to address the challenges of their low-scoring executive functioning skills and explore whether one person's strategies might appeal to someone else. How about giving them a try and seeing what happens?

Many kids articulate how similarities with their parents affect them:

"I have another person at home who's just like me: Mom. But she's not hyper at all. Her brain wanders. I just know that I have someone else who knows how I feel sometimes. She had it when she was a kid too. . . . If Dad gets mad that I don't remember something, Mom knows what that's like."

—Ruby, age 9

"My dad has ADD. Sometimes we talk about what it's like to have it and disorganization. That's pretty cool. But sometimes we get into fights about me having to clean my room. He'll say ADHD makes me messy but that's not an acceptable excuse. I just have to 'bear it and do it.'"

—Clay, age 11

"My dad and I, we talk about ADHD all the time, but we don't get along. He's super hypersensitive to me having it. He always says, 'I'm so tough on you because I don't want you repeating my mistakes.' Sometimes it'll feel like he's unnecessarily pointing out my flaws. Then I don't do what he says."

—Lila, age 17

RECOGNIZING EXECUTIVE FUNCTIONING strengths and challenges in yourself assists you in relating to what your child deals with each day.

Trouble Getting Started:
Dealing with Procrastination and Time Management

Everyone puts things off. In Chapter 7, you saw how kids with ADHD often struggle with flagging motivation when they have to tackle unpleasant tasks related to school. With lower amounts of dopamine in their brains, it just takes them longer than their non-ADHD peers to get moving. They usually need an external reward to encourage them until the satisfaction of doing it—an internal reward—kicks in. The "because I said so" intimidation approach of our parents' generation may get the job done, but it does not build any lasting skills. **Co-created, incentive-based plans** work best to improve motivation for home responsibilities just as they do for school-related assignments.

Procrastination kicks in when kids with ADHD are faced with an unappealing project like helping you rake the leaves, folding the laundry, or taking out the trash. It quickly teams up with *overwhelm* and *avoidance*, making it tough to start anything. What pops up is negative self-talk: *"Why bother doing the dishes? It will take forever"* or *"If I keep playing my computer game, Mom will do it and I won't have to."* This internal commentary becomes an excuse to keep your child or teen from embarking on what they need to do.

Another big obstacle is the internal challenge with understanding and effectively using time. For ADHD brains, time is divided into "NOW" or "NOT NOW." They may not grasp how five minutes feels. Either they tend to underestimate how long things take and wait until the last minute, or they overestimate how long something will take and are too daunted to start. Time management is a readily teachable skill that you can begin imparting as early as age six by using the method of Backward Design. This means planning in reverse to get to where you want to be in the future. It relies on being able to estimate how long things take by beginning with your ideal arrival or finishing time. You work backward and assign increments of time to the various steps along the way. *"Okay, I need to leave for work by 7:45, and before that, I have to feed the cat, which takes about five minutes; make and eat breakfast, which takes about twenty minutes; and get dressed and brush my teeth, which takes twenty-five minutes, so that totals fifty minutes. That means that I have ten extra minutes if I wake up at 6:45. Is that enough time to deal with unpredictable things, returning phone calls, or checking my email?"*

Using Backward Design requires an accurate assessment of how long tasks actually take, which can be tough for many folks, especially those with ADHD. Developing the capability for your son or daughter to estimate time and monitor how they spend it requires giving direct instruction. When you are not rushing around, sit down together and slowly go through the steps necessary for a given sequence of activities, such as budgeting time for homework or practicing piano before dinner. Listen to their estimates of allocating time. Give them feedback about how long things really take based on your observations. Together, set up alarms on phones or iPods to alert them about time. This can be quite helpful.

Although estimating time is one important part of procrastination, the other major aspect is being overwhelmed. Feeling swamped makes it hard to know where to begin. When the size of the job seems too big, avoidance kicks in. Sofia, age sixteen, describes this phenomenon:

> Like a lot of people, I don't love doing my laundry and would rather do anything else. I put it off day after day, until my laundry pile is really crazy and I have nothing to wear. By the time I finally do it, the mountain of laundry amounts to a much bigger chore than it would have been if I done it earlier. Instead of one or two quick loads, it takes all day. Dirty laundry isn't life or death, but it's how I procrastinate and make things worse for myself.

Sofia misjudges the time and size of the laundry chore until it mushrooms into a job that fulfills her worst fears. **Breaking the task down** into smaller pieces would have aided her greatly. If the laundry became smaller chunks of chores—like washing only shirts and then only pants, she would probably have completed it sooner—one step at a time. Instead, she left the unpleasant task until the last minute, when she desperately needed clothes. She ended up losing a whole day in the process.

Unlike their younger peers, many teenagers no longer have parental assistance to keep them on track, and they procrastinate more than they would like.

> "I wait till the last minute or not do it at all. I try to do everything as quickly as I can so I have time for other fun things, for myself, to hang

out with my friends, other last-minute stuff. I've been a procrastinator for a very long time." —Nadia, age 15

"Sometimes I just don't know where to start. I look at something my mom wants me to do, like clean the kitchen after dinner, all the dirty dishes, the pots, the food to put away. It's too much. So I go on my phone, but it's still there when my dad yells at me to get off and do it." —Meg, age 13

"I'm the best procrastinator ever. I push everything off to the last minute. If I had an essay due Friday, I'll do it Thursday night, 2:00 in the morning. Just lazy, kind of. I work better under pressure 'cause it just puts heat under me to do it. My dad says, 'Hey, don't feel bad about the procrastination because me and your mom do the same thing.'" —Marcus, age 15

OF COURSE, THE big question for you as a parent is: *"How do I create tasks that are the right size for them to start on?"* Collaborate with your child or teen to set up a plan that fits their capabilities. Listen to their input about when and how they become overwhelmed, staying as specific as possible to establish guidelines for a chore. Follow through with support and acknowledgment when you see a desired outcome. If your seven-year-old son's room is trashed by bedtime and he gets distracted when he tries to clean it, try a different approach. Maybe agree that you and your son will each pick up five items so the tidying stays on track. Perhaps offer to dry the pots from dinner and keep your daughter company while steering her along the path to a clean kitchen. Your participation instructs them to learn how to do tasks independently and competently.

Here's how you use the Five C's to conquer procrastination in your house:

1. Before sitting down to talk with your son or daughter at a specific time, ask yourself: How long can they really focus on a chore before

getting distracted or bored? What types of negative self-talk do they engage in? Then, ask them these same questions.

2. Talk about the difference between homework and chores. With homework, it is often good to do the hardest thing first when your concentration is the strongest. With chores, it's better to start with something easier and get it over with so you can feel accomplished before moving onto bigger stuff.

3. Just like with homework, make a list of appealing activities for your child that will act as incentives. Discuss whether a break will be necessary and, if so, for how long. If needed, create together a game plan of where to start and what to do next. Be specific about start and end times so the chore doesn't last too long.

4. Encourage their progress, however small. If they cannot complete the task, then it is still too big: make it smaller. Use *self-Control* or take a time-apart if you become upset. Whatever chore they are doing is not worth an explosion.

5. When the job is finished, take a minute to notice its completion *positively*.

Making things fun goes a long way toward engaging your child and reducing procrastination. Your youngster will be more willing to do a routine chore if there is an element of play. Can you time how fast you and your son pick up the floor and make it an amusing contest? What about asking your daughter to put on her favorite tunes while she washes the dishes and you join her in a drying dance? Making tedious jobs more amusing lightens up their drudgery and increases willing participation. Who knows? There might even be laughter along the way.

Giving Directions That Work: The Rule of Three

An important part of getting things done is following instructions. Parents and teachers frequently complain to me that kids with ADHD don't remember things they are told. Listing things all at once—get dressed, make your bed, brush your teeth—is a prescription for failure. Kids either can't recall the steps required to follow the sequence you just told them or they are distracted by something else. Your son may put on his pants but then start playing with the Transformer on the dresser next to his shirt. Your daughter may go into the bathroom to brush her teeth but then spend five minutes letting water run on her hands because it feels good. They have long abandoned what they were supposed to do next. This forgetfulness happens for a number of reasons—challenges with working memory, internal or external distractions, trouble putting tasks into steps, anxiety about forgetting. Changing how you talk to a young person about the task at hand can improve all these things.

Using the **Rule of Three** assists you in delivering instructions more effectively. It starts with the premise that you need your child's full attention when you instruct them. This means that you do not yell from the kitchen to the upstairs or give reminders as you walk out the front door. Instead, the **Rule of Three** entails looking, listening, and speaking as you must make direct contact with your child. Here's how it works:

1. Get down to your child's *eye level*, touch them gently on the shoulder, and say their name. If they are taller than you are, then you both sit down. Make sure they are *looking at you*, listening, and engaged. If their eyes are wandering or their bodies are moving, gently help them focus on you by saying "Your eyes on my eyes." [**Looking**]

2. *State* your task clearly and calmly. ("Tyler, I want you to clear your plate from the table" or "Sally, go get your shoes from your room and bring them downstairs.") [**Listening**]

3. Ask them to *repeat your request exactly* twice. ("What did I ask you to do? One more time, please.") [**Speaking**]

By giving directions this way, you activate several areas of the brain— sight, touch, sound, and speech—to help the director get everyone on board to work. It improves the likelihood that the task is remembered and completed. When the first task is finished, you can give another one in exactly the same manner. You may need to keep an eye on what is happening and give a prompt. If you find that they are dragging on doing the task, it might be too complex; break it down. Single directions for simple tasks are the way to go for kids with ADHD. Getting dressed may be one whole task, or it may need to be broken down into component parts: put on your shirt, put on your pants, etc. It's one thing at a time, especially when they are younger, until they have demonstrated that they are ready for two things at a time, usually by adolescence.

Home Routines Make Things Happen!

Just as you learned about the importance of routines with homework, routines for life at home reduce conflict and reminders while promoting accomplishment. Leaving the house in the morning and getting everyone settled at night are prime times for disagreements and irritation. Carol is a grandmother who lives with her daughter, Stephanie, and her two grandchildren, Winnie, age fourteen, and Greg, age ten. Carol paints a common scenario of mornings with Greg, who was diagnosed with ADHD a few months before:

> Every day his mother wakes him up before she leaves. Then he stays in bed until I yell at him three times to get up. [She imitates Greg.] "Well, now that I am awake, I'll stand at my drawers for a while until I pick out my clothes by tossing them in the air. Oops, they're on the floor. I'll sit on the bed with my pants and fiddle with some LEGOs for a while." He just delays and dawdles like nobody's business. When I go in and holler at him, he puts one sock on and I put on the other. He really needs my constant supervision just to get dressed and then I'm not even talking about breakfast, or teeth, or walking out that door. I have things to do. I have to get ready for work too.

As much as Carol is unhappy, Greg told me that he, too, hates the mornings: *"I'm in trouble before I even get to school."* Structuring the morning with a routine based on a checklist and incentives would dramatically help them.

You can use the **Rule of Three** for specific tasks, but for a chain of events like preparing for the school day or going to bed, you need more than single directions. This is where lists or charts of these single items come into play. When your youngster can see the steps that they need to follow, laid out in words or pictures, they can follow them more successfully than being told those same things repeatedly by you. Their retention is better and bolstered by the incentives you have already established, and so is their motivation. Many kids with ADHD simply have not yet developed the ability to hold a sequence of things to do in their minds, and a list helps them follow through. In fact, many older teens keep lists on their phones because they can't remember things as much as they would like.

Successful morning and evening routines are ones that you establish by talking with your child. You know what has to be done, how long it takes, and when it has to be finished. But they may have their own system for doing things that likely clashes with yours. You may think it makes sense for them to eat breakfast first, followed by getting dressed, brushing teeth, and packing the backpack. They might prefer getting dressed first followed by eating. Perhaps it would be easier to brush teeth before breakfast. This is where the negotiating takes place. You hold the goal and the elements needed to meet it, but they interject parts that make sense to them. Their participation in creating that order (and later choosing the incentive) will bring a positive outcome. Maisie, age ten, tells me: "*I want to have a say about how I do things. No one in the house respects me or listens to me. Whenever I try to say my ideas people yell or laugh.*"

I encourage you to enlist your child in making whatever list or chart you use. Some families use whiteboards that change daily according to family schedules. Eric, the father of Sheena, age twelve, tells me: "*The big board in the kitchen is a godsend. I am reinforcing it because I am actively writing on it—art, piano, basketball.*" You do not have to use words for this. If your child struggles with reading or prefers images, use pictures—hand-drawn or cut from magazines. One mother I know took pictures of her daughter when she was ready for school and assembled them into a poster. She hung this on the refrigerator with the words "Do you look like this? Do you have everything you need?" Evening routines can follow in the same way.

Lists with concrete steps tied to incentives are the key to freedom. If your child likes to read with you before bed, add two extra stories as the draw for putting clothes in the hamper, showering, and teeth brushing in a timely fashion. Maybe a game or fifteen minutes of texting privileges is appealing. Whatever you decide, make sure you figure it out beforehand. Within a month, your child may become bored by the chosen incentive: add something new and renegotiate. In fact, the chores themselves may get tedious, so think about switching folding the laundry for vacuuming the living room.

Here's an example of a checklist for neatening a bedroom.

YOUR ROOM IS CLEAN WHEN YOU . . .

Task	Completed!
Put your books away.	
Gather up and put pens and pencils in your desk.	
Pick up your clothes from the floor and put them in the hamper or drawers.	
Put away your toys, dolls, and stuffed animals.	
Make the bed.	
Empty the trash.	
YOU'VE EARNED→	

———

YOU WILL STILL have to remind your son or daughter to use the list. This is better than telling them what to do. When kids with ADHD make and refer to lists, they strengthen their executive functioning skills for planning, sequencing, and completing tasks by going back, seeing everything laid out, and marking their own progress. Carter, age eleven, shared how he uses them:

> When I get home from school, Mom helps me make a list of what I have to do, like unpack backpack, take out my lunch box on the counter, eat snack, do homework. Sometimes I check it by myself, but most of the time she asks me to do it.

On the other hand, Carly, age twelve, stopped making lists because they overwhelmed her. She told me: *"My list kept growing and growing. It went on and on. I mean, it looked like the deep sea scrolls."* If your son or daughter balks at creating or following lists, perhaps use Post-it reminders like Tonya does.

However you can, reinforce that the family goal is less arguing and more independence—both of which matter to kids. With practice and repetition, they will see the benefits of outlining tasks. Xavier, age fifteen, spoke about how he shifted from resisting the structure of lists to embracing them:

> At first they were challenging because I felt like I didn't have the freedom to express myself, but now, in high school, I realize I love structure and it works for me very well. I learn a lot more, and I stay more focused. That's why I like to write everything down in my book, doing my own routines where I go home and I do this, this, and that. I plan ahead, and so far everything's been working out better for me than ever before.

Xavier shows us how learning to make lists helps him accomplish what he wants. Ivan, age seventeen, shared how doing certain chores now comes naturally:

I always clean my room on Sunday, because that's my mom's cleaning day. Clean my room, bring the clothes down. Take out the trash when you can. My mom tries not to say, "Do this or do that." It's more like, "I told you this when you were younger, so now you should have the responsibility to know to just do it." See the trash getting full? Just take it out. Like that, it's normal to me now, because I've been used to doing them so long.

Where once Ivan followed the routines his parents set up, now they have become his own.

Curing Clutter Trouble

Every child or teen shared stories about their challenges with disorganization or messiness.

It's actually easier to find stuff when it's messy. I don't have to take it out, fold it, and put it back. I have piles for jeans, and today I pulled out two pairs of capris and a pair of shorts before I found these."

—Tiana, age 9

"If you saw my backpack, it's pretty bad. My room's pretty clean, but not my backpack. When I get a paper, I shove it in there. At nighttime, I'll be like, 'Where's that paper?' I'll take out fifty papers and flip through all of them. I'll make a deal with myself to be more organized and it works for like a day, but then it's a mess."

—Oscar, age 15

"I'm super messy, not just with my room, but everything I do seems to just get messy somehow. If I'm drawing something or trying to make something neat for a project, it just will end up being not that nice. It's so frustrating. I'll try to keep my room clean, and then a week later it'll be disgusting. I'll be like, 'How did this happen? I don't remember making it messy.'"   —Brianna, age 17

WHETHER IT'S PILES of clothes, chaotic backpacks, or untidy projects, these kids all struggle with putting things in their places and keeping them there.

Organization makes life at home easier. Think about your own methods for managing your stuff. While being tidy may be easy for some people, for others, it feels like a fifty-ton albatross around their neck. When you completed the Understanding Your Family's Brains exercise on page 169, were there any similarities between you and your child in terms of organization? It's helpful to know this information before you get started trying to organize, because it allows you to feel genuine *Compassion* about the challenges your youngster faces.

There is no question that it's much easier to create systems of organization than to maintain them, but it is maintenance that teaches the lasting skills that your child with ADHD likely needs. Start with a program that you can actually monitor over time and they can truly follow. As much as possible, keep common spaces like the kitchen or living room uncluttered. This reduces their general sense of feeling overwhelmed. Carly, age twelve, tells me that she lives every day feeling like she can never catch up: *"It's like a file comes in my head but then paper goes everywhere and then you have to look through everything to find one thing. All this time, more files are coming in with more paper that goes everywhere."* With this mayhem in her brain, it is tough to think straight about sorting through anything.

If everything has a place, kids with ADHD are more likely to put them away. When you set up labeled bins in visible places where specific items are placed, you guide your youngster in the right direction. Using a cubby or box for hats and gloves, you can say, "Put your hat and gloves *in your cubby*," instead of "*away*." The clearer the direction, the better the understanding and follow-through. Consider reducing the number of toys, books, and gadgets that your child can see and access. They do not need twenty-five things to choose from. Pick some, put the others out of sight, and rotate them back into use in a month or two. It will be like another birthday when they reencounter them. Working together, designate a spot for important things like keys, a school identification card, a wallet, or a favorite water bottle. This will prevent a frantic search for them later on.

What surprised me was how often these kids had their own ways of keeping track of their stuff—what I like to call Self-Smart Systems. Sometimes their parents responded positively and worked with them to incorporate their ideas; other times, they did not. Celeste, age seventeen, begged her mother to let her put her clothes on bookshelves instead of in drawers. She explained that she could not see her clothes so she pulled them out on the floor. Her mother, Sylvia, refused, believing that Celeste could just keep her drawers neater. They battled for six months until Sylvia finally agreed to try it, overriding her own unhappiness with how the room would look. Ultimately, the shelf solution was a success: Celeste's clothes remained neater and mostly off the floor.

Here are some of the organizational methods kids reported that worked for them:

- **Having a parent or caring adult keep them company or guide them:** Ramon, age 12, says: "*Papi tells me, 'Go pick up all your shirts,' and I'll be like, 'Nah, it's a big mess, I can't find them.' 'Doesn't matter, just pick up all your shirts.' I put the dirty ones in a pile and we fold the clean stuff.*"

- **Using systems that make sense to them:** Tiana, age 9, explains: "*Color coded for my clothes was easier than pants and tops because I like to wear what I'm feeling. If I was happy, then I might want to wear* *my happy colors—purple, yellow, and orange. If I have to organize something, then I want to organize it in a way that I'll be able to find it.*

- **Having a specific place to put things:** Maria, age 13, says: "My mom says the laundry basket with my clean clothes is actually the dirty clothes basket. I just have to empty it, but I want a basket that I can fill and take it with me to the bathroom so when I get undressed to take a shower, it's right there."

- **Using technology to keep organized:** Henry, age 16, shares: "I could not live without my iPhone. I organize everything with it. Everything. I write notes about all sorts of stuff, like what to take with me in the morning. I use the clock on my phone to set alarms, and tons of scheduling."

Fostering Order and Productivity

Applying the Five C's to organizational and chore challenges at home makes life calmer. Using *self-Control* to monitor your frustration and *Compassion* to empathize with your child's perspective, you find workable, lasting solutions together. You ask questions and listen to their ideas, integrating some of them into household tasks. You hold on to your standards about what is acceptable, but you offer them meaningful participation in how to accomplish chores. By adding appealing incentives, this *Collaboration* inspires your child's willingness to buy into the programs you want to establish. To keep things moving, you apply *Consistency* by observing their efforts and giving simple directions they can follow. Although you might initially wrestle with their suggestions, as Sylvia did with Celeste, you could be pleasantly surprised in the long run. If not, regroup and try something different. Either way, a *Celebration* of their progress as they keep track of their stuff and get things done is in order.

Chapter 12

You've Gotta Have Friends

The Social Lives of Kids with ADHD

MEET ELIJAH, JASMINE, and Carter as they navigate peer relationships:

"I don't like most of the kids at school. They come up and try to annoy me and ask me stupid things. I am what people call 'weird.' I don't act the same way as them, do the same things. There are sixteen ways people don't like me: five involve me being a nerd. I don't watch or do any team sports, so when people talk about the big game last night, I'm not. I like anime and have some friends who aren't the most popular. The only time I talk to them is at school. No one comes over my house. I don't invite them, and they don't ask."   —Elijah, age 13

"If you throw me in a party, I'm extroverted, charming, and charismatic. I'm totally not shy or afraid. I have a lot of friends and a boyfriend. They're really, really important to me. They are my life. Honestly, I'm so f**king social that I don't think about other things. One problem is I end up blabbing secrets. But my friends know me so well and they're patient with my quirks. They know I care a lot and I'll do anything for you."

—Jasmine, age 17

"When I think about making friends, I wouldn't want to be friends with myself. I get really annoying, really upset about everything, and really loud. I get a strange feeling when I go over someone's house. I'm just worried if they play with me too much they'll start getting sick of it, like sometimes people just need patience to play with you again."

—Carter, age 11

WE ALL NEED friends. People who laugh at our jokes, comfort us when we feel low, and rejoice with us in good times. These relationships sustain us. When people don't like us, those rejections shape us too. Living a rich, satisfying life means having people to interact with and knowing how to weather the ups and downs that inevitably arise between you. For some kids with ADHD, like Jasmine, forming fulfilling relationships comes naturally. For others, like Elijah or Carter, it's a lot harder. Either way, your child or teen needs your guidance to help them make good choices, manage sticky situations, and build confidence as they engage with the world. In this chapter, as kids share both positive and frustrating experiences with peers based on in-person interactions, you will learn how to help them cultivate and maintain social relationships.

Figuring Out Your Role

Most parents assist their youngsters in forming early peer relationships. By sending them to daycare or preschool or arranging playdates, you created contact with other children. You taught them to play fairly, to stop themselves from saying or doing hurtful things, to share their toys, and to go along with the rules of the group. As children grow older, though, their peer relationships occur more and more outside of parental purview—at school, sports, or other activities. Kids with ADHD who may miss facial and physical cues may struggle with empathy and lack *self-Control* around others. They often benefit from learning social skills directly but resist doing so. It can be confusing for caring adults to know when and how to step in when their child experiences peer challenges.

EXERCISE 6:
Reflection On Your Relationships

Do you have satisfying personal relationships in your life right now?
If not, what prevents you from forming these connections?
Have you ever struggled with friendships or relationships with significant others?
Does interacting with people come naturally to you? Why?
What were your friendships like as a child or teen?

WHEN YOUR CHILD or teen has friendship issues, your own history with relationships can combine with your natural, protective parental instincts to send you through the roof. Friendship struggles are a great opportunity to use the Five C's. Instead of rushing to call the parent of the boy who teased your daughter on the playground, *Stop, Think, Act*. Take a minute to settle down and breathe. Offer verbal or physical comfort to your child, and listen to what happened. These choices will simultaneously calm your brain and help your child settle. Together, wonder about options, brainstorm responses, and decide on next steps.

EXERCISE 7:
Reflection On Friendship With Your Child Or Teen

In a quiet moment, perhaps at bedtime, start a casual conversation with your son or daughter on the general topic of friendship: *"How are things going with so-and-so? Who are you hanging out with at recess or lunch? How are you getting along with so-and-so?"* Check out the possibility of loneliness or awkwardness. Explore what it means to be a friend, and inquire about any challenges they might be experiencing. Low-key chats like this provide you with a clearer picture of their social world.

CHALLENGES WITH WORKING memory, focus, impulse control, and self-understanding commonly propel kids with ADHD to miss critical aspects of social dynamics. Seth, age nine, told me: *"You don't notice when you're doing something that people want you to stop."* Fatima, age sixteen, stated: *"I'm not always very good at telling what other people are thinking and feeling. I'll stay quiet because either I don't want to mess up or don't have much to say. Some people just know what other people like to talk about; I don't."* You can help your son or daughter improve how they read social cues and what to say to people by practicing with you and other family members. Point out body language and facial expressions: *"Your brother was telling you no and kicking you. What message was he communicating?"* or *"My arms are crossed and I am waiting for you to tie your shoes. What are my body and face showing you?"* Use meals as times to build conversational skills. If your cousin from Atlanta comes to visit, give your daughter some sample questions beforehand: *"How do you like Atlanta?"* *"What do you do for work?"* Help her translate those inquiries to her interactions with peers: *"Did you think that test was hard? I didn't like the essay part."* *"What do you do after school? I get paid to walk my neighbor's dog."* These rehearsals set up your child or teen for the real thing in the hallway.

Left Out

Some kids with ADHD struggle with understanding what friendship means. They do not fully understand that each of us interacts with others in a range of ways: acquaintances, friends, best buddies, and, later, significant others. Some folks are better suited for the acquaintance category: you say "Hi" in the hallways. Those who qualify as friends probably sit at your lunch table, work on a project with you or play on your hockey team. You pour out your heart and soul to best buddies in your inner circle. These nuances can be challenging for kids with ADHD whose brains think more concretely. They may not comprehend how to invite companionship appropriately or how they might unintentionally alienate others. I asked Marlon, age fifteen, about his definition of a friend:

> Honestly, just somebody who puts up with me. You have to understand me. I'm a goofy person who likes to have fun. I always tell myself, "Live every day like it's your last." So I'm always goofing around, making good memories with people. If I walk up and tickle you and you didn't know me, you'd be like, "What's wrong with him?" but if you knew me, you'd be like, "That's just Marlon being Marlon." Once you take the time to understand me, you'll know I'm a cool person.

Marlon confuses appropriate levels of intimacy with people. While a good friend wouldn't mind being tickled, a stranger probably would.

While certain kids struggle with reaching out and connecting to peers, others don't think people are interested in them.

> "The other kids don't let me play in games 'cause I get out of control when I'm happy. I'm way too different with my ADHD, my color, and being new. It makes me feel bad. It's mostly white here, and I speak Spanish. I'm like Ruby Bridges. I'm not as normal."   —Camilla, age 10

> "No one's ever told me that they want to hang out with me; I've always told them. I worry about saying the wrong thing that I can't take back. Last week, this kid I know from the musical asked if I wanted to get coffee but I had to babysit my sister. He said we could do it another time. I really hope so. This is probably one of the first times someone's been like, 'Hey, Dustin, do you wanna go hang out?'"   —Dustin, age 16

> "The only friends I have are people who appreciate me. I'm the jerk, the idiot, the crazy lady, the artist: always kinda on the outside of the box. My friends are outside of the box–ers too. We're like the dweebs. Inside the box–ers—they're perfect and cool, everybody likes them. Not a lot in the

box are nice to me, but I don't want to be inside the box. It's boring. When you're outside of the box, you're in the adventure." —Bree, age 11

WHILE THESE CHILDREN and teens report not fitting in or feeling lonely, Camilla's struggles are compounded by racism. Bree has cleverly crafted a box metaphor to reframe her situation and protect herself. By seeing herself as an artist who lives outside of the box with her like-minded cohort, she transforms feeling excluded into something positive and adventurous. Like Maya from Chapter 3, who laughs at her bullet brain and accepts her mistakes, Bree has courageously figured out how to surround herself with a few similar kids and form her own group.

You can help your son or daughter be more like Bree and create friendships. When kids with ADHD struggle socially, they tend to have fewer opportunities to practice the relationship skills they most need to develop. This can lead to further social awkwardness over time. Talk with your son or daughter about who, if anyone, is a potential new friend. Go over how, what, and where to connect with them appropriately, including tag lines they can remember. Just like you teach them to break down a chore, encourage them to start small: maybe a "Hello" one day, a "Nice T-shirt" the next. With younger kids, offer to call a parent and set up a playdate. With older ones, review possible activities that they could pursue with new friends. Greet each step with encouragement to keep trying. If something goes poorly, remind them that friendships take time. Trust builds through conversations and shared activities, and bumps in the road are inevitable. When you nurture social confidence and resiliency at home like this, you give your youngster the tools to do it independently later on.

Face-to-Face Bullying

When difficult social situations and unhealthy peer relationships cross the line into bullying or aggression, your thoughtful involvement is warranted. Bullying incidents are power fights: they occur in the presence of bystanders who empower the aggressor either overtly or silently. Many kids engage in this behavior to gain social status and become cool, which only perpetuates the cycle. Sometimes bullying others acts as a defense against people attacking you. There is a big difference between *teasing* (a lighthearted joke made with friends or family) and *taunting* (an aggressive act against someone you dislike). Teasing means you are laughing *with* the person; taunting means you are laughing *at* the person. With taunting, a form of bullying, the goal is to cause damage through humiliation, cruelty, or bigotry. All forms of bullying impact a child or teen significantly and require adult intervention at school and home.

Here are a few of the aggressive situations kids described:

"Ryan is a bully. He mostly makes fun of me. You know how teasing is okay if you do a little, but once it crosses into insulting, it's not okay. He crosses that line a lot. If something bad happens, he blames it on whoever's closest to him. He slipped on the doormat and said I pushed him. I wished I had. My teacher makes sure we are never at the same table."

—Levi, age 9

"When I was in sixth grade, this girl Hannah bullied me. She was a real b*tch, callin' me names, pushin' me in line at lunch, and laughin' with her skanky friends. She said all kinds of sh*t about me. I told my guidance counselor about it, like, five times, but she did nothing. Well I got sick of it. So me and my friend Jess took things into our own hands. We paid Max, this big kid in seventh grade, to scare her, nothin' serious. Somehow the principal found out before it happened and we got suspended. Then me and Jess couldn't be friends."

—Esme, age 15

"It's like a comedy routine for them to make fun of me. I've been called stupid, annoying, and every curse word. I try to ignore them. Kids have stolen my lunch, taken my science book. Gym class is the worst. I got smashed into the lockers last year, and I punched the kid in the face. I

think he got the message, but I got sent down to the principal, who called
my dad. . . . [Laughs.] Yeah, I fantasize about something bad happening to
them and going away."   —Drew, age 12

WHEN BILL, DREW'S father, heard about what is happening at school,
he immediately asked for a meeting with the principal, Mr. Chen. Together, all three of them discussed what was going on, who the main
players were, and a plan to protect Drew:

> If something bad is going on, I can leave and go to the office. I can also
> raise my water bottle in the air at lunch and Mr. Chen will come to my
> table. Also, I am supposed to write down the "incidents" on my iPad that
> I carry around and tell him once a week, but small things happen all the
> time that I can't remember. I mean, I try to forget it as soon as it happens.

Although Drew felt doubtful about this plan and worried about retri-
bution, he was surprised that it helped. He went to the office once and
made a few lists of things people said to him. After that, the harass-
ment subsided. He still didn't have many friends, but he was happy not
to be targeted anymore.

Learning the specifics of situations like these assist you (and the school)
to address whatever bullying is indeed occurring. Unfortunately, kids do
not often share this information. Perhaps they feel ashamed, fear retalia-
tion, or believe that no one can help. Maybe they want to avoid tattling,
minimize the seriousness of the situation, or think they may have de-
served it. All these things impede a child or teen from opening up.

SIGNS OF BULLYING

If you suspect that your child might be a victim of bullying, watch for
these signs:
- Social withdrawal or excessive time alone
- Recent disinterest in school or sudden drop in grades

- Negativity when talking about classmates or peers
- Physical symptoms of distress like headaches, stomachaches, or fatigue that would prevent attending school, family events, or extracurricular activities
- Reduction in cell phone or computer use

If you observe that several signs of bullying are occurring, enlist the Five C's. Manage your concern with *self Control* and stay as centered as you can. Then embark on *Compassion*. Talk about what behaviors you are noticing, and wonder aloud if something is going on. Ask if kids are saying or doing mean things to them and what they are. Find out what, if anything, your child did in response. Reassure them that bullying (or the offending behaviors) is not okay and that they are not alone in dealing with it. Together, take a look at the options. Not fighting back and ignoring may work with teasing, but they are often not forceful enough tools to address the seriousness of bullying in the long run.

Your *Collaboration* goal is to find something that works better than whatever they have been doing so far. If they protest sharing any information with the school or extracurricular organization, remind them that there are laws to protect victims of bullying, which is why involving the school is important. Then, with all concerned, patiently navigate a strategy that involves the *Consistency* of *efforting* on all sides—you, the school, and your child all have something to do. No matter what, do not take the situation into your own hands by calling parents or solving the problem for your child. Work with official channels that have a mandate to protect children and teens. Eventually, when things start to improve, like they did for Drew, take some time to review (*Celebration*) how that happened.

When Friendships Come Easily

Many kids with ADHD are comfortable socially and have rewarding peer relationships. For some of them, making friends and being with people is as easy as drinking a glass of water. Others had to overcome awkwardness to reach out to peers. Some kids prefer to hang out with people who share their interests, while others prefer those who do not. Friends are trusted companions and crucial supports for living with ADHD.

> "I like finding friends who are the opposite. I'm dating somebody who literally has the exact opposite of ADD. Zach is meticulous about his schoolwork and driven to finish what he's doing and then move on to the next thing. I think being around that all the time, it's helped me. When we study together, if I ever get off task, he throws a pencil at me and brings me back, which is so nice."   —Lila, age 17

> "I have known my friend Paul since preschool. We sort of act the same exact way. He thinks of the same things that I do. We both are so happy and off the wall. Sometimes we get in fights, not big fights but just like, 'No, that's wrong.' 'No, that's right.' 'No, that's wrong.' It's just how we are. We are really close friends."   —Sanjay, age 10

> "I definitely tend to find people that are like me—a little scatter-brained. It's nice having that community. We don't usually have to talk about it, but they get it. When I'm frustrated, they know why 'cause they go through similar experiences. Then when I'm excited about something, they get it too. I wrote this paper that's two pages long. Woo hoo!"   —Ella, age 16

THESE KIDS SHOW us how much they value their friends, even when they hit bumps like Sanjay and his buddy, Paul. Their friends steer them back on course when they veer off, support them by sharing idiosyncrasies, and offer company during rough moments.

Sanjay also told me that he has trouble leaving his playdates with Paul. Many children with ADHD share this challenge when they have to leave a social activity they enjoy. It can be tough to shift from something they enjoy to anything else. Hiding, having a tantrum, kicking the tires of your car—these behaviors can be frustrating and embarrassing for everyone. Avoiding them requires making a plan before the playdate or gathering begins. Frustrated with unpleasant departures, Sanjay's parents wanted to make a change. Sanjay thought something could be better too.

We explored the components of an easy departure: no arguing, no whining, no physicality. While there may be natural disappointment that things are ending, they all wanted more cooperation. Sanjay commented that it is hard to leave because *"I don't know when you are coming and then you show up and whatever is next will be boring."* His parents decided to warn Sanjay when they were on their way to pick him up. Dad said: *"I can text the parents to ask them to please let Sanjay know. This will give him a ten-minute warning, but when I get there, it's time to roll."* Sanjay thought this would really help him. We explored what incentive might further motivate him to behave more appropriately at the time of a departure. His parents agreed that if Sanjay leaves something calmly and cooperatively, they would play a game of his choice for ten minutes when they get home or soon thereafter. If he does not follow the plan, Sanjay will spend ten minutes doing a task of his parents' choosing. One month later, the family reported that this system had been working. Sanjay smiled: *"Now they know how to play UNO!"*

Risky Business: When Teens' Social Choices Go Awry

Although the social lives of teens with ADHD are usually fun, enriching, and satisfying, sometimes they swerve into undesirable and even dangerous directions. When your teen makes dicey choices, it can be worrisome and frightening. All too often, adolescents in the United States face risks for using tobacco, marijuana, and alcohol, and illegal substances as well as for inappropriate or early sexual activity. For kids with ADHD whose brains lag in maturity, who struggle with impulsivity, and who focus on the pleasure of "now" more than the consequences of "later," these risks can be especially serious. Studies have found that teens with ADHD from all backgrounds are more apt to try cigarettes, alcohol, and marijuana earlier than their peers and are four to five times more likely to "escalate heavy cigarette and marijuana use after trying these substances once."[1] These behaviors can also decrease their chances of graduating from high school on time.[2] Both boys and girls with ADHD tend to engage in earlier sexual activity than their peers, before the age of fifteen, often with more partners and sometimes leading to unwanted pregnancies.[3] While dealing with suggestions about direct interventions related to addiction, illegal activities, and teen pregnancy is beyond the scope of this book, let's look carefully at why these dicey choices can be attractive to kids with ADHD. Listening to their reasons for pursuing drinking, smoking cigarettes or marijuana, or early sexual behavior provides insights into their behaviors beyond simple gratification. Many of them pursue these activities as another way to gain acceptance, act cool, or compensate for feeling inadequate.

Teens speak to me candidly about these issues and other types of rule-breaking behaviors. They often realize that they have made poor choices in the past or are still making them now. Sometimes they fail to see other options for themselves. Sometimes they don't care; they just want to do what they feel like.

"My dad says I make bad choices. He doesn't like my friends, thinks they're trashy people. Yeah, one of them got suspended last week for bringing vodka to the football game on Friday night, but they're my friends. After school or on the weekends, sometimes we get high. It's not a big deal. Everyone smokes. Some kids do other things but, nah, that stuff ain't for me." —Jaden, age 15

"I used to have a lot more sex when I was drunk or high. My friends were big partiers. When I'm sober with my ADHD, I don't think that clearly to begin with. I slept around a lot just because I felt like it. It was fun. I liked that people wanted me. I wouldn't think about how I feel in the future."

—Rose, age 17

"Around the end of ninth grade I started drinking with my friends just because it was fun. We even drank on the bus on the way to school, which in hindsight was really, really stupid. Then I stopped drinking and started smoking weed. That's how I could get out of my brain. My brain doesn't like to stop thinking. It's always working and jumping from subject to subject. When you're high it's just kind of quiet and relaxed."

—Anthony, age 16

"If I'm running late and my clothes aren't right and I'm doing my hair wrong, I get set off. It's stupid, but I get more and more angry and eventually I'm in a freak-out. That's when I feel like, 'Oh man, I should smoke a bowl to keep myself out of this place.' Like it's covering up the feeling of hating my ugly body but I'm okay with that because it works."

—Sofia, age 16

WHETHER IT'S SMOKING marijuana or drinking with friends, these kids all struggle with curbing their impulses and lacking resources to make alternative choices. They privately confided their wishes that they had made other choices but those felt impossible at the time. Some of their parents took them to therapy; others told me that their parents did not know what they were doing.

Of course, there is no single way to address risky behaviors like the ones described here. The best options involve maintaining a positive connection with your teen and nurturing their self-confidence. It can be very confusing for you to know how to best respond to your child's undesirable or unsafe choices, especially if you are upset. *Cool off before you talk to your teen*, and turn to your partner or trusted family and friends for support. Perhaps someone you know has been through something like this before and their child is doing well now. They may have a few tidbits of sage advice for you. Before moving forward, though, make sure you and your partner are on the same page about your intended conversation with your son or daughter.

Calmly gather information from your teen: the what, where, when, and how of an event that has brought these unsafe behaviors to your attention. Clarify the options they saw for themselves, their reflections, if any, about their decisions, and any other choices they could have made. See if you can find an aspect of their predicament with which you can empathize. Maybe like Jaden or Rose, they felt peer pressure. Maybe like Anthony, they wanted their brain to calm down. Ask them what they think should happen now. This is a key point. Most kids are well aware when they have erred, and they have interesting ideas about what the next step should be.

If you have a family rule forbidding smoking marijuana in your house and your son lights up on the porch one Saturday with some friends, refrain from immediately taking away his phone. Instead, talk about your value of creating a substance-free home and the violation of trust that has occurred. Parent-teen trust is like a bank account with breaches resembling overdraws. Kids understand this metaphor and what it means to go from twenty-five to negative five. Try saying something like: *"We have agreed to no drinking or smoking on our property. I'm very disappointed that you broke that agreement and my trust. I am curious about why you did that. What was going on? What do you think should happen now?"* Perhaps your son will suggest that he is grounded for a month; perhaps he will suggest that his curfew moves from midnight to 10:30. Listen to his ideas and take some time to consider them. There is no law that says you have to tell him right then what you have decided about the situation, but you must *offer him ways to earn back your trust* as part of your decision, and whatever you do, stick with your plan. Otherwise, he won't take you seriously.

> Parent-teen trust is like a bank account with breaches resembling overdraws.

Despite whatever typical adolescent snarkiness or reaction you may receive, your teen still needs and wants your support. Being available to listen, comfort, and talk through things is essential for keeping them on a positive track and addressing risky behaviors. Feeling competent in some areas, being accepted by peers, and liking aspects of themselves also reduces adolescent substance use. When teens are busy with sports, extracurricular activities, a part-time job, or a religious group, they build confidence and resilience. They develop a wider network of friends, so they don't have to rely on one group of kids who like to drink or smoke. Even though adolescents with ADHD who take medication have shown a lower likelihood for substance abuse, many teens on stimulant or nonstimulant prescriptions are still using them.[4] If you are concerned about issues like substance use and sexuality for your son or daughter, *I strongly encourage you to seek professional help.* There is no award for handling these kinds of challenges alone. Seek out support if you need it.

Chapter 13

Plugged In

Crazy About Technology

MEET JOSIE, KYLE, and Destiny as they talk about technology in their lives:

"I love my tablet. It's my favorite thing. I like Google Maps because if you type in sixteen zero zero you can see the White House. I like Cool Math Games 'cause it gets me better at math and Mama lets me play whenever I want. When I get mad or frustrated, my iPad calms me down."

—Josie, age 10

"Papa is mad most of the time, which is why I am on the computer to avoid him. My favorite games are Mortal Kombat and Halo 5. Usually, he has to yell at me to get off. First, he tells me to stop and I'm like, 'Okay. Let me just finish this game.' Then it takes like another thirty minutes. Then he yells and he's really mad and I get kind of shocked and get off. If there's something better to do, then I could get off better. If I can't watch TV, then I lie on my bed. Maybe chew on my fingers or go to sleep."

—Kyle, age 12

"I need to have my phone with me 24/7. I live around my phone. I use it for apps, texting, talking to my friends. I check Instagram, Snapchat, Facebook, I don't know, maybe twenty-five times a day. I wonder what everybody else is up to, if they are saying anything about me, how many likes I have. I just feel naked without it."   —Destiny, age 15

LIKE MOST AMERICAN youngsters, kids with ADHD use technology for entertainment, socializing, and relaxing. Sometimes it helps them escape from daily stress, express themselves creatively, or build academic skills. With its countless options, the internet and the devices that access it are a gold mine for kids with ADHD. They can instantaneously satisfy their natural distractibility by doing several things simultaneously: music, videos, socializing, homework, and more. While finding stimulation anytime, anywhere can be exciting, it can also lead kids further away from themselves into numbing out. As parents, the breadth of online and social media options and activities for our youngsters can seem mind-blowing. It is almost impossible to keep up with every new game or site and know which ones are appropriate. It is equally daunting to know how to monitor kids' online activities. In this chapter, we will examine why technology is so appealing for kids with ADHD and how the Five C's helps you successfully handle their activities.

Our Networked Lives

The influence of technology pervades all our lives. Whether it is television, computers, tablets, or cell phones, people around the world are more connected today than ever before. From preschool to the senior center, everybody has screens in their lives. Your son or daughter was born into a world already filled with technology. They grasp it with uncanny speed and dexterity, zipping here and there while you likely lag behind. Online is also their social world: the cool locale for today's kids. Whereas you went to the mall, corner store, or community center, they now go online to hang out (socialize), develop special interests (music, videos, or alternative reality games), or just mess around (surf the internet, look at funny YouTube videos).[1] The ubiquity of mobile devices makes internet activity a constant presence in their lives. Almost 75 percent of thirteen-to-seventeen-year-olds possess smartphones, and 54 percent admit that they go online several times a day.[2] Many kids, especially girls, now create their sense of identity based on how many likes, retweets, or followers they have instead of developing an internally based self-esteem. Most young people over the age of twelve admit to checking their phones twenty-five to thirty times per day to see who texted them, what peers are doing, and others' opinions of them. Studies have found these estimates to be low, with Americans of all ages checking their phones an average of forty-six times per day.[3]

Many parents acknowledge that too much media exposure is risky. While today's kids have a digital prowess for manipulating a wide variety of gadgets, they are far less adept at applying ethical standards to what they do. Girls tend to spend extra time on social media; boys focus more on gaming. Research has found significant associations between too much media usage and obesity, tobacco, alcohol and marijuana use, sexual permissiveness, and low academic achievement.[4] You can help your son or daughter create a healthy media diet, reduce the behavioral risks, and create a balance between "in-person" life and life "in the cloud."

The online world of websites, social media platforms, and blogs, to name just a few, has taken things that used to be private and personal and made them public and tangible. Whatever you say or do in the networked world leaves a mark—a digital footprint. Adults often forget this, and kids, who may have never learned it in the first place, certainly do not seem aware of the dangers. If you add the impulsive aspects of ADHD into the mix, the likelihood of considering the consequences of writing snarky words on someone's wall or friending someone from Norway in a computer game, is quite low. Even more than their peers, kids with ADHD simply do not possess the developed capacity to stop themselves when something seems like fun. You must explicitly teach them online safety over and over again, and *it is never too late or too early to start*. Clear, consistent ground rules about technology lead to safe and healthy choices.

It can be daunting to convey to children and teens why and how they should monitor their digital activities when everybody is so plugged in. A large study of diverse American adults showed that 90 percent of them own a computer, 74 percent own an internet-connected smartphone, and 65 percent use social media.[5] It is no longer considered rude to turn our attention away from someone during a conversation to respond to our cell phone—it is usually considered perfectly normal. How often have you turned away from your child to check your phone, showing them silently that they matter less than an incoming message?[6] The parts of our brains that detect novelty activate every time there is a ping, urging us to shift our awareness to the potential pleasure of an incoming message. These constant pulls on our attention can be addicting for anyone, but for kids or adults with ADHD who are naturally drawn to new stimuli, they are particularly seductive. Although one study showed that 72 percent of parents believe they model a healthy relationship to technology for their children, approximately 67 percent admitted to behaviors that indicated the opposite: often or constantly checking personal email, text messages, and social media wherever they were.[7]

Your kids notice your actions and when you do exactly what you have told them not to. J.J., age thirteen, explains what happens when he and his dad work at the kitchen table:

> What I can't stand is what Dad does when I ask him a question and he's typing on the computer. He turns his head to look at me, but he's still looking at the computer. It drives me crazy. It's like he's not even paying attention. Dad gets mad at me when I am gaming and I don't look at him to answer, but I can't say anything to him.

While you may be working, figuring out family finances, or planning a vacation, your son or daughter sees no difference from their online activities. The adult is on a screen when they are not. Carly, age twelve, told me why time limits on her phone are not fair:

> My brother is in his room on his phone, or computer, or doing home-work. Papa's on his computer doing spreadsheets, and Mama's on Face-book or working or cleaning, so there's no one to socialize with. That's why I want to text my friends.

Carly, bored and alone, wants entertainment and cannot understand why her phone time is curtailed when everyone else can be online. This perspective suggests that you (and your partner) reflect on your own patterns of using phones and computers before you start to address the issue of technology in your family. Sixty-five percent of parents agree that unplugging is important for mental health, but only 28 percent actually do it.[8]

EXERCISE 8:

Reflections On How You Use Technology

Before you begin to teach digital citizenship, honestly reflect on how you use technology.
How often do you get on your computer or phone?
Is it too much?
Are you modeling using technology in ways you feel good about?
What, if anything, would you like to do differently?

JUST AS YOU explicitly instruct children not to lie, steal, or punch, you have to impart your values regarding digital manners and online safety. Online etiquette refers to how you act toward people in the digital world. If you wouldn't say something in person, then you prob-ably shouldn't say it online. Establishing what netiquette means in your family is a crucial family discussion that will have to be repeated periodically as your child matures. Online safety deals with your digital footprint: the lasting legacy of where you go online, what you do, and with whom you do it. It's an ongoing process with many reminders. Instruct or remind your child about basic internet security: They should never share passwords with peers, enter personal information without parental guidance, meet a stranger in person whom they contacted online, or deal with cyber-bullying or inappropriate behavior alone. Insist on being their friend/follower and having access to all their media accounts, including passwords. With their "now/not now" brains, your child or teen with ADHD especially has to absorb that their internet behavior can follow them for years.

These lessons begin with considering the role you (and your partner) want technology to play in your family's life. What websites, games, and apps are appropriate for their age and maturity? Where and when can they use their devices? Are they powered down at night and if so, where are they kept? Setting these boundaries can be tricky because many kids think they should have whatever access they desire. The American Academy of Pediatrics recommends keeping computers, TVs, and other electronic media out of your kids' bedrooms (especially before the ages of sixteen or until your child has demonstrated maturity and dependability about technology use).[9] Using technology is a privilege, not a right. It is not predetermined by some higher power that your son can play Battlefield or your daughter can have Instagram. Like driving, access to certain privileges comes when you have demonstrated readiness through developed skills and sound judgment.

> Using technology is a privilege, not a right.

With this clarity about the role of technology in your home and the boundaries you want to establish, begin a fruitful discussion with your family. You may receive pushback as you set limits about what sites or apps your child can access, and that is *okay*. You are changing their assumption that they are as entitled to technology as food, clothing, shelter, and love. You want the option of monitoring the frequency and content of their internet activity, and it is a lot easier when the device lives outside the bedroom. With younger kids, plan what they can watch or play and when they can do it. Try to create family computer time, when they do their stuff and you pursue yours. Maybe stream a show and watch it together, talking later about the images and messages you see. I encourage you to make a written contract based on your family discussion about technology to ensure a healthy media diet. Excellent age-appropriate media contracts are available at www.commonsensemedia.org. Have everyone sign it to show that you are taking this seriously, and monitor it regularly.

Finally, consider family times to unplug and connect with one another. After work, plan to spend the first hour at home reconnecting with your family. If you are "just checking [your] phone," then you are checking out. Kids, even teens, will act out to get your attention, so give it before any drama occurs. Try scheduling screen-free days and do something else together. Use meals as times for interaction without phones or television.[10]

Easy On, Easy Off

Although logging onto devices happens easily, logging off can be an ordeal for everyone. Masters of delay maneuvers, kids with ADHD seem incapable of resisting the appeal of the computer, phone, or tablet. Whether the goal is avoiding boredom, reaching that magic level of a favorite game, or texting about a friendship drama, they feel a pressing, passionate desire to be on a screen, no matter what. One of the major obstacles for shutting off screen activities is the perception that nothing else seems as interesting. Ending a game of Minecraft to do homework or clean your room pales in comparison to the action online.

> "My favorite game is Zombies Call of Duty. If I'm playing and then all of
> a sudden I have to stop right when I am about to kill the monster zombie,
> I get frustrated. I'll go, 'Mom, come on, please.' It's better when, like,

they'll actually play with me. I like to play board games. Connect Four and Sorry are the best." —Christian, age 9

"I try to interact, but I have nobody to interact. Everyone is busy. Last night, I sneaked my iPod. I was in the bathroom with it, and after, Mom said, 'Didn't you just have your iPod in the bathroom?' and I said, 'No.' And she said, 'You're lying,' and I said, 'You're right.' Mom said, 'You should stop going over screen limits.' I said, 'Why don't you do something with me? There's nothing for me to do.'" —Taylor, age 12

"If I don't get off, Dad starts taking things away. It doesn't work because I will keep on asking for screens or do other things that annoy him because he might give it back. Sometimes I give up when he doesn't. If my games get taken away, I'll be pretty frustrated with that and keep bugging him." —J.J., age 12

PARENTS REGULARLY CONFIDE to me that they threaten things they cannot enact or have no plan to enforce to get their kids off devices. Do you ever do this? One father was so mad at his daughter for not getting off her phone and making them late for church that he threatened to take away her birthday party. She was quite hysterical by the time they arrived, and they couldn't enter the service. Ultimately he relented and she had her party. Every time you threaten and do not deliver, your credibility slides down a notch. Upping the ante to make a punishment mean something—like taking away the computer for a month because your son didn't clean his room—seems severe and, frankly, meaningless. Many kids with ADHD can't grasp what a month means anyway: it just feels like forever. Furthermore, when kids are not part of the discussion about what would help them stop gaming, messaging, or texting, they lack real investment in cooperating. They focus solely on avoiding negative consequences and learn nothing about transitioning off screens. It's much more effective to replace threats and punishments with the Five C's.

Easy On/Easy Off involves setting a baseline for screen time and using meaningful incentives. Before doing anything, you (and your partner) need to decide the total amount of screen time per day you want your child (or children) to have. Kids do better when they have an automatic baseline of screen time that is nonnegotiable: they get this regardless of anything they do. It's their gimme: they don't have to jockey for technology, and you don't have to negotiate it on a daily basis. Perhaps you want your son to have a total of one and a half hours per day. The first hour is the automatic baseline. It is a given for him, not to be removed due to misbehavior, disrespect, low grades, etc.

The other thirty minutes—the golden carrot of bonus time your son or daughter really wants—serves as the valuable incentive behind motivation and cooperation for *Easy On/Easy Off*. If your son completes his hour and gets off the computer *with no arguing* to practice violin or set the dinner table, he can earn the extra thirty minutes, beginning at a time you choose. Discuss with your son or daughter what should happen if they have trouble getting offline from bonus time, write down their ideas, and incorporate them into your plan. I have seen these clear expectations and the desire for this extra time lead kids with ADHD to do many responsibilities with less arguing.

Another valuable incentive that you can use with bonus time or by itself is time with you. Just as incentives propel kids with ADHD to complete homework and chores, they also motivate your child or teen to get offline. Time and again, I have seen families orchestrate *Easy On/Easy Off* plans when parents offer themselves as an option for post-screen activity—even for teens. Similar to identifying incentives for doing chores, collaborate on a written list of enjoyable shared activities that you post in the kitchen. Explain that they will have two options following screen time. Option One, if they practice *Easy On/Easy Off*, means they can pick something from the activity list; Option Two, if they don't practice *Easy On/Easy Off*, means you pick the household helping activity.

Now you are ready to run the *Easy On/Easy Off* program. Follow these steps:

1. At the beginning of a time-limited screen session, set up two timers: one for you and one for them. Tell them they will have two warnings, at five minutes and at two minutes before the stop time. Use the *Rule of Three* for both warnings.
2. When the five-minute warning arrives, go to your son or daughter and say, *"That's your five-minute warning. I will come back in two minutes."* Then reset the timers.
3. Come back in two minutes and state, *"This is your two-minute warning. I am reminding you to start saving your stuff now."* Make sure they repeat your reminder. Set the final alarm.
4. When the alarm beeps, if your child manages an *Easy Off*, commend them on their transition. Either do their chosen activity immediately, or tell them they've earned the bonus time and when they can begin it.

Whatever your do, avoid negotiating. Keep breathing; remember this is tough for everyone and stick with your *Collaboration* plan.

Remember Malik, who threw his eggs in Chapter 10? His parents adopted the *Easy On/Easy Off* method, with him and his sister giving key input into their family's plan. In their agreement, computer or tablet *Easy Offs* were rewarded with fifteen minutes of extra phone time to text or talk. Arguing about getting off, procrastinating, or throwing a controller eliminated the phone time. The kids then offered an idea: if they violated that fifteen minutes by going over, then they would lose their phones for the next day. Their parents, unsure initially about having technology after computer time, opted, in the spirit of *Collaboration*, to try it out. This system was easier for everyone to remember and reduced arguments about fairness and begging for more time. Everybody was pleasantly surprised.

This method may seem labor intensive to you. When I suggested it to J.J. and his father, J.J. smiled and said, "*I like that. I could do that.*" His father, however, balked:

> So now every time he puts electronics down I'm supposed to play cruise director? No. I don't have time for that. The issue is doing the hard, boring stuff of life. There's no problem with transitioning to the computer. It's getting off to do something he doesn't like. He has to learn to do that.

While it's true that J.J. should learn to do the "boring stuff of life," his frequent arguments with his father and subsequent punishments won't teach him how. J.J. is smart: he knows that his overworked father will forget what he threatened or grow tired of enforcing the rule. This is why many kids with ADHD do not take their parents seriously. These tactics may work when they are younger, but by high school, teens are savvier and less scared.

Promising to withdraw a technology privilege may temporarily change a behavior, but it rarely has lasting effects. It fails to teach necessary lifelong executive functioning skills. How will a threat help youngsters learn to end their games and study for a geometry test the next day? How will they eventually be able to switch tasks and meet deadlines at their jobs? Kids with ADHD need extra assistance as they mature to develop these skills related to transitions, flexibility, and regulation.

When your child or teen is using technology or social media inappropriately, taking away devices makes sense. Playing games that you do not approve of, visiting unsuitable websites, or texting or posting inappropriate material (among other things) means that your child is misusing their devices. Using the Five C's, these situations invite conversation and consequences that teach about digital citizenship and online safety. When you see a picture on Instagram of your fifteen-year-old daughter at a party with a beer, you are justifiably concerned. Use *Stop, Think, Act* and plot your course of action.

After a conversation where she explains the situation and how she feels about it, remind her about digital footprints. Future colleges and employers routinely go online to gather information about prospective students and workers. Express your own feelings calmly, and talk together about the breach of trust and how to restore it. Take the time you need to consider your choices, and when you've made a decision, make sure all adults in the house are on the same page. Then reconvene with your daughter and discuss your plan. Whether it's deleting Instagram or restricting phone use, also give her a chance to make amends and rebuild trust. Notice her *efforting* when she brings her phone to your room each night before bed and texts you regularly with her whereabouts. When she follows your agreement, she makes valuable deposits in the trust bank account.

The Lure of Computer Games

Computer games particularly appeal to kids with ADHD because they provide fun and interesting activities where they meet specific objectives and feel accomplished. Using a mix of fantasy, music, and plot intricacies, computer and video games offer a variety of compelling challenges to keep their minds and hands engaged. Seth, age nine, told me: *"When I get to play Mario Kart or Xbox, I just calm down and focus. It's really interesting, like you can actually learn real stuff."* In a life where a child with ADHD and possibly a learning challenge may feel frustrated by a lack of achievement at school, they meet with success every time they reach a designated level. An immediate feeling of competency ensues.

Of course, the seduction of computer or video games lies in the lure of attaining the next level. It is never enough to finish one thing: the games entice you to keep moving on. Your son or daughter can quickly become caught in the vortex of "just one more thing." This temptation is hard to resist for most kids. For kids with ADHD who tend to overfocus, misunderstand time, and live predominantly in the present, it can be almost impossible. When the "now" of the game is totally captivating, there is no "later." Having a single goal of moving from one level to the next fits perfectly with the overfocus that comes naturally to kids with ADHD. Kieran, age ten, tells me: "*I might get zoned in, you know, games and levels. They're so frustrating to beat: I can't stop. I just shut down everything around me and focus on that one thing.*" Kieran is caught up in the thrill of the game. His mother adds: "*Even when I give him a five-minute warning and I tell him over and over that he needs to be done and come to dinner, he's just lost. He can't move on to the next thing.*" When he is playing, Kieran's director cannot summon the motivation and control to stop: he is in his own world.

Healthy gaming is part of a balanced life that includes non-screen activities, caring friends, and proficiency at school, sports, or hobbies. Sometimes your child's fascination with gaming may lead to a career in designing or implementing them. You never know. If you have never played the games your child loves, try them out. Your participation, even if it is the last thing on earth you want to do, shows that you care enough to be interested in what matters to them. It gives you a leg to stand on when you attempt to monitor or set limits on certain games later on.

Games serve a social purpose: kids play them with friends or connect with other players online. Sharing their passion for virtual worlds, they create a twenty-first-century friendship that parents may not understand. Elijah, age thirteen, who shared his social struggles at the beginning of Chapter 12, told me that he does not see the difference between computer friends and real-life friends.

> It's safer on the computer; people are nicer than most people I know. On the computer you are judged by your actions, not just by what you like. I'm not wearing the latest fashion or into sports, so I'm not cool. But on the computer, I'm good at gaming so I'm cool.

His computer friends are the ones he trusts because they accept him.

Friendships also form around shared interests in gaming. Marcus, age fifteen, shared his plans for the summer: "*Finish the Darksiders series and Hitman: Absolution. See if I can beat Max and get to a higher level before he does. He's gonna come over and we'll play at the same time. As long as we can play, we're happy."* While on the one hand, such relationships do not build typical friendship skills, on the other, they offer these boys a valuable sense of belonging and safety.

While gaming provides entertainment or a much-needed break from a stressful day, at other times, when overused, it may mask underlying issues like anxiety, loneliness, or low self-esteem. Many parents tell me that they believe their child is addicted to computer games. There is a huge difference between gaming as a supplement to daily living and gaming as the focus of daily living. I frequently see "addicted" kids with ADHD for whom gaming is their preferred free-time activity. They are doing fine in school, play a sport, and have a few friends. When they have no commitments, they go online or play video games, but they possess limited abilities to get off co-operatively. They appear, to their parents, as addicted and may, in fact, be overly engaged in screen activities. But when gaming takes priority over all other activities (school, friendships, extracurricular activities) despite significant negative consequences (academic failure, social isolation, etc.), then computer gaming has become unhealthy and your child may well be addicted. This requires professional attention.

Connected to One Another 24/7

"Am I cool? Do people like me? Am I attractive?" For the older children and teens who spoke to me, online social life *is* real social life. Celeste, age seventeen, explained:

> I think it's all part of one big thing, because you can't really separate out your actions on one platform to another. It's still part of who you are. It's not like you get to detach yourself completely from your online presence.

Social media platforms such as Facebook, Instagram, and Snapchat provide a constant gauge of popularity, belonging, and connection. Kids use profiles to boost popularity or comment on one another's status, for better or worse. They can look a certain way or play parts that they may not be able to do in person: fun, sexy, brave, nasty, caring.

> "Well, I used to present myself a lot differently in general. Not a lot of people knew a lot about me, so my social media portrayed that straight hair, contacts, makeup all the time. When in reality, I'm usually with curly hair, glasses, and no makeup." —Sonya, age 17

> "I definitely always post my best self. Everything I post is either of a picture of me or a picture of my friends. We always look super good, and I look super cool. Even though I don't always feel that way."
> —Jackson, age 14

KIDS ALSO SAY or do things via text or online that they would not in person. Without seeing a peer's reactions, they feel little or no impact from their words or deeds. Rating is a perfect example. Destiny explained how she (and her friends) rate *"how someone looks more honestly than what I would say to their face because I don't have to deal with them."* Every post, every like, every follower gives our kids information about where they stand with their peers. The pressure to maintain the image they have created, keep up with what is going on, and stay in touch is enormous. It breeds insecurity and anxiety. For kids with ADHD who may already struggle with peer issues, the intensity of social media elevates their stress.

Social media platforms certainly have benefits. In the same way that many youngsters may feel freer to say mean things to one another online, they seem to feel more comfortable to stand up for what they think is right. These venues allow for displays of affection around birthdays or holidays and provide a place to show caring and approval. Kids often tell me how they rally online in defense of someone. Pablo, age fifteen, explains:

> If someone posts something that is offensive to a certain community, I say something. I might not do it in person, but I will on Facebook. A lot of my friends who don't even identify in that community will go off on this other person. Yeah, they're a lot more likely to stand up for someone Hispanic or Black or someone who's gay or transgender than I think they would be in person.

If being supportive face-to-face feels awkward, the internet provides a safer opportunity to step up.

Just as kids with ADHD are susceptible to overfocusing on computer and video games, they are vulnerable to relying too heavily on their devices, social media, and texting for distraction and engagement. Both boys and girls, ages thirteen and older, reported going on their phones upward of twenty-five times per day to check for notifications or texts.

> "I go on maybe fifty times a day? I don't necessarily always go onto my phone, but I always check it for notifications. Sometimes I don't have any notifications and I'll just go look on social media. I usually check everything. Instagram, Twitter, and Snapchat." —Henry, age 16

> "Probably twice an hour on average. Maybe more. I usually check my texts, email, and Snapchat. Just to see if people have contacted me because it doesn't always pop up. I use Facebook Messenger to communicate with some of my friends, and I use Snapchat just for little cute things I find throughout the day." —Amari, age 17

> "I am addicted to stimulus, as they say. If I am feeling unoccupied in a moment, I will reach for my phone, watch something, read something. I need that visual stimulus. I'm constantly on stupid social media sites, constantly looking at stuff. I need input all the time." —Jasmine, age 17

NOT HAVING THEIR phones means being bored and disconnected. Ana, age fifteen, remarks: *"When I don't have my phone, I'm more anxious than normal because I have it all the time, so it's like I'm missing my underwear or something."* Without their phones, kids feel unrooted, separated from their peer lifelines, and worried about missing out.

For some kids with ADHD, going online to see what other people were doing helped them feel involved; for others, it led to feeling left out. Ethan, age seventeen, described his online choices:

> I would say I mostly go on Instagram to look at photos of hair since I am studying cosmetology. Also cute boys and dogs and stuff. When I'm on Twitter and Snapchat, I feel I'm more in a close web of people. I know most of the people I follow, so I go to see what they're posting about. I'm looking for what Morgan's doing or what my other friend's doing, stuff like that. . . . I have Facebook, too, but I don't really go on it because I don't like the crowd that posts on it.

Although he spends more time now looking rather than posting, Ethan has changed what he posts over the years:

> I used to talk about stupid stuff I was doing. Like if I had drama with my friends I would tweet about that or if I broke up with my boyfriend I would Instagram a picture with a sappy caption. Probably inappropriate for the whole world to be seeing and not something everybody needs to know about. I wouldn't do that now.

As his frontal lobes mature, Ethan has developed the capacity for more impulse control and interpersonal understanding. He no longer feels the need to discuss personal matters online the way he did before.

Sadly, studies show that most parents are inadequately trained in the fast-paced, shifting world of social media.[11] They simply cannot keep up with what is new and hot, periodically misjudging what their kids are doing online and how much fun they are actually having. You may be friends with your thirteen-year-old daughter on Facebook, see a smiling photo of her with friends at the beach, and think everything is fine, but you might miss the slight that all the other girls are tagged in the photo but your daughter is not. This omission, while seemingly innocent, might well be a purposeful maneuver to demonstrate exclusion. Sounds paranoid? Yes, but these kinds of subtle tactics confront our kids daily.

Across the board, parents and kids speak to me about their recurrent arguments related to social media usage. Many parents restrict time spent online by keeping their child's phone, tablet, or computer in their room at night. Others limit certain sites, control passwords, and follow/friend their child. While you may not comprehend the ins and outs of your teen's engagement with social media, your presence and monitoring have been found to lower youngsters' online conflicts and distress.[12] When parents keep track of what is occurring online, it seems that kids try harder to create more appropriate content. Meg, age thirteen, talked about this:

> I have to be careful because I am friends with my parents on Facebook, Instagram, and Snapchat. There's always been "everybody's gonna see this." I think at first it made me a little sneakier. I had a fake Instagram account for a couple of months. I've had my share of arguments with people on Facebook, but knowing my parents are gonna see that, it always makes me think more about the words I'm gonna say, which is hard for me, with my ADD and all.

Despite her challenges with cause-and-effect thinking, Meg tries to edit her words and actions. She told me that she has made some mistakes: posting an ugly picture of a friend or writing something mean about her ex-boyfriend. When her parents saw these, they talked with her about *"acting better and how we don't treat people like that in our family and then I lost my phone for, like, a day. I mean, they were right."*

Being a part of your teen's online life is your best entry into their world and what they deal with. It also allows you to monitor their posts for suitability. Ask your son or daughter to show you around Instagram or Snapchat if you don't have an account. Look at the people or organizations they follow on Twitter and talk about what makes them interesting. You want your child or teen to come to you instead of fishing around online for information when social issues or peer skirmishes arise. Being part of their social media web keeps you in the loop and encourages them to use better netiquette. When you remember that learning digital citizenship takes time and practice, then you can approach missteps with *Compassion*, *Collaboration*, and *Consistency* and good choices with *Celebration*.

Final Note

Hope and Confidence

THIS BOOK ENDS where it began—with the voices of kids with ADHD. They've shared stories about school challenges, medication issues, learning differences, organization, friendships, and technology. They've also given me sound advice for other families based on helpful things their parents do.

"Just know your kid. Be as patient as possible. It definitely gets hard; it did. They would tell me those kinds of things, too, and stuff like 'You're not dumb,' 'It's going to be fine, it's totally okay. A lot of people go through it.'"
—Hunter, age 17

"I have less arguments with Dad now after coming to therapy, so I would say counseling helped us even though I really didn't want to go. Dad's starting to trust me more. Before I would say, 'I don't know how to do this,' and he'd think I was trying to get out of work, but he believes me more now."
—Drew, age 12

"My mom is the main person I talk about this stuff with. She's super helpful and is always telling me to write stuff down. She makes sure I get everything done more by myself now than I used to."   —Nadia, age 15

"My grandpa, my grandma, and my mom, they listen to me. I know they understand that I have the ADHD. . . . Sometimes I feel really slow and sad. Cuddling with my mom makes this better. My sad feeling goes away."   —Kieran, age 10

"My dad was probably the biggest person because he was always helping me to figure out ways to advocate for myself. He never stepped in the way, unless he needed to or I asked him. He would also help me with a lot of breathing techniques and remind me, 'Hey, let's try to focus.' It would get annoying, but now I realize that he was just trying to help me and get me into this zone of remembering to refocus."   —Sonya, age 17

PATIENCE, LISTENING, AFFECTION, trust, and redirection—these types of parent support comprise my Five C's of ADHD parenting that you have learned here. Instead of raised voices, painful misunderstandings, fruitless ultimatums, and unilateral problem-solving, you now rely first on monitoring yourself before dealing with your son or daughter, listening to their words and actions, and figuring out what is going on. Together, you make agreements to tame the homework monster, clean their room, and shut off the computer, based on appealing incentives that include interactions with you. They improve their cooperation because they want to participate. As you see their efforts, you praise them. With *self-Control, Compassion, Collaboration, Consistency*, and *Celebration*, you nurture connection, teach life lessons, and build your child's self-esteem.

It may seem impossible to help your daughter talk back to that negative voice when she can't write her looming history paper; to remember to **Stop, Think, Act** when your son angrily takes apart his sister's castle; or to rely on *Easy On/Easy Off* when faced with a screaming child who will not turn off their computer game. I know that you *can* do all these things. Using the Five C's takes practice, and you may stumble before they become habits. Keep trying anyway. Whatever initial stress you face will fade as your family begins to achieve your desired intentions—together. Making adjustments to charts and agreements and holding your support in place longer than you think you should guarantees those executive functioning skills will click and the director is ready to call "Action!"

Kids repeatedly tell me that they want to feel heard. Listen to your child or teen. You don't have to accede to their wishes, but you do need to acknowledge their concerns to clinch their participation. Having their buy-in, along with your love, understanding, and confidence, makes all the difference for lasting success.

Despite whatever challenges you and your son or daughter may be facing now, things *will* improve. I followed up recently with several of the children and teens from my initial interviews and was happy to see the ways in which their lives had improved. Camilla, age thirteen, who talked about social loneliness, enrolled in an arts magnet school with a diverse population where she pursues dance and has found friends she can relate to. Jose, now fourteen, attends middle school, where he has an IEP, gets A's and B's on his report card, and plays soccer year-round. He no longer meets with the tutor who suggested taking pictures of the homework written on the board. Maisie, whose anxiety about sleep kept her and her parents awake, took acting classes and now, at thirteen, performs in a community theater production each year. She still gets anxious about tests but generally sleeps better. Malik, now fifteen, hasn't been sent to the office at his performing arts charter school in six months and "loses it" much less often at home. He loves being the beatboxer in the school's a cappella singing group.

Kayla, age twenty, started at two different four-year colleges before transferring to a third that finally feels like the right fit. She has received accommodations for note-taking and tests, which she had to arrange and coordinate on her own. Ethan, age twenty, attended cosmetology school and now works happily as an assistant hair stylist. Henry, age nineteen, failed his first semester at a local community college and decided to take a break from academics, moving to a nearby city, where he works in retail and supports himself. Proud of his independence, he hopes to return to college next year, taking a few classes at a time. Overcoming obstacles and learning as they go, all these kids are successfully finding their way in the world.

Finally, I leave you with the kids' advice to other young people with ADHD. Their words reflect brave journeys through struggles at school, at home, and with peers. May their stories inspire you as much as they propelled me to write this book. I encourage you to share them with your son or daughter.

"Keep trying hard. With some teachers, if you really put your neck out there and you show them you're trying hard, most of them will respond well to you. They might not give you the biggest breaks in the world, but they're usually out there to help. Even as a person of color you can still expect to get ahead and to follow the power culture that we live in, if you're able to put your neck out there. It's going to work out for you."

—Carlos, age 15

"There's just going to be bumps in the road, but you can get through it. No one's perfect, you're not perfect, and that's okay. Hey, it's life. As long as you have people to help you like teachers or parents and you have good friends, you can get through it. You have to just learn how to control your anger."

—Kia, age 12

"There's some times when you need to fight back and say, 'Even though I have this distraction, problems with this concentration, I'll try even harder.' There are some parts of ADHD you learn to live with. It's part of your identity and what you're made of. You start to figure it out a little more. It's always a challenge, but it definitely gets better."

—Oscar, age 14

"You're not different from nobody, just your attention. You should understand that you're going to grow up having to work around some things and find your own strategies, just like everyone else, to succeed. It doesn't mean you're stupid. It's just you have trouble doing things like focusing. Feeling different is always going to be there, but just don't think negative on it. You're a human being, you're equal to everybody, and you can accomplish what you want, when you want. You just really have to work for it."   —Ivan, age 17

Acknowledgments

First and foremost, I would like to acknowledge all the young people and their families whose stories made this book possible. It's been a great privilege to talk with you and work together. Your bravery, humor, and persistence are a constant inspiration.

Many people helped shaped this project. Thank you to Janine Roberts, EdD, and Carol Saline for your tireless editing and ongoing support and for showing me what it means to be a writer. My gratitude goes out to Drs. Jane Cross, Jamie Bell, and Jonathan Schwab and their pediatric practices for making arrangements for me to meet with interested families. Thank you to Sam Intrator, PhD, and Dr. Jo Glading-DiLorenzo for orchestrating interviews with kids from Project Coach. Jonathan Lichtenstein, PsyD, offered sage consultations about neuropsychiatry. Melinda Messeck, Rae Maltz, Maggie Peebles-Dorin, Isabel Snodgrass, and Jonah Hahn provided excellent research assistance; Sarina Hahn created original drawings; and Drs. Kyle and Marsha Pruett, Julie Mencher, Dr. Aaron Beck, Rachel Simmons, the folks at Big Yellow, and Elaine Taylor-Klaus offered early and continued support of this undertaking. Joann Levin, John Joelson, and Kathy Eckles gave me quiet, beautiful places to think and write.

The insightful feedback of my dedicated readers—Kathy Casale, MA; Margaret Miller, EdD; and Kenneth Hahn—improved this book immensely. I am very lucky to have a wonderful circle of friends whose encouragement often came when it was most needed. A special thank-you to Dr. Laura Markham, who is one of those truly generous people who nurtures success in others. She's been a champion of my work, supporting me in every possible way, including introductions to the folks at TarcherPerigee.

To Marian Lizzi and her incredible team at TarcherPerigee, thank you for believing in my work and for taking it to a new level. It's been a great pleasure to collaborate with you throughout this project. I am very grateful for your discerning edits, genuine enthusiasm about this book, and continued patience with my many questions. To Suzy Evans, my agent, your guidance and support have been a valuable touchstone. To Christina Veal, I am extremely appreciative for your constant kindness, PR work, and marketing knowledge.

My deepest gratitude goes out to my family. Kenny, Jonah, and Sarina, you have taught me the true meaning of love, patience, and connection. You constantly underscore the precious anchor that families can provide and bring so much light into my life. I'm a better person, parent, and spouse because of you. A truly heartfelt thanks to my husband, Kenny, my rock and best friend, for the innumerable ways you've believed in me and cheered me on.

Lastly, I am grateful to all the researchers who study ADHD and share their important information with the rest of us. Without your work, this book would never have come to pass.

Resources for Parents

ORGANIZATIONS

Children and Adults with Attention-Deficit/Hyperactivity Disorder (CHADD), www.chadd.org: Provides information, local support groups, and monthly magazine.

Learning Disabilities Association of America, www.ldaamerica.com: Provides programs, resources, advocacy, and research about learning disabilities.

Common Sense Media, www.commonsensemedia.org: Offers independent articles, reviews, and ratings about television, games, books, movies, and apps.

ADHD Coaches Organization, www.adhdcoaches.org: Presents information about ADHD coaching, newsletter, and programs.

ADHD-RELATED WEBSITES

www.drsharonsaline.com: Monthly blog, informational videos, podcast, and free support for parents based on practical, integrative strategies for attention, behavior, and learning.

www.additudemag.com (ADDitude magazine): Newletters and monthly magazine about everything related to ADHD.

www.impactadhd.com: Blog, free support, resources, videos, trainings, and coaching for parents.

www.understood.org: A range of information, blog, and supportive community for parents about learning and attention issues for kids between three and twenty.

www.drhallowell.com: News, articles, apps, and blog about living with ADHD from a strength-based approach from international ADHD expert and best-selling author Dr. Edward Hallowell.

www.brownadhdclinic.com: Books, articles, resources, and blog by leading ADHD expert and researcher Dr. Thomas Brown.

www.russellbarkley.org: Books, the *ADHD Report* newsletter, fact sheets, and courses by international ADHD authority Dr. Russell Barkley.

www.smartbutscatteredkids.com: Blog and books about building executive skills in children and teens by Drs. Peg Dawson and Richard Guare.

HELPFUL PARENTING WEBSITES

www.ahaparenting.com: General parenting advice, blog, videos, and resources with an empathic, mindful perspective by international parenting expert and popular author Dr. Laura Markham.

www.lynnlyonsnh.com: Support, advice, and blog for helping families dealing with anxiety from author and clinician Lynn Lyons, LICSW.

www.livesinthebalance.org: Resources, newsletter, workshops, videos, and advocacy for parents and educators about children with behavioral challenges from author, clinician, and researcher Dr. Ross Greene.

www.thefamilydinnerproject.org: Tips, blog, resources, and recipes to help parents create fun and successful family dinners.

Notes

CHAPTER 1

1. Greene, R. W. (2008). *Lost at School: Why Our Kids with Behavioral Challenges are Falling Through the Cracks and How We Can Help Them.* New York: Scribner.
2. Taffel, R. (2009). *Childhood Unbound: Saving Our Kids' Best Selves—Confident Parenting in a World of Change.* New York: Free Press.
3. Baumrind, D. (1967). "Child Care Practices Anteceding Three Patterns of Preschool Behavior." *Genetic Psychology Monographs, 75*(1), 43–88.
4. Honig, A. S. (1985). "Research in Review. Compliance, Control, and Discipline." *Young Children, 40*(2), 50–58.
5. Kohn, A. (2005). *Unconditional Parenting: Moving from Rewards and Punishment to Love and Reason.* New York: Atria.
6. The Mindful Classroom. (2012). "Self-Regulation One Breath at a Time." Retrieved from https://themindfulclassroom.wordpress.com/tag/mindful-breathing.
7. Markham, L. (2012). *Peaceful Parent, Happy Kids: How to Stop Yelling and Start Connecting.* New York: Perigee Book.
8. Shaw, P. et al. (2007). "Attention-Deficit/Hyperactivity Disorder Is Characterized by a Delay in Cortical Maturation." *Proceedings of the National Academy of Sciences, 104*(49), 19649–54.
9. Dalai Lama. (1998). *The Art of Happiness: A Handbook for Living.* New York: Riverhead Books.
10. Hallowell, E. M., and Jensen, P. S. (2008). *Superparenting for ADD: An Innovative Approach to Raising Your Distracted Child.* New York: Ballantine.

11. Baumeister, R. F. et al. (2001). "Bad Is Stronger Than Good." *Review of General Psychology, 5*(4), 323–70.
12. Fredrickson, B. L. (2009). *Positivity: Top-Notch Research Reveals the Upward Spiral That Will Change Your Life.* New York: Three Rivers Press, 32.

CHAPTER 2

1. Hallowell and Jensen. *Superparenting for ADD.*
2. Douglas, V. I. (1972). "Stop, Look and Listen: The Problem of Sustained Attention and Impulse Control in Hyperactive and Normal Children." *Canadian Journal of Behavioural Science/Revue canadienne des sciences du comportement, 4*(4), 259–82.
3. *Diagnostic and Statistical Manual of Mental Disorders: DSM-5.* (2014). Washington, DC: American Psychiatric Publishing.
4. Faraone, S. V. et al. (2003). "The Worldwide Prevalence of ADHD: Is It an American Condition?" *World Psychiatry, 2*(2), 104–13; Polanczyk, G., et al. (2007). "The Worldwide Prevalence of ADHD: A Systematic Review and Metaregression Analysis." *American Journal of Psychiatry, 164*(6), 942–8.
5. Willcutt, E. G. (2012). "The Prevalence of DSM-IV Attention-Deficit/Hyperactivity Disorder: A Meta-Analytic Review." *Neurotherapeutics, 9*(3), 490–9.; Visser, S. N., et al. (2014). "Trends in the Parent-Report of Health Care Provider–Diagnosed and Medicated ADHD: United States, 2003–2011. *Journal of the American Academy of Child and Adolescent Psychiatry, 53*(1), 34–46.
6. Centers for Disease Control and Prevention. (2017). "Attention-Deficit/Hyperactivity Disorder (ADHD)." Retrieved from http://www.cdc.gov/ncbddd/adhd /data.html.
7. Rucklidge, J. J. (2008). "Gender Differences in ADHD: Implications for Psychosocial Treatments." *Expert Review of Neurotherapeutics, 8*(4), 643–55.
8. Centers for Disease Control and Prevention, "Attention-Deficit/Hyperactivity Disorder (ADHD)."
9. Barkley, R. A. (2013). *Taking Charge of ADHD: The Complete, Authoritative Guide for Parents* (3rd edition). New York: Guilford Press, 112–13, 258–60; Wilens, T. E. et al. (2003). "Does Stimulant Therapy of Attention-Deficit/Hyperactivity Disorder Beget Later Substance Abuse? A Meta-Analytic Review of the Literature." *Pediatrics, 111*(1), 179–85.
10. Watts, V. (2016). "ADHD Diagnoses Climb Across Racial/Ethnic Groups." *Psychiatric News.* American Psychiatric Association.
11. Starck, M., Grünwald, J., and Schlarb, A. A. (2016). "Occurrence of ADHD in Parents of ADHD Children in a Clinical Sample." *Neuropsychiatric Disease and Treatment, 12,* 581–8; Larsson, H., et al. (2014). "The Heritability of Clinically Diagnosed Attention Deficit Hyperactivity Disorder Across the Lifespan." *Psychological Medicine, 44*(10), 2223–9.

12. Biederman, J. et al. (1995). "High Risk for Attention Deficit Hyperactivity Disorder among Children of Parents with Childhood Onset of the Disorder: A Pilot Study." *American Journal of Psychiatry, 152*(3), 431-5.
13. Barkley, *Taking Charge of ADHD*, 112-13, 258-60; Banerjee, T. D., Middleton, F., and Faraone, S. V. (2007). "Environmental Risk Factors for Attention-Deficit Hyperactivity Disorder." *Acta Paediatrica, 96*(9), 1269-74.
14. Arnsten, A. F. (2009). "Toward a New Understanding of Attention-Deficit Hyperactivity Disorder Pathophysiology: An Important Role for Prefrontal Cortex Dysfunction." *CNS Drugs, 23*(Supplement 1), 33-41; Rubia, K., Alegria A. A., and Brinson, H. (2014). "Brain Abnormalities in Attention-Deficit Hyperactivity Disorder: A Review." *Revista de Neurologia, 58*(Supplement 1), 33-318.
15. Monastra, V. J. (2014). *Parenting Children with ADHD: 10 Lessons That Medicine Cannot Teach* (2nd edition). Washington, DC: APA LifeTools.
16. Volkow, N. D. et al. (2009). "Evaluating Dopamine Reward Pathway in ADHD: Clinical Implications." *JAMA: The Journal of the American Medical Association, 302*(10), 1084-91.
17. Brown, T. E. (2013). *A New Understanding of ADHD in Children and Adults: Executive Function Impairments.* New York: Routledge; Gallo, E. F., and Posner, J. (2016). "Moving Towards Causality in Attention-Deficit Hyperactivity Disorder: Overview of Neural and Genetic Mechanisms." *The Lancet Psychiatry, 3*(6), 555-67.
18. Brown, *A New Understanding of ADHD in Children and Adults.*
19. Woltering, S. et al. (2015). "Executive Function in Children with Externalizing and Comorbid Internalizing Behavior Problems." *Journal of Child Psychology and Psychiatry, 57*(1), 30-38. http://doi.org/10.1111/jcpp.12428.
20. Brown, *A New Understanding of ADHD in Children and Adults.*
21. Mayes, S. D., and Calhoun, S. L. (2006). "Frequency of Reading, Math, and Writing Disabilities in Children with Clinical Disorders." *Learning and Individual Differences, 16*(2), 145-57. http://doi.org/10.1016/j.lindif.2005.07.004.
22. DuPaul, G. J., Gormley, M. J., and Laracy, S. D. (2012). "Comorbidity of LD and ADHD: Implications of DSM-5 for Assessment and Treatment." *Journal of Learning Disabilities, 46*(1), 43-51. http://doi.org/10.1177/0022219412464351; Larson, K., et al. (2011). "Patterns of Comorbidity, Functioning, and Service Use for US Children with ADHD, 2007." *Pediatrics, 127*(3), 462-70; Mayes and Calhoun, "Frequency of Reading, Math, and Writing Disabilities in Children with Clinical Disorders."
23. Medina, J. (2017). "Specific Learning Disorder." Psych Central. Retrieved from https://psychcentral.com/disorders/specific-learning-disorder.
24. Sexton, C. C. et al. (2012). "The Co-occurrence of Reading Disorder and ADHD." *Journal of Learning Disabilities, 45*(6), 538-64. http://doi.org/10.1177/0022219411407772.
25. Shaywitz, S. E., Gruen, J. R., and Shaywitz, B. A. (2007). "Management of Dyslexia, Its Rationale, and Underlying Neurobiology." *Pediatric Clinics of North America, 54*(3), 609-23.

26. Kutscher, M. L., Attwood, T., and Wolff, R. R. (2014). *Kids in the Syndrome Mix of ADHD, LD, Autism Spectrum, Tourette's, Anxiety and More!: The One-Stop Guide for Parents, Teachers and Other Professionals.* London: Jessica Kingsley.

27. Mayes, S. D., and Calhoun, S. L. (2007). "Learning, Attention, Writing, and Processing Speed in Typical Children and Children with ADHD, Autism, Anxiety, Depression, and Oppositional-Defiant Disorder." *Child Neuropsychology,* 13(6), 469–93; Yoshimasu, K. et al. (2011). "Written-Language Disorder Among Children with and Without ADHD in a Population-Based Birth Cohort." *Pediatrics, 128*(3), e605–12.

28. These patterns can be called "oppositional defiant disorder," usually emerging in childhood and often reflecting relationship difficulties as well. Sometimes, these problems develop into more serious issues in adolescenece to include stealing, property destruction, or persistent lying. See: Barkley, R. A. (2015). *Attention-Deficit Hyperactivity Disorder: A Handbook for Diagnosis and Treatment.* (Fourth edition). New York: Guilford Press, 184–218; Larson et al., "Patterns of Comorbidity, Functioning, and Service Use for US Children with ADHD, 2007."

29. Hoza, B. (2007). "Peer Functioning in Children with ADHD." *Ambulatory Pediatrics,* 7(Supplement 1), 101–6.

30. Barkley, *Attention-Deficit Hyperactivity Disorder*; Elia, J., Ambrosini, P., & Berrettini, W. (2008). "ADHD Characteristics: I. Concurrent Co-morbidity Patterns in Children and Adolescents." *Child and Adolescent Psychiatry and Mental Health,* 2(1), 15.

31. Masi, L., and Gignac, M. (2015). "ADHD and Comorbid Disorders in Childhood Psychiatric Problems, Medical Problems, Learning Disorders and Developmental Coordination Disorder." Clinical Psychiatry. Retrieved from http://clinical-psychiatry.imedpub.com/adhd-and-comorbid-disorders-inchildhoodpsychiatric-problems-medicalproblems-learning-disordersand-developmental-coordinationdisorder.php?aid=7487.

32. Bunford, N., Evans, S. W., and Wymbs, F. (2015). "ADHD and Emotion Dysregulation Among Children and Adolescents." *Clinical Child and Family Psychology Review, 18*(3), 185–217.

33. DuPaul, Gormley, and Laracy, "Comorbidity of LD and ADHD"; Subcommittee on Attention-Deficit/Hyperactivity Disorder Committee on Quality Improvement (2001). "Clinical Practice Guideline: Treatment of the School-Aged Child with Attention-Deficit/Hyperactivity Disorder." *Pediatrics, 108*(4), 1033–44. http://doi.org/10.1542/peds.108.4.1033.

34. U.S. Department of Education. (2006). "Building the Legacy: IDEA 2004." Retrieved from https://sites.ed.gov/idea/.

35. U.S. Department of Education. (2015). "Protecting Students with Disabilities." Office of Civil Rights. Retrieved from http://ed.gov/about/offices/list/ocr/504faq.html.

36. The MTA Cooperative Group. (1999). "A 14-Month Randomized Clinical Trial of Treatment Strategies for Attention-Deficit/Hyperactivity Disorder." *Archives of General Psychiatry, 56*(12), 1073–86.

37. Jensen, P. S. et al. (2001). "ADHD Comorbidity Findings from the MTA Study: Comparing Comorbid Subgroups." *Journal of the American Academy of Child and Adolescent Psychiatry, 40*(2), 147–58.

38. Jensen, C. M., and Steinhausen, H-C. (2015). "Comorbid Mental Disorders in Children and Adolescents with Attention-Deficit/Hyperactivity Disorder in a Large Nationwide Study." *Attention Deficit and Hyperactivity Disorders, 7*(1), 27–38.

39. Biederman, J. et al. (2010). "A Naturalistic 10-Year Prospective Study of Height and Weight in Children with Attention-Deficit Hyperactivity Disorder Grown Up: Sex and Treatment Effects." *The Journal of Pediatrics, 157*(4), 635–40.

40. Kohls, G., Herpertz-Dahlmann, B., and Konrad, K. (2009). "Hyperresponsiveness to Social Rewards in Children and Adolescents with Attention-Deficit/Hyperactivity Disorder (ADHD)." *Behavioral and Brain Functions, 5*(1), 20.

41. Therapy with a cognitive focus that also includes mindfulness has been shown to improve acknowledging and understanding emotions with less judgment. It can also reduce negative family interactions and improve emotional regulation for both parents and their child with ADHD. See: Shaw, P., et al. (2014). "Emotion Dysregulation in Attention Deficit Hyperactivity Disorder." *American Journal of Psychiatry, 171*(3), 276–93.

42. Meppelink, R., de Bruin, E. I., and Bögels, S. M. (2016). "Meditation or Medication?: Mindfulness Training versus Medication in the Treatment of Childhood ADHD: A Randomized Controlled Trial. *BMC Psychiatry, 16*(1); Schmiedeler, S. (2015). "[Mindfulness-based Intervention in Attention-Deficit/Hyperactivity Disorder (ADHD).]" *Zeitschrift für Kinder- und Jugendpsychiatrie und Psychotherapie, 43*(2), 123–31.

43. Den Heijer, A. E. et al. (2016). "Sweat It Out?: The Effects of Physical Exercise on Cognition and Behavior in Children and Adults with ADHD: A Systematic Literature Review." *Journal of Neural Transmission, 124*(Supplement 1), 3–26. doi:10.1007/s00702-016-1593-7.

44. Cortese, S. et al. (2016). "Neurofeedback for Attention-Deficit/Hyperactivity Disorder: Meta-Analysis of Clinical and Neuropsychological Outcomes from Randomized Controlled Trials." *Journal of the American Academy of Child and Adolescent Psychiatry, 55*(6), 444–55; Barkley, R. A. (2015). Research Findings. *The ADHD Report, 23*(8). Retrieved from https://guilfordjournals.com/loi/adhd.

CHAPTER 3

1. Hallowell and Jensen, *Superparenting for ADD*.

CHAPTER 4

1. Lawrence-Lightfoot, S. (2004). *The Essential Conversation: What Parents and Teachers Can Learn from Each Other*. New York: Ballantine Books.

2. DuPaul, Gormley, and Laracy, "Comorbidity of LD and ADHD."
3. DuPaul, Gormley, and Laracy, "Comorbidity of LD and ADHD."
4. Lahey, J. (2015). *The Gift of Failure: How the Best Parents Learn to Let Go So Their Children Can Succeed.* New York: HarperCollins.

CHAPTER 5

1. Goleman, D. (2013). *Focus: The Hidden Driver of Excellence.* New York: HarperCollins, 203.

CHAPTER 6

1. Nadeau, K. G., Littman, E. B., and Quinn, P. O. (1999). *Understanding Girls with ADHD: How They Feel and Why They Do What They Do.* Silver Spring, MD: Advantage.

CHAPTER 7

1. DuPaul, Gormley, and Laracy, " Comorbidity of LD and ADHD."

CHAPTER 10

1. Goleman, D. (1995). *Emotional Intelligence: Why It Can Matter More Than IQ.* New York: Bantam Books.
2. Thomas, E. (2015). "The Amygdala & Emotions." Retrieved from http://www.effective-mind-control.com/amygdala.html.
3. Brown, T. E. (2013). *A New Understanding of ADHD in Children and Adults: Executive Function Impairments.* New York: Routledge, 36.
4. Schmeichel, B. J., Volokhov, R. N., and Demaree, H. A. (2008). "Working Memory Capacity and the Self-Regulation of Emotional Expression and Experience." *Journal of Personality and Social Psychology, 95*(6), 1526–40.
5. Hallowell and Jensen, *Superparenting for ADD,* 77.
6. Hallowell and Jensen, *Superparenting for ADD,* 77–80.
7. Pratt, K. (2014). "Psychology Tools: What Is Anger? A Secondary Emotion." Retrieved from https://healthypsych.com/psychology-tools-what-is-anger-a-secondary-emotion.
8. Chansky, T. E. (2008). *Freeing Your Child from Negative Thinking: Powerful, Practical Strategies to Build a Lifetime of Resilience, Flexibility, and Happiness.* Cambridge, MA: Da Capo Press, 36–38.

9. Kemp, C. (2017). "Many Parents Use Time-Outs Incorrectly." Retrieved from http://www.aappublications.org/news/2017/01/24/TimeOut012417; Morgan, A. (2017). "Why Traditional Time-Outs Don't Work and What to Do Instead." Retrieved from http://www.notimeforflashcards.com/2017/01/time-outs-dont-work.html.
10. Geurts, H. M., Luman, M., and van Meel, C. S. (2008). "What's in a Game: The Effect of Social Motivation on Interference Control in Boys with ADHD and Autism Spectrum Disorders. *Journal of Child Psychology and Psychiatry,* 49(8), 848–57. http://doi.org/10.1111/j.1469-7610.2008.01916.x; Sergeant, J. (2005). "Modeling Attention-Deficit/Hyperactivity Disorder: A Critical Appraisal of the Cognitive-Energetic Model." *Biological Psychiatry,* 57(11), 1248–55. http://doi.org10.1016/j.bps.2004.09.010.
11. Wilson, R., and Lyons, L. L. (2013). *Anxious Kids, Anxious Parents: 7 Ways to Stop the Worry Cycle and Raise Courageous & Independent Children.* Deerfield Beach, FL: Health Communications, Inc.

CHAPTER 11

1. Inspired by the work of Peg Dawson and Richard Guare in their book *Smart but Scattered.* Dawson, P., and Guare, R. (2009). *Smart but Scattered: The Revolutionary "Executive Skills" Approach to Helping Kids Reach Their Potential.* New York: Guilford Press.

CHAPTER 12

1. Nadeau, Littman, and Quinn, *Understanding Girls with ADHD;* Lee, S. S. et al. (2011). "Prospective Association of Childhood Attention-Deficit/Hyperactivity Disorder (ADHD) and Substance Use and Abuse/Dependence: A Meta-Analytic Review." *Clinical Psychology Review,* 31(3), 328–41.
2. Brown, *A New Understanding of ADHD in Children and Adults,* 155.
3. Flory, K. et al. (2006). "Childhood ADHD Predicts Risky Sexual Behavior in Young Adulthood." *Journal of Clinical Child & Adolescent Psychology,* 35(4), 571–7; Babinski, D. E., and Waschbusch, D. A. (2016). "The Interpersonal Difficulties of Women with ADHD." *The ADHD Report,* 24(7), 1–8. http://doi.org/10.1521/adhd.2016.24.7.1.
4. Bertin, M. (2011). *The Family ADHD Solution: A Scientific Approach to Maximizing Your Child's Attention and Minimizing Parental Stress.* New York: St. Martin's Griffin, 162–4.

CHAPTER 13

1. Ito, M. et al. (2013). *Hanging Out, Messing Around, and Geeking Out: Kids Living and Learning with New Media*. Boston, MA: The MIT Press.
2. Lenhart, A. (2015). "Teens, Social Media & Technology Overview 2015." Retrieved from http://www.pewinternet.org/2015/04/09/teens-social-media-technology-2015.
3. Eadicicco, L. (2015). "Americans Check Their Phones 8 Billion Times a Day." Retrieved from http://time.com/4147614/smartphone-usage-us-2015.
4. Nunez-Smith, M., et al. (2008). Media + Child and Adolescent Health: A Systematic Review." *Common Sense Media*.
5. American Psychological Association. (2017). "Stress in America: Coping with Change."
6. Steiner-Adair, C., with Barker, T. H. (2014). *The Big Disconnect: Protecting Childhood and Family Relationships in the Digital Age*. New York: Harper. See pp. 4 and 17 for an analysis of how these behaviors impact parent/child relationships.
7. American Psychological Association, "Stress in America: Coping with Change."
8. American Psychological Association, "Stress in America: Coping with Change."
9. Chassiakos, Y. R. (2016). "Children and Adolescents and Digital Media." *Pediatrics, 138*(5), e1–e18. Retrieved from http://pediatrics.aappublications.org/content/138/5/e20162593.
10. TheFamilyDinnerProject.org: Food, Fun and Conversation About Things That Matter. Retrieved from https://thefamilydinnerproject.org.
11. Underwood, M. K., and Faris, R. (2015). "#Being Thirteen: Social Media and the Hidden World of Young Adolescents' Peer Culture". Retrieved from https://assets.documentcloud.org/documents/2448422/being-13-report.pdf.
12. Underwood and Faris, "# Being Thirteen."

Bibliography

American Academy of Pediatrics, and National Initiative for Children's Healthcare Quality. (2002). *Caring for Children with ADHD: A Resource Toolkit for Clinicians*. Chicago: McNeil. http://www.nichq.org/childrens-health/adhd/resources/vanderbilt-assessment-scales.

Anderson, A. K. (2007). "Feeling Emotional: The Amygdala Links Emotional Perception and Experience." *Social Cognitive and Affective Neuroscience*, 2(2), 71–72.

Anderson, P. (2002). "Assessment and Development of Executive Function (EF) During Childhood." *Child Neuropsychology*, 8(2), 71–82.

Barkley, R. A. (2011). *Barkley Deficits in Executive Functioning Scale: Children and Adolescents*. New York: Guildford Press.

———. (2012). *Executive Functions: What They Are, How They Work, and Why They Evolved*. New York: Guilford Press.

———, and Murphy, K. A. (2006). *Attention-Deficit Hyperactivity Disorder: A Clinical Workbook*. New Haven, CT: Yale University Press.

Baweja, R. et al. (2016). "The Effectiveness and Tolerability of Central Nervous System Stimulants in School-Age Children with Attention-Deficit/Hyperactivity Disorder and Disruptive Mood Dysregulation Disorder Across Home and School." *Journal of Child and Adolescent Psychopharmacology*, 26(2), 154–63.

Biederman, J. (2000). "Age-Dependent Decline of Symptoms of Attention Deficit Hyperactivity Disorder: Impact of Remission Definition and Symptom Type." *American Journal of Psychiatry*, *157*(5), 816–18.

—— et al. (2012). "Predictors of Persistence in Girls with Attention Deficit Hyperactivity Disorder: Results from an 11-Year Controlled Follow-up Study." *Acta Psychiatrica Scandinavica*, *125*(2), 147–56.

Brown, T. E. (2005). *Attention Deficit Disorder: The Unfocused Mind in Children and Adults*. New Haven, CT: Yale University Press.

——. (2014). *Smart but Stuck: Emotions in Teens and Adults with ADHD*. San Francisco: Jossey-Bass.

Buitelaar, J. K. (2017). "Optimising Treatment Strategies for ADHD in Adolescence to Minimise 'Lost in Transition' to Adulthood." *Epidemiology and Psychiatric Sciences*, *26*(5), 448–52.

Coloroso, B. (2016). "15 Clues Your Child Is Getting Bullied & What to Do About It." Retrieved from http://impactadhd.com/manage-emotions-and-impulses/child-is-getting-bullied.

Conners, K. (2008). *Conners*. (3rd edition). Toronto: Multi-Health Systems.

Cooper-Kahn, J., and Dietzel, L. (2008). *Late, Lost, and Unprepared: A Parents' Guide to Helping Children with Executive Functioning*. Bethesda, MD: Woodbine House.

Cortese, S. et al. (2012). "Toward Systems Neuroscience of ADHD: A Meta-Analysis of 55 fMRI Studies." *American Journal of Psychiatry*, *169*(10), 1038–55.

Davidson, R. J., and Begley, S. (2012). *The Emotional Life of Your Brain: How Its Unique Patterns Affect the Way You Think, Feel, and Live—and How You Can Change Them*. New York: Hudson Street Press.

Dawson, P., and Guare, R. (2010). *Executive Skills in Children and Adolescents: A Practical Guide to Assessment and Intervention*. (2nd edition). New York: Guilford Press.

——. (2012). *Coaching Students with Executive Skills Deficits*. New York: Guilford Press.

——. (2013). *Smart but Scattered Teens: The "Executive Skills" Program for Helping Teens Reach Their Potential*. New York: Guilford Press.

Dendy, C. A., and Ziegler, A. (2007). *A Bird's Eye View of Life with ADD and ADHD: Advice from Young Survivors*. (2nd edition). Cedar Bluff, AL: Cherish the Children.

Early Childhood Australia, Inc. (2012). "Collaborating with Families: Not a Problem!" *Every Child*, *18*(1), 28–29.

Ellison, K. (2010). *Buzz: A Year of Paying Attention*. New York: Hyperion.

Epstein, T., and Saltzman-Benaiah, J. (2010). "Parenting Children with Disruptive Behaviors: Evaluation of a Collaborative Problem Solving Pilot Program." *Journal of Clinical Psychology Practice*, 27–40.

Ferrer, E. et al. (2015). "Achievement Gap in Reading Is Present as Early as First Grade and Persists through Adolescence." *Journal of Pediatrics*, 167(5), 1121-25.

Gillberg, C. et al. (2004). "Co-Existing Disorders in ADHD—Implications for Diagnosis and Intervention." *European Child + Adolescent Psychiatry*, 13(Supplement 1), i80-i92.

Gold, A. L., Morey, R. A., and McCarthy, G. (2015). "Amygdala–Prefrontal Cortex Functional Connectivity During Threat-Induced Anxiety and Goal Distraction." *Biological Psychiatry*, 77(4), 394-403.

Greene, R. W. (2011). "The Aggressive, Explosive Child." In M. Augustyn, B. Zuckerman, and E. B. Caronna, eds., *The Zuckerman Parker Handbook of Developmental and Behavioral Pediatrics for Primary Care*. (2nd edition). Baltimore: Lippincott, Williams, & Wilkins, 282-84.

—— et al. (2004). "Effectiveness of Collaborative Problem Solving in Affectively Dysregulated Youth with Oppositional Defiant Disorder: Initial findings." *Journal of Consulting and Clinical Psychology*, 72(6), 1157-64.

Hallowell, E., and Ratey, J. (2011). *Driven to Distraction: Recognizing and Coping with Attention Deficit Disorder from Childhood to Adulthood* (2nd edition). New York: Anchor.

Harty, S. C. et al. (2017). "Anger-Irritability as a Mediator of Attention Deficit Hyperactivity Disorder Risk for Adolescent Alcohol Use and the Contribution of Coping Skills." *Journal of Child Psychology and Psychiatry*, 58(5), 555-63.

Hosain, G. M. et al. (2012). "Attention Deficit Hyperactivity Symptoms and Risky Sexual Behavior in Young Adult Women." *Journal of Women's Health*, 21(4), 463-68.

Johnson, M. et al. (2012). "Attention-Deficit/Hyperactivity Disorder (ADHD) with Oppositional Defiant Disorder in Swedish Children: An Open Study of Collaborative Problem Solving." *Acta Paediactrica*, 101(6), 624-30.

Kapalka, G. (2010). *Counseling Boys and Men with ADHD*. New York: Routledge.

Kok, F. M. et al. (2016). "Problematic Peer Functioning in Girls with ADHD: A Systematic Literature Review." *PLOS ONE*, 11(11), e0165119.

Kooij, S.J.J. et al. (2010). "European Consensus Statement on Diagnosis and Treatment of Adult ADHD: The European Network Adult ADHD." *BMC Psychiatry*, 10(1).

Lange, K. W. et al. (2010). "The History of Attention Deficit Hyperactivity Disorder." *Attention Deficit and Hyperactivity Disorders*, 2(4), 241-55.

Loe, I. M., and Feldman, H. M. (2007). "Academic and Educational Outcomes of Children with ADHD." *Ambulatory Pediatrics*, 7(Supplement 1), 82-90.

Mautone, J. A., Lefler, E. K., and Power, T. J. (2011). "Promoting Family and School Success for Children with ADHD: Strengthening Relationships While Building Skills." *Theory into Practice*, *50*(1), 43–51.

Merikangas, K. R. et al. (2010). "Lifetime Prevalence of Mental Disorders in U.S. Adolescents: Results from the National Comorbidity Survey Replication—Adolescent Supplement (NCS-A)." *Journal of the American Academy of Child & Adolescent Psychiatry*, *49*(10), 980–89.

Miller, V. A. (2009). "Parent-Child Collaborative Decision Making for the Management of Chronic Illness: A Qualitative Analysis." *Families, Systems, & Health*, *27*(3), 249–66.

Molina, B. S. et al. (2013). "Adolescent Substance Use in the Multimodal Treatment Study of Attention-Deficit/Hyperactivity Disorder (ADHD) (MTA) as a Function of Childhood ADHD, Random Assignment to Childhood Treatments, and Subsequent Medication." *Journal of the American Academy of Child & Adolescent Psychiatry*, *52*(3), 250–63.

——. (2009). "The MTA at 8 Years: Prospective Follow-Up of Children Treated for Combined-Type ADHD in a Multisite Study." *Journal of the American Academy of Child & Adolescent Psychiatry*, *48*(5), 484–500.

——, and Pelham, W. E. (2003). "Childhood Predictors of Adolescent Substance Use in a Longitudinal Study of Children with ADHD." *Journal of Abnormal Psychology*, *112*(3), 497–507.

Moya-Albiol et al. (2013). "Psychophysiological Responses to Cooperation: The Role of Outcome and Gender." *International Journal of Psychology*, *48*(4), 542–50.

Mrug, S. et al. (2012). "Peer Rejection and Friendships in Children with Attention-Deficit/Hyperactivity Disorder: Contributions to Long-Term Outcomes." *Journal of Abnormal Child Psychology*, *40*(6), 1013–26.

Murray-Close, D. et al. (2010). "Developmental Processes in Peer Problems of Children with Attention-Deficit/Hyperactivity Disorder in the Multimodal Treatment Study of Children with ADHD: Developmental Cascades and Vicious Cycles." *Development and Psychopathology*, *22*(4), 785–802.

Newcorn, J. H. et al. (2001). "Symptom Profiles in Children with ADHD: Effects of Comorbidity and Gender." *Journal of the American Academy of Child & Adolescent Psychiatry*, *40*(2), 37–146.

Nigg, J. T. (2013). "Attention-Deficit/Hyperactivity Disorder and Adverse Health Outcomes." *Clinical Psychology Review*, *33*(2), 215–28.

Ollendick, T. H., et al. (2016). "Parent Management Training (PMT) and Collaborative & Proactive Solutions (CPS): A Randomized Control Trial for Oppositional Youth." *Journal of Clinical Child and Adolescent Psychology*, *45*(5), 591–604.

Peterson, R. L. et al. (2017). "Cognitive Prediction of Reading, Math, and Attention: Shared and Unique Influences." *Journal of Learning Disabilities*, 50(4), 408–21.

Polderman, T. J. et al. (2010). "A Systematic Review of Prospective Studies on Attention Problems and Academic Achievement." *Acta Psychiatrica Scandinavica*, 122(4), 271–84.

Pollastri, A. et al. (2013). "The Collaborative Problem Solving Approach: Outcomes Across Settings." *Harvard Review of Psychiatry*, 21(4),188–99.

Quinn, P. O., and Nadeau, K. G., eds. (2002). *Understanding Women with AD/HD*. Silver Spring, MD: Advantage.

Reynolds, C. R., and Kamphaus, R. W. (2015). *Behavior Assessment System for Children* (3rd edition). New York: Pearson.

Riley, A. R. et al. (2017). "A Survey of Parents' Perceptions and Use of Time-Out Compared to Empirical Evidence." *Academic Pediatrics*, 17(2), 168–75.

Rubia, K., Alegria, A., and Brinson, H. (2014). "Imaging the ADHD Brain: Disorder-Specificity, Medication Effects and Clinical Translation." *Expert Review of Neurotherapeutics*, 14(5), 519–38.

Seidman, L. J. et al. (2005). "Impact of Gender and Age on Executive Functioning: Do Girls and Boys with and Without Attention Deficit Hyperactivity Disorder Differ Neuropsychologically in Preteen and Teenage Years?" *Developmental Neuropsychology*, 27(1), 79–105.

Sesma, H. W. et al. (2009). "The Contribution of Executive Skills to Reading Comprehension." *Child Neuropsychology*, 15(3), 232–46.

Shaywitz, S. E., and Shaywitz, B. A. (2005). "Dyslexia (Specific Reading Disability)." *Biological Psychiatry*, 57(11), 1301–9.

Siegel, D. (2013). *Brainstorm: The Power and Purpose of the Teenage Brain*. New York: Jeremy P. Tarcher/Penguin.

Sobanski, E. et al. (2010). "Emotional Lability in Children and Adolescents with Attention Deficit/Hyperactivity Disorder (ADHD): Clinical Correlates and Familial Prevalence: Emotional lability in ADHD." *Journal of Child Psychology and Psychiatry*, 51(8), 915–23.

Spencer, T. J. et al. (2013). "Effect of Psychostimulants on Brain Structure and Function in ADHD: A Qualitative Literature Review of Magnetic Resonance Imaging-Based Neuroimaging Studies." *Journal of Clinical Psychiatry*, 74(9), 902–17.

Stasik, D. et al. (2008). "[Graphomotor Functions in Children with Attention Deficit Hyperactivity Disorder (ADHD).]" *Psychiatria Polska*, 43(2), 183–92.

Stiles, J., and Jernigan, T. L. (2010). "The Basics of Brain Development." *Neuropsychology Review*, 20(4), 327–48.

Swanson, E. N., Owens, E. B., and Hinshaw, S. P. (2014). Pathways to self-harmful behaviors in young women with and without ADHD: a longitudinal examination of mediating factors. *Journal of Child Psychology and Psychiatry, 55*(5), 505–515.

Swanson, E. N., Owens, E. B., and Hinshaw, S. P. (2001). "Clinical Relevance of the Primary Findings of the MTA: Success Rates Based on Severity of ADHD and ODD Symptoms at the End of Treatment." *Journal of the American Academy of Child & Adolescent Psychiatry, 40*(2), 168–79.

Talan, J. (2007). "ADHD Brains Lag in Development, New Study Finds." *Neurology Today, 7*(24), 1.

Tough, P. (2012). *How Children Succeed: Grit, Curiosity and the Hidden Power of Character.* New York: Houghton Mifflin Harcourt.

Tuckman, A. (2012). *Understand Your Brain, Get More Done: The ADHD Executive Functions Workbook.* Plantation, FL: Speciality Press.

Uchida, M. et al. (2015). "Adult Outcome of ADHD: An Overview of Results from the MGH Longitudinal Family Studies of Pediatrically and Psychiatrically Referred Youth with and Without ADHD of Both Sexes." *Journal of Attention Disorders,* 1–12.

University of Michigan. (2015). "Slow to Mature, Quick to Distract: ADHD Brain Study Finds Slower Development of Key Connections." Health System University of Michigan. Retrieved from http://www.uofmhealth.org/news/archive/201409/slow-mature-quick-distract-adhd-brain-study-finds-slower.

Volkow, N. D. et al. (2011). "Motivation Deficit in ADHD Is Associated with Dysfunction of the Dopamine Reward Pathway." *Molecular Psychiatry, 16*(11), 1147–54.

Willcutt, E. G., Doyle, A. E., Nigg, J. T., Faraone, S. V., and Pennington, B. F. (2005). Validity of the Executive Function Theory of Attention-Deficit/Hyperactivity Disorder: a Meta-Analytic Review. *Biological Psychiatry, 57*(11), 1336–1346.

Willcutt, E. G. et al. (2010). "Etiology and Neuropsychology of Comorbidity between RD and ADHD: The Case for Multiple-Deficit models." *Cortex, 46*(10), 1345–61.

Wolraich, M. L. (2005). "Attention-Deficit/Hyperactivity Disorder Among Adolescents: A Review of the Diagnosis, Treatment, and Clinical Implications." *Pediatrics, 115*(6), 1734–46.

Zwi, M. et al. (2011). "Parent Training Interventions for Attention Deficit Hyperactivity Disorder (ADHD) in Children Aged 5 to 18 Years." In the Cochrane Collaboration, ed., *Cochrane Database of Systematic Reviews.* Chichester, UK: John Wiley & Sons, Ltd.

Index

About the Author

Photograph of the author: Shauna Surek

SHARON SALINE, PSY.D., a licensed clinical psychologist in private practice, is a top expert in how ADHD, learning disabilities, and mental health issues affect children, teens, and families. In addition to maintaining a busy private practice, Dr. Saline has worked extensively with schools on mental health issues in the classroom, tools for alternative learners, and teacher/parent communication. Her unique perspective, namely growing up in a household with a sibling who wrestled with untreated ADHD, combined with decades of clinical experience, assists her in guiding families through the maze of information, emotions, conflict, and stress toward successful dialogue, interventions, and connection.

As an internationally sought-after lecturer, workshop facilitator, and clinician/educator trainer known for combining her knowledge about psychology with a background in theater, she addresses a variety of topics from understanding ADHD and executive functioning in children and teens to making sense of the teen brain to working with different kinds of learners and raising digital citizens. A magna cum laude graduate of Brown University, she received her master's degree in psychology from New College of California and her doctorate in psychology from the California School of Professional Psychology.

A regular contributor for *ADDitude magazine*'s new Dear Parent Teen Coach series and a popular speaker at many ADHD and parenting conferences, Dr. Saline also shares valuable insights and recommendations in her free parenting tools via her newsletter, blog, and social media presence. More information is available at www.drsharonsaline.com, Facebook @DrSharonSaline, and Twitter @DrSharonSaline.